GUERRILLA MARKETING
—TO—
HEAL THE WORLD

The success of Chicken Soup is because most people want to help others and want to do the right thing. Jay and Shel show that not only do people want to change the paradigm toward people-centered, planet-friendly behavior, but that they can lift people out of poverty and profit handsomely by doing so. I'm delighted to recommend *Guerrilla Marketing To Heal the World*—the world needs more of this.

—**Jack Canfield**, co-creator, *Chicken Soup for the Soul* series, co-author, *The Success Principles*, and CEO, Canfield Training Group, JackCanfield.com

Like all of the best Guerrilla Marketing books, this one is powerful, direct and simple. Unlike the other ones, this book also heals our communities, fortifies the planet and helps you build an enterprise for the long haul. Just in time.

—**Seth Godin**, author and blogger, SethGodin.com

For decades, I've supported the idea that business has a higher purpose. *Guerrilla Marketing to Heal the World* offers practical examples and fresh insights into how business can address poverty, war, and climate—profitably and collaboratively. I'm delighted to recommend this book.

—**Ivan Misner, Ph.D.**, founder of BNI (Business Network International), BNI.com

A wonderful combination of guerrilla marketing chockfull of practical green and social change marketing tips—and first-hand advice from two pros.

—**Jacquelyn Ottman**, Author of *The New Rules of Green Marketing*, GreenMarketing.com/

The tools that wire the social web are perfect for driving interest and action around sustainability and bringing people up out of poverty. Jay Levinson and Shel Horowitz have a clever blend of ideas, recipes, and thoughts for the future. Their ideas might just become your blueprint, if you want to see the successful greening of the world and empowerment of its citizens.

—**Chris Brogan**, co-author of *Trust Agents*, ChrisBrogan.com

As consumers use their own guerrilla techniques to hold companies accountable, *Guerrilla Marketing to Heal the World* levels the playing field, a playbook for companies that want to succeed in a world where integrity and transparency trump slick slogans. This is a gem that should be required reading—not just for so-called green marketers, but for any marketer who wants to succeed in today's economy, and tomorrow's.

—**Joel Makower**, Executive Editor, GreenBiz.com,
and author of *Strategies for the Green Economy*

Guerrilla Marketing to Heal the World proves marketing and making the world a better place are not mutually exclusive. Jay Conrad Levinson and Shel Horowitz demonstrate how you can build a better business based on ethical, Green and value-centered principles.

—**Michael Port**, New York Times best-selling author of
The Think Big Manifesto, MichaelPort.com/

Taking a long-overdue holistic approach, *Guerrilla Marketing to Heal the World* shows business how to heal the world—not through guilt and shame, but by weaving the profit motive into this work and honorably embracing core business values that honor humanity and the planet.

—**Alicia Bay Laurel**, author of *Living On the Earth*, AliciaBayLaurel.com/

In a world filled with shameless self-promoters and hype-filled hucksters, Shel Horowitz and Jay Conrad Levinson stand out as honest, ethical marketers. I like the clear, high-content, value-based, forthright approach to selling with integrity they teach in *Guerrilla Marketing to Heal the World*, and from experience, I know their ideas can generate highly profitable results.

—**Bob Bly**, author of 80+ books and the man
McGraw-Hill calls "America's top copywriter," Bly.com

Green, social change marketing is here for good. This book will show you how to market, influence others and resonate with the times. The advice is simple and the premise is compelling—read this and join the 21st century.

—**Tim Sanders**, author of *Saving The World At Work*,
Love is the Killer App, etc., TimSanders.com

When it comes to finding your voice online or offline, it takes much more than transparency and authenticity. It takes connectivity and inspiration. Jay and Shel are no strangers to helping brands and entrepreneurs build creative and effective channels to reach and attract customers. Now they're helping businesses increase profitability through green, socially conscious, and eco-friendly strategies and services that also benefit our environment. Build in a higher purpose or go home!

—**Brian Solis**, leading digital analyst and best-selling author, @briansolis

In Jay Levinson's and Shel Horowitz's world, people do matter. The book combines the best of marketing and relationship theory with real-world examples and practical advice to create a winning, inspirational package. If we all adopted their advice to create value for others in everything that we do, the world would be a better place.

—**Melanie Rigney**, former Editor of Writer's Digest magazine/Editorial Director of Writer's Digest Trade Books, author of *Sisterhood of Saints*, MelanieRigney.com/

Guerrilla Marketing to Heal the World is a clear call to action and a magnificent mandate for the rewards of our better nature. Jay Conrad Levinson and Shel Horowitz enlighten you with a bright new world and give you a clear manifesto for feeling good about yourself as you reap bigger profits and create a better, more ethical place to live and work in. This book will IMPACT!

—**Ken McArthur**, best-selling author of *Impact: How to Get Noticed, Motivate Millions and Make a Difference in a Noisy World* and founder of JVAlertLive.com

No message could be more timely than Jay Conrad Levinson's and Shel Horowitz's. In the long run, only an ethical approach to marketing works.

—**Al Ries**, author of several best-selling marketing books including *Positioning, The 22 Immutable Laws of Marketing, and The Fall of Advertising and the Rise of PR*, Ries.com

Good marketing is about doing things right, but more importantly about doing the right thing. *Guerrilla Marketing to Heal the World* will show you how to be more successful by doing both.

—**Brian Jud**, Executive Director of the Association of Publishers for Special Sales, BookAPSS.org/

A course in marketing for mensches. Stop wallowing in the sleazy world of dog-eat-dog business and learn how making the world better will actually improve your bottom line! *Guerrilla Marketing to Heal the World* is the wave of the future. Books on green, ethical, socially beneficial business practices, like this one, are sorely needed in today's world. This is one of the best books on the topic that I've seen. Buy it for your CEO.

—**Fern Reiss**, Director of PublishingGame.com

Very wise words from very wise men. Shel and Jay are seasoned marketing pros who not only talk the talk, but walk the walk...of business both making a real difference in the world—and making a profit. Their brilliance shines through and their methods will not only help you to make lots of money, but to feel great while doing so. And that, in essence, is free enterprise—that the money you make is directly proportionate to how many people you serve and how well you serve them. Follow the advice of *Guerrilla Marketing to Heal the World*. Your current customers, your new customers, and your bank account will be richer for it.

—**Bob Burg**, author of *Endless Referrals*, co-author of *The Go-Giver*, Burg.com/

The essential key to marketing is making friends, creating relationships. My friend and competitor Shel Horowitz explains in clear terms why those two roles are in harmony and not conflict, and how serving the most underserved can build on this idea. A must read for anyone who wants to understand the new way of doing business and doing it well.

—**John Kremer**, author of *1001 Ways to Market Your Books*, BookMarket.com

It's about time someone wrote a book about the way things REALLY work at the values, ethics, and service levels in the marketplace. Yes, there are scandals and scoundrels in business. But they're truly in the minority. Because the people who last... the people with whom others most want to do business... the people who set the pace for the rest... are quietly and consistently principled individuals operating to help the world overcome its hardest problems. This book spells out what those people are doing and why it's to your advantage to follow their lead.

—**David Garfinkel**, best-selling author of *Breakthrough Copywriting*, DavidGarfinkel.com/

Jay Conrad Levinson and Shel Horowitz show, on every page, that not only can business succeed by tackling hunger, poverty, war, and climate change, but that doing so can change the world. Doing the right thing not only feels good, it works. *Guerrilla Marketing to Heal the World* should be required reading in every marketing class.

—**Mary Westheimer**, Marketing Director of Kevin Caron Studios, L.L.C., kevincaron.com

Creating socially responsible businesses is not only a good thing to do, but it will give you company a unique competitive advantage. And *Guerrilla Marketing to Heal the World* shows you how to do that. This book will give you dozens of new and fresh green ideas about how to not only market your business responsibility, but break new ground in solving the world's most pressing problems—AND beat the pants off your competitors.

—**David Frey**, author of *The Small Business Marketing Bible*, MarketingBlogger.com

This is a refreshing, wonderful, and practical book. Jay Conrad Levinson and Shel Horowitz tell you that integrity is not naiveté and that you can stand up for what you believe in and still make a profit. I'd like to thank the authors… Bravo!

—**Jeffrey Eisenberg**, New York Times best-selling co-author of *Waiting for Your Cat to Bark, Call to Action,* and other books, @JeffreyGroks

GUERRILLA MARKETING

– TO –
HEAL
THE WORLD

*Combining Principles and Profit
to Create the World We Want*

JAY CONRAD LEVINSON
AND SHEL HOROWITZ

New York

GUERRILLA MARKETING TO HEAL THE WORLD
Combining Principles and Profit to Create the World We Want

Published in New York, New York, by Morgan James Publishing. Morgan James and The Entrepreneurial Publisher are trademarks of Morgan James, LLC.
www.MorganJamesPublishing.com

The Morgan James Speakers Group can bring authors to your live event. For more information or to book an event visit The Morgan James Speakers Group at
www.TheMorganJamesSpeakersGroup.com.

A **free** eBook edition is available
with the purchase of this print book.

CLEARLY PRINT YOUR NAME ABOVE IN UPPER CASE

Instructions to claim your free eBook edition:
1. Download the BitLit app for Android or iOS
2. Write your name in **UPPER CASE** on the line
3. Use the BitLit app to submit a photo
4. Download your eBook to any device

ISBN 978-1-63047-658-8 paperback
ISBN 978-1-63047-659-5 eBook
Library of Congress Control Number:
2015907450

Cover Design by:
Rachel Lopez
www.r2cdesign.com

Interior Design by:
Bonnie Bushman
The Whole Caboodle Graphic Design

In an effort to support local communities and raise awareness and funds, Morgan James Publishing donates a percentage of all book sales for the life of each book to Habitat for Humanity Peninsula and Greater Williamsburg.

Get involved today, visit
www.MorganJamesBuilds.com

Habitat
for Humanity®
Peninsula and
Greater Williamsburg
Building Partner

DEDICATION

I dedicate this book to Al Gore, who has put his heart where his mind is.

—**Jay Conrad Levinson**

To the wonderful visionary activists who have spent their lives working for peace, environmental/social justice, especially those I've known personally, including Wally and Juanita Nelson, Dave Dellinger, Frances Crowe, George Lakey, and many others. And to the practical visionaries who show over and over again that business can and should be part of the solution. Some of you are cited in these pages, including Amory Lovins, Janine Benyus, Sir Richard Branson, Ray Anderson, John Todd, Ben Cohen and Jerry Greenfield, Barbara Waugh, Van Jones, Majora Carter, Bob Burg and John Kremer, among others.

And to my wonderful children, Alana Horowitz Friedman, Rafael Horowitz Friedman, and Bobby Hirtle. Carry the torch forward!

—**Shel Horowitz**

TABLE OF CONTENTS

LIST OF ILLUSTRATIONS

SPECIAL BONUSES
FOR READING THIS BOOK

Congratulations on picking up this book. It will be your guide to establishing or expanding a business that has a mission to help transform one or more of our biggest problems into a win-win-win—for the people facing those issues, for your profitable business, and for the planet. *Guerrilla Marketing to Heal the World* contains plenty of wisdom from "practical visionaries" who walk their talk and make profits by making changes.

But we wanted to give you even more. And so, we offer you these extra bonuses, just for sharing this journey with us.

1. A no-charge fifteen-minute consultation with Shel, on any aspect of social change or green business profitability and marketing, green business/green lifestyle, social entrepreneurship, or book publishing. NOTE: You must fill a questionnaire and show that you're serious. Also, to maximize your benefit from this free consultation, please read the entire book and set a clear goal for what you'd like to accomplish. You'll find instructions on claiming this bonus later in the book.

2. A free copy of Shel's $9.95 ebook, Painless Green: 111 Tips to Help the Environment, Lower Your Carbon Footprint, Cut Your Budget, and Improve Your Quality of Life—With No Negative Impact on Your Lifestyle, offering easy free/inexpensive tips to save energy, water, and other resources.

3. Seven Tips to Gain Marketing Traction as a Green Guerrilla (immediately on confirming your subscription, Seven Weeks to a Greener Business (once a week for seven weeks), and Shel's monthly Clean and Green Business newsletter. Each issue of the newsletter includes a main article with powerful strategies or profile of a successful conscious business, as well as a review of a recommended book. Shel has been publishing a marketing newsletter online all the way back to 1997, making him one of the longest-running marketing newsletter publishers on the Internet. Of course, you can unsubscribe at any time—but we think you're going to want to read this one. In fact, if you use Gmail, we suggest that you drag your first issue from the Promotions folder to Primary, and say yes when Gmail asks if it should do that from now on.

4. An 18-page Special Report, Practical Tools for Effective Marketing, that guides you through working with mainstream media, using social media effectively, traditional direct mail, and even marketing with apparel.

Claim your gifts at http://impactwithprofit.com/giftsforreaders (yes, you'll need to give your name and email address).

ACKNOWLEDGMENTS

I owe acknowledgements to many enlightened souls, the most important of whom is co-author Shel Horowitz, who braved the battles of apathy and ignorance in causing this book to rise from the ashes and alight in your consciousness and indeed, the consciousness of all citizens of planet earth, our home sweet home.

—Jay Conrad Levinson

"It takes a village" to make a book. Thanks to (in alphabetical order within each category)…

- Those sources who kindly gave permission for me to quote or reprint large chunks of their material: Eric Anderson, Kare Anderson, Tom Antion, Stefan Apse and Susan Witt of the Schumacher Center For New Economics, Bill Baue of CSRWire, Christopher Bauer, Mary Boyle of Common Cause, Mike Brady and Katherine M. Harris of Greyston Bakery, Bob Burg, Patrick Byers, Melissa Chungfat of Ecopreneurist, Beth Craig of Webcom, Seth Godin, Hazel Henderson, John Kremer, Wendy Kurtz, Amory Lovins, Perry Marshall, Myelita Melton, Robert Middleton, Terry Mollner, B.L. Ochman, Jacquelyn Ottman, Martin

Ping, Jode Roberts of Ecojustice, John Todd, Al Vital of Fidlar-Doubleday, Barbara Waugh, David Wood.

- David Hancock, Margo Toulouse, Nickcole Watkins, Jim Howard, Terry Whalin, Rich Frishman, and Jessica Howard at Morgan James Publishing—and especially David, for his unflagging championing of this book from the moment he heard it might be a possibility. Also Cynthia Frank of Cypress House for providing advice on rendering screenshots at high enough quality to reproduce in print.

- The many smart and creative people who have added so much to the world's understanding of Green principles, the role of business in social change, people-centered marketing strategies, and social media in the years since I wrote *Principled Profit* and *Guerrilla Marketing Goes Green*.

- The late Jay Conrad Levinson, for being an enthusiastic supporter of our original collaboration, his widow, Jeannie Levinson, for facilitating this updated collaboration, and his daughter, Amy Levinson, for keeping the Guerrilla Marketing community in the loop. And all the Guerrilla Marketing co-authors for helping to create a savvy and successful brand that stands the test of time.

- The more than 100 people who have endorsed, blurbed, or favorably reviewed *Guerrilla Marketing to Heal the World* or its two predecessors.

- My wife, novelist D. Dina Friedman, for 37 years of encouragement, constructive criticism, and love

—**Shel Horowitz**

If you've already read *Principled Profit: Marketing That Puts People First* or *Guerrilla Marketing Goes Green*

Guerrilla Marketing to Heal the World is based heavily on our earlier book, *Guerrilla Marketing Goes Green*—which, in turn, is based on Shel's earlier book *Principled Profit: Marketing That Puts People*. But fear not! First, there's a great deal of new material here. Each time, the book has been updated, expanded, and refocused, with more than 20,000 words of fresh content. Eight chapters have been added, and almost every chapter includes new examples, new research—and often, whole sections. We expect that you will receive substantial value from this book, even though some of it will be familiar.

GREEN MARKETING IS A MANDATE FROM NATURE

I've believed from the start that marketing is part of evolution. It helps the world go round and is part of mass communications, so it greases the skids of progress inside and outside the mind.

Imagine my delight to team up with Shel and be able to generate the green ideas that will help evolution, which does not exclude the generating of more greenbacks for your paperless bank account. In fact, that's the whole purpose of this book—to prove that successful green guerrilla marketing can contribute to your financial well-being as well as the well-being of your entire planet, now and in the future.

It isn't as though you have a choice of green guerrilla marketing and standard guerrilla marketing. Instead, it's to prove to you that the two go hand in hand in a mutual effort towards making the best of two worlds while making both worlds the best they can be.

When I wrote the first Guerrilla Marketing book in 1984, this was an alien concept. But life has changed since that date. Finally, civilization has caught on to the idea that we can do something about the deteriorating state of the environment and about beautifying our planet. Amazingly, at the same time, you can do your part to beautify your own bottom line.

What we say in this book is not theory. It is a call to action. It is a mandate from nature.

TASTES GREAT AND GOOD FOR YOU

You start with a fresh organic mesclun salad, savor your beautiful healthy entrée, lick your lips to get the last crumb of that amazing vegan brownie, and wash it all down with a few sips of all-natural premium beer. It's hard to imagine that just a few decades ago, if you wanted to dine out, you were told you had to choose between healthy and tasty. Either your plate was full of unappetizing piles of healthy mush, or with something delicious but deadly. But now, the world knows that great food can also be healthy.

Similarly, in marketing, we've been told most of our lives that we had to choose between *value* and *values*. But like the choice between healthy and scrumptious, that's a false choice. It turns out that when we create companies based in core values of green awareness, high standards of ethics, cooperation, and service, *our marketing actually works better—and costs much less*. And when we go beyond our own bottom lines to create businesses that actively heal the world, we can do even better.

This book is designed to redefine what the business world thinks of as possible, and to show through hundreds of powerful examples that not only can we *succeed by baking our values into our business practices*, the path of success is noticeably easier.

It's not new with us; wise people at least as far back as Confucius have recognized that a social conscience makes business better, and conscious business makes the world better. Napoleon Hill studied the most successful people of his day for 25 years. He wrote in *Think and Grow Rich*, published in 1937,

> No wealth or position can long endure, unless built upon truth and justice, therefore, I will engage in no transaction which does not benefit all whom it affects. I will succeed by attracting to myself the forces I wish to use, and the cooperation of other people. I will induce others to serve me, because of my willingness to serve others. I will eliminate hatred, envy, jealousy, selfishness, and cynicism, by developing love for all humanity...[1]

In this book, you'll learn to set a course for the smooth channel of success, instead of the rocky shoals of stress—by helping customers and ecosystems meet or surpass their goals.

(We primarily use "customers" as a generic term for "the people you serve," "prospects" for those considering doing business, and "consumers" to describe people who purchase products and services. In our own practices, we—like other providers of professional services—have clients. Other organizations have students or patients. Substitute whatever term works for you.)

Beyond operating your own successful business, this book will show over and over again that business can shape the world: developing profitable offerings that turn hunger and poverty into sufficiency, war and violence into peace, and catastrophic climate change into planetary balance—possibly the most exciting set of tasks the business world has ever taken on, and well within the realm of possibility.

Fasten your seat belts; it's an exciting ride!

---

1   *Think and Grow Rich*, Chapter 3—Faith Visualization of, and Belief in Attainment of Desire, as step 5 in a five-step Self-Confidence Formula, appearing on p. 45 of a PDF facsimile edition with no marks identifying the publisher or the year. It can also be heard at just about the two-hour mark in the audio version found at http://gazpo.com/video/ motivational/1061/napoleon-hill-think-and-grow-rich-video, accessed 2/9/15.

PART I

THE WAY OF
THE GOLDEN RULE

CHAPTER 1

BECAUSE PEOPLE MATTER

People *do* matter—as do animals, plants, ecosystems, and Planet Earth. You can be a successful marketer while keeping your actions ethical, aligned with environmental principles, and fostering a greater good: the end of hunger, poverty, war, and catastrophic climate change. Not only don't you have to be crooked or mean-spirited to succeed in business, the success strategies of a business formed in an attitude of abundance and grounded in ethics and cooperation, respect for nature, and a big-picture vision of a society that works are powerful and long-lasting. These values also help you feel good about yourself as you bring in profits.

Your parents and teachers probably taught you to treat others the way you want to be treated, play fair, and cooperate. Make these principles a cornerstone of your business, and that design marketing that not only follows this precept, but brings success and abundance into your life.

Too many businesses see marketing as a weapon of war. They think that to succeed, they have to climb over their competitors, fool their customers, and herd their employees into constricted conformity. We think that's just plain wrong.

Our whole premise is that when businesses embrace the world's abundance, stop seeing their competitors as a threat, protect the planet, and take on a higher purpose, magic can happen. We invite you to stop thinking of business as win-lose and begin to think of it as win-win-win; design that business so that you, the community of stakeholders (customers, competitors, abutters, suppliers, etc.), and Earth all win. Think of your business not only as a stand-alone entity, but as part of an industry, a town, a region, human culture, and the whole planet.

BUSINESS CAN—AND WILL—CHANGE THE WORLD

Business has enormous potential to better the world—to overcome the huge problems that have plagued human society since the beginning of time. For the first time in history, we don't have to let ourselves be hammered down by the threats of poverty, war, and environmental disaster. *We have the technology, the know-how, to fix these things.* And this book is your road map.

We make some assumptions about this throughout the book, and we want to share them with you right from the start:

- While we may differ on what that means, we all want to preserve and improve our world, which is at risk
- The measures we take to preserve and improve humanity and the planet turn out to be very profitable—and that's a good thing
- The Triple Bottom Line (combining financial, environmental, and social metrics) and corporate social responsibility (CSR) are business success strategies—and we can go beyond them to create the world we want
- Business, creativity, and community are our three most powerful tools to eliminate or sharply reduce hunger and poverty, war, and catastrophic climate change—when we join them together, we can achieve this wonderful new world
- We are empowered individuals, and each of us can make a difference; changemakers throughout history were just as ordinary as we are; we make a bigger difference when we work with others

We'll be exploring these ideas throughout the rest of the book.

MARKETING AS COURTSHIP

Marketing is a series of partnerships—of courtships, really. Businesses that succeed with this model understand that they have to woo their customers, just as a suitor woos for the chance to marry. And just as a successful marriage is built on years of mutual communication and meeting each other's needs, successful marketing looks for a deep and long-lasting relationship based on meeting the needs and wants of everyone involved. That means your customers, your employees, your suppliers, and, yes, even your competitors. You can knock someone's socks off on the first date, but if you betray that trust afterwards, you become your own biggest obstacle on the road to success.

And just like a courtship, you want to go as fast as possible but as slow as necessary. The singles scene is littered with the carcasses of relationships that never went anywhere because on the first contact, one person came on too heavy, too fast, or too self-involved. Many businesses fail when companies spend so much time crowing about how great they are, they forget to listen to their prospects.

Always remember that, like successful romance, successful marketing is about how you can add value for the other person. And the most effective way to add value is by developing a long-term positive relationship with the customer.

So stay out of marketing divorce court; be there for the long term. It takes work to achieve a successful, long-lasting marriage, but the rewards are worth it. Similarly, you have to work at successful long-term mutual-benefit relationships with all the other interest groups that interact with your business.

Remember too that in our Internet era, scandals and problems never go away. In 2015, a Google search for "business scandals 2014) turns up more than 15 million articles, with results involving Walmart, Hewlett-Packard, the National Football League, and General Motors all on the first page.[2] That number goes up to 36 million if we remove the date.

---

2   Accessed 3/9/15.

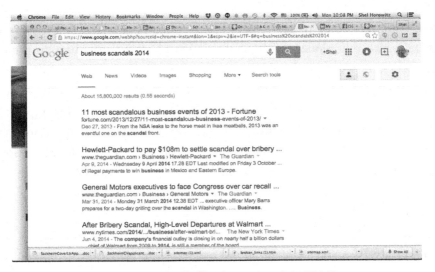

Google search for "business scandals 2014"

Just as a romance that's based on false promises and miscommunication is doomed to failure, business relationships based on greed and backed by false promises aren't going to work long-term. But the good news is that if you treat others well, they'll become your best marketers. The better you treat others, the more they will not just to *do* business with you, but to *bring business to you.*

You make your own success by helping others succeed—you succeed without selling your soul. Think about this style of business as a practical, day-to-day expression of the old Golden Rule: Do unto others as you would like others to do unto you—a precept found in every major religion.[3]

Although both Jay and Shel believe very strongly in the Golden Rule, this is not a religious book. Rather, it's based on a code of ethics. Your ethics might or might not be religiously based; the important thing is that you have an ethical basis for your professional or business behavior.

The modern business world doesn't always assume that business should be based on ethics. But we do. We'll assume that you're reading this book because

---

3   Stephen Apatow of the UK-based Humanitarian Resource Institute, in his "The Golden Rule Principle: Global Religious Leaders Called to Re-Focus on This Universal Objective of the Interfaith Community," cites 13 examples from primary religious texts, from Buddhism to Zoroastrianism http://www.humanitarian.net/interfaith/goldenrule.html, verified 4/5/15.

you really want to do what's right; but perhaps you've been steeped in so many years of Nice Guys Finish Last that you aren't sure it's really possible to succeed, thrive, and be profitable while doing the right thing. We're here to tell you that you *can* succeed and still keep your conscience. In this book, you'll encounter many success stories that put a practical handle on this philosophy. You'll see that others are doing very well by doing good, and that you can too.

Spend an hour or two with this book, and you may find that you no longer need to live in a dog-eat-dog world—and that in fact, when the dogs learn to work together, they can accomplish much more than any of them could on their own. Think of the incredible weight a team of sled dogs can comfortably pull across the snow—far greater than any single dog could manage. And thus, when you join forces with others—even those you've been trained to think of as your competitors—truly amazing things can happen.

This is an opinionated and personal book; we make no pretense otherwise. It is based on our combined 80+ years in marketing. We've built thriving decades-old businesses using the principles in this book. And we want you to do at least as well.

LESSONS
- Marketing is a like a romance: subtlety works better
- The Golden Rule actually works in business
- Success is not only compatible with ethics, it's easier
- For the first time in history, we have the power to end poverty, hunger, war, and catastrophic climate change

ACTIONS
- Think about three times when you did the right thing even if it felt hard.
- Replay a time you didn't do the right thing, and describe how you would do it differently.

CHAPTER 2

BASIC CONCEPTS

THE ROAD TO YOUR SUCCESS: PROVIDING VALUE TO OTHERS

In the business world, we hear a lot about cutthroat competition and gaining advantage over the enemy. In some circles, it seems to be a game to see how best to cheat your customers.

These are the concepts of win–lose marketing, which leads eventually to lose-lose marketing. This "dinosaur thinking" won't survive.

This book is about Marketing That Puts People First. Most of the time, everyone can win—nobody has to lose. Not only can you succeed in business by doing the right thing—with every person and business that interacts with you—but often, it's the only way to succeed.

Don't take our word for it—listen to some experts:

Consumers Prefer to Buy from Companies That Support Their Social Agenda

In 2014, a series of studies by Havas PR found that worldwide, 34 percent of consumers actually make purchasing decisions based on social responsibility[4]—

---

4   http://havaspr.com/?page_id=2343, accessed 2/11/15.

that's one in three consumers. By December, 2014, that number had leapt to 43 percent, according to a survey by Tiller, LLC.[5]

The Tiller study offered several other fascinating results, among them:

- 83 percent of Americans are seeking opportunities to go greener
- 85 percent want to leave the world greener for their children
- 90 percent feel recycling and conservation are important
- 60 percent are worried about a major environmental catastrophe in the future
- 78 percent want corporations to adopt green behaviors—and 72 percent don't care about companies' motivation for going greener; they just want them to get on with it[6]

When price and quality are equal, 76 percent of consumers would switch brands or retailers to a company associated with a good cause. Criteria frequently cited by consumers as affecting their purchasing decisions include environmental responsibility, community philanthropy, and avoiding the use of "sweatshop" or child labor.[7]

Interestingly, one study found that the best predictor of whether a person will respond to eco-products even if they're more expensive is not income or education, but current or past contributions to environmental groups.[8]

Even research conducted during the late 2000s recession shows massive swings toward social consciousness. A remarkable November 2008 study by the PR superagency Edelman, long an advocate of trust-building, surveyed

5   Tiller, LLC, "Nationwide Survey Finds: Americans Believe Environmental Issues Pose Greater Long-Term Threat To Their Health and Well-Being than Terrorism or Global Epidemics like Ebola," press release at http://www.tillerllc.com/wp-content/uploads/2014/12/Tiller-Green-Survey-Press-Release-Final.pdf, accessed 4/6/15.
6   Tiller, LLC, op. cit.
7   Business for Social Responsibility's "Marketplace" White Paper, op. cit. (referencing a 1997 study by Walker Research).
8   Ottman, Jacquelyn, *Green Marketing: Opportunity for Innovation*, 2d Ed. (New York, J. Ottman Consulting, 1997), p. 20, citing Baugh, Keith, Brian Byrnes, Clive Jones, and Maribeth Rahimzadeh, "Gren Pricing: Removing the Guesswork," *Public Utilities Fortnightly*, August 1995, p. 27.

6000 consumers across 10 countries, and found extremely high numbers for social consciousness:

- 68 percent of consumers "would remain loyal to a brand during a recession if it supports a good cause"
- 71 percent have donated as much or more time and money to good causes despite the economic downturn
- 42 percent would choose a brand with commitment to a social purpose over design, innovation, or brand loyalty, if price and quality are equal
- 52 percent would recommend a brand that supports a good cause over one that doesn't, and 54 percent would actually promote the product to support the cause
- An astonishing 87 percent feel an obligation to contribute to a better society and environment; 83 percent would change their own consumption habits to help create that better world
- 76 percent prefer to buy from brands that give to worthy causes [9]

Equally fascinating: a Washington Post study ranked 498 major corporations for social responsibility and compared market performance during the 2008-09 downturn. Performance among the top-rated companies equaled or surpassed the whole market. But even more remarkably, the lowest ranked companies— Eastman Chemical, Lockheed Martin, and ExxonMobil—"turned out to be less interested in talking about the limitations of corporate responsibility than explaining what they were doing to achieve it." [10]

Also in 2014, we learned from Commit Forum that 71 percent of Americans would prefer to be employed by "a company whose CEO is actively involved in

---

9   "Despite Economic Crisis, Consumers Value Brands' Commitment To Social Purpose, Global Study Finds: Strong Personal Beliefs in Making a Difference Signal Opportunity for Marketers," http://www.prnewswire.com/news-releases/despite-economic-crisis-consumers-value-brands-commitment-to-social-purpose-global-study-finds-65450537.html, verified 4/5/15.

10   Flavelle, Christopher, "Responsibility Is Still Good For Business," Washington Post, February 15, 2009, http://www.washingtonpost.com/wp-dyn/content/article/2009/02/14/AR2009021400094.html, verified 4/5/15.

corporate responsibility and/or environmental issues."[11]—and that 53 percent reward eco-friendly companies with repeat purchases.[12]

And green concepts have clearly entered the public consciousness; a Google search for "global warming" (exact match) plus 2002 yields 5,740,000 hits; by 2008, the results multiply almost five-fold, to 25,100,000. That had almost doubled again by 2015, to 49,800,000. Searching for "climate change" shows similar gains, from 8,180,000 for 2002 to 36,100,000 for 2008,[13] and 105,000,000 (almost three times as much) by 2015.[14]

This awareness not only permeates consumers, but reaches business school students, too. A fascinating article in Business Week documents a strong trend among students at top-flight b-schools toward not just caring about green and socially conscious values, but looking to start entrepreneurial ventures in line with those commitments, such as a solar-powered trash compactor manufacturer, or a retailer positioning itself as "the Whole Foods of hardware."[15] This social consciousness seems stronger among women[16] and particularly strong among Millennials—who are just beginning their several decades of active adult consumerism.

Many consumers also actively support companies that court business from their ethnic or subculture group. By 2014, African-Americans controlled $157 billion in US discretionary spending and Latino-Americans, $197 billion;[17]

---

11 http://www.commitforum.com/index.php/the-cost-bad-reputation-the-impacts-corporate-reputation-talent-acquisition/, accessed 2/11/15

12 "The State of Sustainability in America Report: Trends & Opportunities," Natural Marketing Institute, 2014, p. 28. PDF of highlights: http://www.nmisolutions.com/opt/excerpts/1502/NMI-2015-State-of-Sustainability-in-America-Excerpts-1-19-2015.pdf, accessed 2/20/15.

13 Searches conducted 12/31/08

14 2015 searches conducted 2/11/15.

15 http://www.businessweek.com/smallbiz/content/sep2008/sb2008098_742970.htm, verified 4/5/15.

16 Ibid.

17 http://www.marketingcharts.com/traditional/african-americans-and-hispanics-combine-for-one-fifth-of-estimated-national-discretionary-spending-41922/, accessed 3/10/15.

people with disabilities controlled $220 billion as far back as 2001.[18] A more recent study estimates gay and lesbian purchasing power at $835 billion.[19]

In the online world, male Americans and Western Europeans who embraced the Internet early are being supplanted by users of color, often female, often from non-Western countries: Women are now a majority of Net users—and of the 29 million new Internet users that joined the online community from 2008 to 2011, 54 percent were likely Hispanic, African American, or Asian.[20] Marketers who ignore this massive demographic shift do so at their peril.

These types of loyalties extend beyond mere demographics—into values:

Another growing area is cause-related marketing, in which companies align with charities or causes in a marketing campaign. Such campaigns have become increasingly common as consumers become more accepting of the concept. For many companies, the question no longer is whether they will engage in cause-related marketing, but which cause to embrace.[21]

Actually, not only have consumers become more accepting of social and environmental responsibility, they've begun to demand it. Companies that refuse to embrace sustainability values will be left to a world of diminishing markets, falling profits, and increasing lawsuits. More than ever before, today's consumer wants to feel a part of solving the world's pressing problems, from global warming to child toy safety, from treatment of farm workers to getting out from under the thumb of foreign oil.

We see this in the enormous growth of Fair Trade and organic products, the Buy Local movement, and the backlash against highly processed foods with their transfats and unpronounceable ingredients.

And we see it in the vast stream of social and environmental responsibility initiatives from the world's largest companies—firms like General Electric,

---

18   Witeck-Combs Communications, "America's Disability Market at a Glance," http://www.witeck.com/wp/files/Americas-Disability-Market-at-a-Glance-FINAL-5-25-2006.pdf, accessed 3/10/15.

19   "Achieving Impressive R.O.I. with The Gay Consumer Market," Howard Buford, president, Prime Access, Inc., http://www.lsu.edu/raceandmedia/gay-consumer-market.pdf, accessed 4/5/15..

20   Basin, Neeta, "Meet the South Asians," Diversity Business, November 2008, http://www.diversitybusiness.com/news/supplierdiversity/45200763.asp, verified 4/5/15.

21   Business for Social Responsibility's "Marketplace" White Paper, op. cit

Siemens, Boeing, Toyota, Walmart, and Dow—to not only initiate cost-cutting initiatives based on green principles but to market the heck out of these commitments.[22]

We see it too in the rapid and widespread worldwide adoption by more than 450 key financial institutions, managing assets totaling $18 *trillion*, of the UN's Principles for Responsible Investment, which require signers to consider "environmental, social and corporate governance (ESG) issues within their investment decisions and processes."[23]

We even see it in the growing shift among MBA and BBA programs toward including ethics and sustainability in the core curriculum, and in the eagerness of such mainstream organizations as the *Wall Street Journal* and the *Financial Times* to rate corporate social responsibility (CSR) in their evaluations of business schools.[24]

Consumers Avoid Buying from—and Put Pressure On— Companies They Perceive As Unethical

As far back as 1998, a study commissioned by the UK-based Cooperative Wholesale Services found that 60 percent of retail food customers, even in the absence of an organized boycott, have avoided a shop or product they associated with unethical behavior. A 1999 survey of consumers in 23 countries by Environics International, in cooperation with The Prince of Wales Business Leaders Forum and The Conference Board, found that 40 percent of consumers had considered punishing a company based on its social actions, and nearly 20 percent had actually avoided a company's products because of its social actions.[25]

---

22 See, among many examples, "Outlook 2008: Marketers Face Challenges from Economy to Ecology," BtoB Magazine, December 10, 2007, and "Walmart Announces New Ethical and Environmental Principles," by Stephanie Rosenbloom, International Herald-Tribune, October 22, 2008, http://www.nytimes.com/2008/10/22/business/worldbusiness/22iht-walmart.4.17172614.html?_r=0, cited by Chris MacDonald in The Business Ethics Blog, http://businessethicsblog.com/2008/10/22/wal-mart-flexes-its-muscles/, both verified 4/5/15..

23 Robins, Ron, "Reminder: Responsible Investing Forum, January 12-13, New York City," email blast from investngfortheosul.com, December 31, 2008

24 McElhaney, Kellie A., *Just Good Business: The Strategic Guide to Aligning Corporate Responsibility and Brand* (San Francisco: Berrett-Koehler, 2008), page ix.

25 Business for Social Responsibility's "Marketplace" White Paper, http://www.bsr.org/BSRResources/WhitePaperDetail.cfm?DocumentID=269. Downloaded Jan. 16, 2003.

Individuals don't just act alone. Shareholder activism and widely publicized boycotts force companies to negotiate from a position of perceived weakness. These have built momentum since at least the 1950s, when the Montgomery, Alabama bus boycott organized by Dr. Martin Luther King, Jr. and others struck a powerful blow against racial segregation. In 2014 alone, IW Financial documented 334 activist shareholder resolutions just on the environment[26]— not even counting other issues ranging from CEO pay to sweatshops.

In an earlier case, a UK-based insurance association that owned shares in ExxonMobil actually sent a press release opposing the reappointment of CEO Lee Raymond on environmental grounds.[27]

If groups like Corporate Accountability International (formerly known as INFACT), the Interfaith Center on Corporate Responsibility, or major labor unions organize shareholder actions or call a boycott, it is not only very bad for the targeted business, but can even bring down governments; divestment campaigns spurred the collapse of the apartheid regime in South Africa.

Be seen as a leader, not a Johnny-come-lately forced to the table by threats. Avoid profit-killing shareholder initiatives and consumer boycotts; take a proactive and very public stance in favor of socially, economically, and environmentally responsible behavior—the "triple bottom line."

Investors Have Shifted 21.4 Trillion into Socially Responsible Companies

In November 1999, the Social Investment Forum reported that more than $2 trillion—an increase of 82 percent from 1997 levels—was invested in the United States in funds identified as socially responsible investing (SRI—also called by

---

This source has been taken down, but another study, conducted in 2003, showed that the $230-billion Lifestyles of Health and Sustainability (LOHAS) demographic accounted for nearly 1/3 of all American households even then, and 51% of these 68 million Americans make values-based buying decisions: http://www.npicenter.com/anm/templates/ newsATemp.aspx?articleid=4469&zoneid=3, verified July 6, 2009.

26 "Companies face record number of shareholder resolutions urging action on environmental issues," http://news.iwfinancial.com/corporate-sustainability/companies-face-record-number-of-shareholder-resolutions-urging-action-on-environmental-issues/, accessed 3/10/15.

27 "CIS Opposes Election of Exxon Mobil Chief for 'Head in the Sand' Approach to Climate Change," http://www.prnewswire.co.uk/cgi/news/release?id=146589, May 23, 2005.

several other terms: "ethical investing", "green investing", "impact investing", "values-based investing", to name a few)—and one of every eight investment dollars was engaged in SRI.[28] By 2013, that amount had more than tripled, to at least $6.57 trillion, and the percentage was up to one in every six investment dollars (16.6 percent).[29]

In fact, the growth in socially screened investment dollars just from $2 trillion in 1999 to $2.7 trillion by 2007 about equaled the $700 billion bailout of the US financial industry in the fall of 2008. World-wide, SRI investments passed $21.4 trillion by early 2014.[30]

On the private investment side, take a look at investment funds set up specifically for SRI (in other words, not counting the much broader picture of investments in socially responsible companies through more general funds). The market went from 55 SRI funds in 1995, with $12 billion in assets, to 201 funds managing $179 billion just a decade later.[31] The following decade, which included the 2007-08 financial crisis, saw a shakeout, and the numbers went down to 159 funds managing $102 billion[32]—still an eight-fold increase in 20 years.

A related trend, microlending, lets investors seed businesses among the poorest of the poor in developing countries, using a circle of borrowers that creates peer pressure to succeed and repay the loan; even with no collateral, microlending pioneer Grameen Bank, founded by Dr. Muhammad Yunus of Bangladesh, achieves 99 percent repayment. Typically, microlending organizations offer loans of $25 to $100. That can be enough to lift a family out of poverty by achieving some specific business goal that had been out of reach. The concept has spread to dozens of organizations, such as Kiva.org,

---

28   Business for Social Responsibility's "Marketplace" White Paper, op. cit.

29   US Sustainable Investment Forum, "SRI Basics," http://www.ussif.org/sribasics, accessed 3/10/15.

30   "2014 Global Sustainable Investment Review," http://www.gsi-alliance.org/wp-content/uploads/2015/02/GSIA_Review_download.pdf, accessed 4/7/15.

31   "The financial facts, figures, and bottom line of socially responsible investing," as posted in this page accessed in 2009 and now only available via archive.org: https://web.archive.org/web/20110425064500/http://www.sristocks.com/Learning/Socially-responsible-investing-facts.html, accessed 4/5/15.

32   Total of $102,146,680,000 obtained by pasting each fund's total from a USSIF/Bloomberg chart at http://charts.ussif.org/mfpc/, accessed 3/10/15.

Accion, Finca, and many others.[33] Meanwhile, Dr. Yunus, who was awarded the 2006 Nobel Peace Prize for his work, has stated a goal of eliminating poverty by 2030.[34]

Does ending poverty sound overly ambitious? We submit that it's totally possible. Environmental consultant and author L. Hunter Lovins, of Natural Capitalism Solutions, points out that we've got plenty of resources, but our priorities could use some adjustment.

> Maybe we're buying the wrong stuff. What we pay for makeup would cover global reproductive health. Pet food could eliminate world hunger. We are using material purchases to meet nonmaterial needs. Nelson Mandela said, "Poverty is not an accident." We created and can uncreate it.[35]

It's not at all surprising that socially responsible investing is growing so rapidly. Here's a little secret: well-managed SRI funds often outperform the market.

- Socially responsible investment funds continue to demonstrate their ability to match or outperform their full market diversified counterparts. For example, the socially responsible MSCI KLD (formerly known as the Domini 400) has outperformed the S&P 500, with 11.75% and 11.21% annualized returns from socially responsible investments, respectively—posting returns of 12.72 percent for 2014, an incredible 36.20 percent in 2013, and 13.24 percent in 2012[36]. The S&P matched this fund with 12.72 percent in 2014, but only 22.11 in 2013 and 9.36 in 2012.[37]

---

33   http://en.wikipedia.org/wiki/Microlending, viewed May 23, 2009

34   Home page banner at http://www.muhammadyunus.org/, seen May 23, 2009. Text: "We will create a poverty museum by 2030. We will start with Bangladesh."

35   Talk by Hunter Lovins at Strengthening Ties for Collective Impact: Campus Sustainability in the Northeast Region conference, University of Massachusetts Amherst, April 9, 2015.

36   http://www.msci.com/resources/factsheets/index_fact_sheet/msci-kld-400-social-index.pdf, accessed 4/5/15.

37   http://dqydj.net/sp-500-return-calculator/, accessed 4/5/15.

- Individual companies with a commitment to social and environmental responsibility also outperform the overall market, even during a recession. Informal indices of firms named in The CRO Magazine's (formerly called Business Ethics) Top 100 routinely outperform the S&P 500, both short- and long-term.[38] The very mainstream consulting firm Booz Allen Hamilton, in partnership with the Aspen Institute, also found high correlation between ethics and financial performance.[39] A.T. Kearney tracked the market from May to November, 2008 (a period of drastic decline), and found:

> In 16 of the 18 industries examined, companies recognized as sustainability-focused outperformed their industry peers over both a three- and six-month period, and were well protected from value erosion. Over three months, the performance differential across the 99 companies in this analysis worked out to 10 percent; over six months, the differential was 15 percent...This performance differential translates to an average $650 million in market capitalization per company.[40]

In other words, not only can you have both values *and* profits, it's actually easier.

Customers, Investors, and Employees Like This Approach

Not only does the socially and environmentally responsible approach win friends among customers and investors, current and potential employees love it too. As

---

38 Among the numerous studies and news articles: Lee, Darren D. and Robert W. Faff, "Corporate Sustainability Performance and Idiosyncratic Risk: A Global Perspective," and Filbeck, Greg, Raymond Gorman and Xin Zhao, "The 'Best Corporate Citizens': Are they good for their shareholders?", both of which were published in *The Financial Review*, Volume 44, No. 2, May, 2009, and accessed March 31, 2009 from http://www. thefinancialreview.org/abstracts/Financial-Review-Abstracts-May-2009.html. MSNBC compared Domini's performance against the S&P in "Cause investing: Do-it-yourself giving Shareholder communities reward companies that champion social change," http://www. msnbc.msn.com/id/24863380/ , May 28, 2008.

39 "New Study Finds Link between Financial Success and Focus on Corporate Values," http:// www.csrwire.com/News/3511.html, verified 4/5/15.

40 A.T. Kearney, Inc., "Green Winners: the Performance of Sustainability-Focused Companies in the Financial Crisis," February 9, 2009, http://www.atkearney.com/ documents/10192/6972076a-9cdc-4b20-bc3a-d2a4c43c9c21, verified 4/5/15..

we've seen, studies that compare stock market performance of ethics-oriented and/or socially/environmentally conscious companies consistently report higher performance than the overall market.

Social Venture Network (http://www.svn.org) is a national membership organization committed to business as an instrument of social justice and environmental improvement—and many of its member companies hire and actively nurture employees who share these core values. In general, they stay profitable, enjoy enormous employee loyalty with minimal attrition, and often find that their employees do their recruiting when they need to fill positions.

And many of these companies approach the employer-employee relationship with the idea that employees have a lot more to contribute than just their labor on the job:

- Clif Bar funds employee community service projects during regular working hours, up to the equivalent of one full-time employee's entire year's work (2080 hours)[41]
- While Ben & Jerry's was still operated by Ben Cohen and Jerry Silverman, CEO pay never exceeded seven times the compensation of the lowest-paid full-time worker in the company[42]
- Greyston Bakery purposely located in a depressed area in Yonkers, New York, so that its success could lift the community, and uses an open hiring system for entry-level jobs, providing employment—and the training and support they need to turn their lives around—to people often seen as unemployable, such as those with disabilities or criminal records[43]

Today's employees are happier working for firms that share their values—but tomorrow's employees demand it. Achieve's 2013 Millennial Impact Research

41 Cohen, Ben and Mal Warwick, *Values-Driven Business: How to Change the World, Make Money, and Have Fun* (Social Venture Network series, San Francisco: Berrett-Koehler, 2006), pp. 36-37.
42 Ibid., p., 34.
43 Hammel, Laury and Gun Dehnhart, *Growing Local Value: How to Build Business Partnerships that Strengthen Your Community* (Social Venture Network series, San Francisco: Berrett-Koehler, 2007), pp. 64-67.

Report found that Millennials are amazingly active, with 83 percent donating to charity, 72 percent expressing interest in participating in a nonprofit-sponsored networking group, and 60 percent sharing stories about successful help-the-world projects on social media.[44]

This trend has been percolating for a while. The International Business Times reports on a November 2008 survey conducted by Top Employers Ltd of more than 1000 students at Britain's prestigious Oxford University and Cambridge University.[45] Just three factors were each cited by more than 70 percent of respondents: Life Balance (74 percent), Ethical Business Practices (72%), and Variety of Work (72%). Public service was tied (with media) for the top choice of industry to work in. Issues like salary and opportunity to advance were much lower on the list.

Interestingly, the study notes that recruitment spending by Britain's top companies has increased; they're having to work harder to recruit these talented grads, and social screens will probably be an ever-growing factor.

In the US, MarketWatch referred to a recent crop of MBA students as "the Zen class of 2010: They are seeking more social, environmental, and economic perspectives built into their education." And 79% would choose a job at an environmentally aware company over a conventional one.[46]

Going even farther, Harvard Business School professors Rakesh Khurana and Nitin Nohria call for businesses to take a "Green Hippocratic Oath": first do no harm—to the environment.[47]

In his book, *The Company We Keep: Reinventing Small Business for People, Community, and Place* (Chelsea Green, 2005), John Abrams describes his decision

---

44 AchieveGuidance.com, 2013 Millennial Impact Research Report , "http://cdn. trustedpartner.com/docs/library/AchieveMCON2013/Research%20Report/Millennial%20 Impact%20Research.pdf, accessed 3/11/15.

45 http://www.ibtimes.com/prnews/20081120/oxbridge-students-choose-work-life-balance-and-ethics-over-a-graduate-career-path.htm (no longer online)

46 Kostigan, Thomas, "MBA students see green as the way to go," http://www.marketwatch. com/news/story/mba-students-see-green-way/story.aspx?guid={50A42E30-51E3-4C7C-BB32-CBF3BFA38060}&dist=msr_1, verified 4/5/15.

47 "Should Managers Have a Green Hippocratic Oath?," Harvard Business Review, April 1, 2008, http://www.hbrgreen.org/2008/04/should_managers_have_a_green_h.html., verified 4/5/15.

to create a values-based construction firm and then eventually turn ownership over to his workers:

> The idea was to spread that control widely, so the voices of all the owners had meaning. You can't steal second without taking your foot off first, and we came to agree that the only protection needed [for Abrams and his wife, who lived on premises] was veto power over issues directly related to the property. (p. 33)

MARKETING FUNDAMENTALS: A QUICK RECAP

This is not a Marketing 101 book; we're assuming you already know the basics. Here's a quick review. If this is unfamiliar, you may want to put this book aside and read a marketing how-to book such as Shel's *Grassroots Marketing: Getting Noticed in a Noisy World*. Successful marketing:

- Attracts long-term customers or clients to you—honestly
- Recognizes that it's five to ten times cheaper—and more profitable— to bring existing customers back to purchase again and refer others than to prospect for new customers—and therefore 1) treats customers and prospects as intelligent, and 2) creates a delightful, high-quality experience
- Works best when it's not intrusive or hostile but speaks directly, as an ally, to prospects' desires and needs
- Goes far beyond paid advertising—using a wide range of strategies and tactics such as media publicity, partnerships, expertise-based marketing, speaking, social media, electronic and postal mail, the Web, and many others
- Paves the way for successful sales conversion

LESSONS
- Social responsibility attracts better employees and customers—and is more profitable

- As problems with the old model continue to surface, capital is shifting toward companies that can be trusted to do the right thing
- Social and environmental responsibility minimizes disruption and conflict and allows you to put resources toward your business goals

ACTIONS

- Examine your marketing materials—are you successfully reaching socially and environmentally conscious consumers? How could you speak more directly to them?
- If you can't answer this question, Shel will give you a 15-minute no-charge consultation—see page xx.

Chapter 3

ADVANTAGES OF DOING THE RIGHT THING

unning an ethical, green, socially conscious business is actually pretty simple (and these days, you can't call your business ethical if it ignores the environment). In fact, Frank C, Bucaro, author of *Trust Me! Insights Into Ethical Leadership* and *Taking The High Road: How To Succeed Ethically When Others Bend The Rules*, boils it down to saying yes to just two questions:

- Does the action meet company's objectives?
- Is it the right thing for the customer? [48]

And when you look at any number of performance indices—customer loyalty, stock performance, employee retention, and more—ethical behavior turns out to be very good for the companies that embrace it.

---

[48] Bucaro, Frank C., " Beyond the Bottom Line! What REALLY Matters Most?" The Ethics Update monthly e-newsletter, May 21, 2008. Bucaro's website is http://www.frankbucaro.com.

WHY RESPONSIBLE COMPANIES PERFORM BETTER

It makes total sense that socially responsible investments do better. Consider these factors:

- Clean-hands companies don't have to pay expensive lawsuit settlements around pollution, safety violations, or discrimination.
- If you tell only the truth, you don't worry about being caught in an embarrassing and profit-killing lie
- When customers believe that you have their best interests at heart, they come back again and again
- When customers fall in love with the way a company does business, they start recruiting other customers—they actually become that firm's unpaid sales force, and that leads to greater profits through reduced marketing expenditures (we'll talk more about this later).
- Ethical, eco-friendly companies are much more likely to build a lasting business, and build it more easily
- Joint ventures are much easier to organize, because the other partners expect that they'll be treated ethically and respected for what they bring
- The high value of goodwill will be factored into the sale price if the business is sold

And the number one reason...

> You never have to worry about seeing
> your picture on the front page, in handcuffs

Not surprisingly, socially and environmentally responsible companies perform well in the financial markets, too.

Merrill Lynch put the value of "values based investing" at $6.57 trillion by the end of 2013.[49] Earlier Merrill Lynch reports noted that "companies that ranked high in responsible economic, environmental, social and corporate governance issues demonstrated lower volatility globally and provided higher dividend yields

---

49   "Values and Impact Investing," https://www.ml.com/articles/values-and-impact-investing.html, accessed 4/5/15.

in the US than those with lower scores"[50] and that "the question, then, is no longer about whether VBI is profitable but about how individual investors can define their priorities around sustainable investing."[51]

In other words, CSR policies reduce investment risk. Which leads to wondering: would Merrill Lynch have gotten into so much trouble in 2007 and 2008 if the company had itself pushed an agenda of economic, environmental, and social responsibility?

The top-tier consulting company Deloitte wrote an entire white paper on the advantages of strong CSR programs and the disadvantages of environmental liabilities during mergers and acquisitions. Risk assessment and due diligence lead to lower prices for companies whose acquisition could bring in toxic "assets" that result in lawsuits and negative publicity—while companies have increased their worth to a buyer by exercising CSR and environmental leadership, especially if they market these virtues properly. For example, a grocery retailer paid more to acquire a company known for its community focus and sustainable approach to procurement, store operations, and distribution, community involvement programs.[52]

BUILDING TRUST

Trust, says Stephen M. R. Covey in his deservedly best-selling book, *The Speed of Trust*, is a key ingredient in business success. When there's trust—in both your character and your competence—people are much more willing to do business with you, they'll come to the deal faster, and the deal itself may well be bigger and will certainly be smoother.

And lack of trust can have serious bottom-line repercussions. United States corporate profits were directly impacted by the Sarbanes-Oxley Act (known colloquially as SOX)—which would not have been seen as necessary without the Enron, WorldCom, and Tyco scandals of the early 2000s:

---

50   http://investingforthesoul.com/08news/september-news-comment.htm, verified 4/5/15.

51   "Maximum Impact: Values-Based Investing Across the Spectrum," http://www.pbig. ml.com/pwa/pages/Values-Based-Investing-Across-the-Spectrum.aspx

52   GreenBiz.com, "How Green is the Deal? The Growing Role of Sustainability in M&A," November 3, 2008.. No longer posted online.

SOX has come at a substantial price. For starters, the amount of time it takes to comply with SOX regulations significantly slows the speed of business operations by adding many extra layers of red tape. It also adds considerable cost. One study estimated the cost of implementing section 404 alone at $35 billion—28 times greater than the SEC's original estimate.[53]

And despite all that expensive compliance, SOX has not convinced the public that business is to be trusted—in the US or elsewhere. Gallup International found that 40 percent of people in 60 different countries have no faith in the honesty of business leaders, and the next year, a Harris poll could find only 13 percent who had high confidence.[54]

Consumer trust in the business community reached a new low a few years ago, as ranked by the 2009 Edelman Trust Barometer. Overall trust in US corporations was at 38 percent: a stunning 20 percent drop in just one year, and lower even than in the Enron era. Information conveyed by CEOs was trusted by 29 percent—but just 17 percent among ages 35-64.[55] The same study noted that 91% of 25-to-64-year-olds worldwide purchased from a trusted company, while 77% chose not to do business with a distrusted company.

Perhaps this is why one study found trust-based advertising can outpull advertising that uses sex—at least for a B2B (business-to-business) audience looking for accounting services.[56]

And when you do have that trust, it goes straight into your positive bottom line. The Great Place to Work Institute notes that trust accounts for fully three-

53 "The Low Trust Epidemic: Why It Matters and What Communicators Can Do About It," December 2008 White Paper issued by Bon Mot Communications, LLC, http://www. bonmotcomms.com/whitepapers/BonMotComms_LowTrust&Communications_Dec2008. pdf, verified 4/5/15.

54 Ibid.

55 Rewers, Angelique. "Drop in Trust Leads to Call for Greater Government Regulation of Business," *The Corporate Communicator* e-newsletter, February 23, 2009, published by bonmotcomms.com; Edelman Trust Barometer 2008, January 2008, https://www.edelman. com/assets/uploads/2014/01/2009-Trust-Barometer-Executive-Summary.pdf, verified 4//515

56 "New Data: How to Maximize Impact of Email Newsletter Ads—4 Takeaways on Ad Recall, Forwards & More," MarketingSherpa.com, March 19, 2008, http://www. marketingsherpa.com/article.php?ident=30391, verified 4/5/15.

fifths of the rankings for Fortune Magazine's list of 100 Best Companies to Work For—and that those companies on the list in 2007 averaged 18.1 percent shareholder return, compared to 10.5 percent for the S&P 500.[57]

Trust is a form of social capital, created in part by the company's sense of who it must be responsible toward, as Dave Pollard points out in *Finding the Sweet Spot*. Those who are only responsible to their shareholders suffer low trust ratings in the marketplace, while those who see themselves as responsible to all stakeholders (and therefore would always include such costs as remediation of pollution or improving poor labor conditions in their cost-benefit analyses) enjoy the trust of all those stakeholders: employees, customers, neighbors, etc.

Pollard identified five bottom-line benefits to companies that have accrued enough social capital:

1. Customers feel good about supporting socially/environmentally responsible businesses, and are willing to pay higher prices
2. Customers become allies in both product development and problem resolution
3. Customers do your marketing for you
4. You'll have an easier time raising capital from nontraditional funding sources, with fewer conditions
5. You'll have lower risk of negative consequences from boycotts to lawsuits[58]

Pete Blackshaw, Executive VP, Digital Strategic Services, Nielsen Online and author of *Satisfied Customers Tell Three Friends, Angry Customers Tell 3,000*, identifies trust as the number one driver of brand credibility (out of six he identified for an article in Marketing Sherpa).[59]

To build that trust, Blackshaw suggests:

---

57 "The Low Trust Epidemic: Why It Matters and What Communicators Can Do About It," Op. cit.
58 Dave Pollard, *Finding the Sweet Spot: The Natural Entrepreneur's Guide to Responsible, Sustainable, Joyful Work*, Chelsea Green, 2008, pp. 174–175
59 "How to Practice Defensive Branding: 6 Key Factors to Build Credibility, Swat Bad Buzz," http://www.marketingsherpa.com/article.php?ident=30850, verified 4/5/15.

- Deliver high value
- Ensure safety
- Dispense straightforward, unambiguous communication
- Respond predictably and appropriately to a crisis: "apologize for any wrong-doing and work to fix problems"
- Provide credible guarantees and warranties

Interestingly, Blackshaw's other five drivers are really subsets of trust-building:

- Authenticity
- Transparency
- Listening
- Responsiveness
- Real data that substantiates the company's claims (e.g., through research or the customer's direct experience); Blackshaw calls this "affirmation," but it would be more accurate to call it "substantiation"

Among many other trust-builders, strong guarantees can jump-start consumer confidence. Want a great example of a powerful guarantee? As jobless rates climbed in the fall of 2008, Hyundai added to its already strong warranty against automotive failure a warranty on the ability of its customers to pay. Anyone who buys or leases a new Hyundai and finances it through the company is eligible to simply return the car if faced with involuntary unemployment, medical disability or loss of driver's license for medical reasons, job transfer out of the country, personal bankruptcy if self-employed, or accidental death.[60]

This very creative risk-reversal strategy won praise from Patrick Byers on the Responsible Marketing Blog:

Any automaker could have done this, but they haven't—yet. And Hyundai did it first.

---

60 http://www.hyundaiusa.com/financing/HyundaiAssurance/HyundaiAssurance.aspx, as of January 21, 2009

Not only will this drive word of mouth, it positions Hyundai as a company that cares—not just another automaker desperately trying to move metal… With this program the car is returned without incident, the customer retains their dignity and Hyundai is the good guy. [61]

Of course, within ten weeks, other automakers offered similar programs.[62]

JOHNSON & JOHNSON: A LESSON IN ETHICAL CRISIS PR

In 1982, seven Chicago-area people died after consuming tampered-with, cyanide-laced packages of Extra-Strength Tylenol—a popular seller for Johnson & Johnson. In an era that was not noted for corporate transparency, Johnson & Johnson broke new ground in the nascent field of corporate responsibility. Even though the poisoning was not J&J's fault, the company's response was nearly immediate and thoroughly centered on protecting consumers. Although the poisonings were localized and specific to one product, the company took no chances. It froze production, recalled all Tylenol products, nationwide—31 million bottles, worth over $100 million—and offered a $100,000 reward for solving the case.[63]

The company clearly put consumer safety ahead of its own profits. Though the loss was substantial, the resulting gain in consumer confidence allowed the company to recover quickly, and gain wide respect.[64]

Johnson & Johnson also set a high standard for corporate crisis response, modeling a new way to face problems squarely and make things right. Smart companies have modeled this in response to crises, and even in supervisor's interactions with employees who made mistakes. And according to *Harvard Business Review*,

61 http://responsiblemarketing.com/blog/?p=876

62 "GM, Ford offer Hyundai-style job-loss protection," http://www.autonews.com/article/20090331/ANA08/903319986/1018

63 Read a detailed description of the case, the company's response, and its rapid recovery at http://www.aerobiologicalengineering.com/wxk116/TylenolMurders/crisis.html, verified 4/5/15.

64 Read a detailed description of the case, the company's response, and its rapid recovery at http://www.aerobiologicalengineering.com/wxk116/TylenolMurders/crisis.html, verified 4/5/15.

The more employees look up to their leaders and are moved by their compassion or kindness (a state he terms elevation), the more loyal they become to him or her.[65]

A particularly striking case of a company stepping forward to ease a crisis happened in the aftermath of Hurricane Katrina, in 2005. When New Orleans and the Gulf Coast were ravaged and the federal and state governments appeared to be dysfunctional, a company that's often been at odds with its host communities[66] stepped in: Walmart trucked in massive quantities of food and water, and is actually credited with saving lives and minimizing looting.[67]

By contrast, when other companies have tried slippery tactics during safety scares—such as, they created PR and sales disasters for themselves.[68]

ONE PART OF CSR: STRATEGIC GIVING

In addition to right behavior, social action (more about that later) and charity are also important parts of CSR. More companies are switching from general corporate philanthropy to supporting social and environmental causes that directly align with their overall mission. For example, Talia Aharoni, founder of Maala, an Israel-based social responsibility index, taught companies to see their donations not as contributions but as investments with fiscal return along with community benefit."[69]

---

65   Emma Seppälä, Why Compassion is a Better Managerial Tactic than Toughness," https://hbr.org/2015/05/why-compassion-is-a-better-managerial-tactic-than-toughness, accessed 5/8/15.

66   See, for example, https://en.wikipedia.org/wiki/Criticism_of_Walmart, accessed 5/8/15.

67   Steven Horwitz, "Wal-Mart to the Rescue Private Enterprise's Response to Hurricane Katrina," *The Independent Review*, 13:4, Spring 2009, p. 512, available at https://www.independent.org/pdf/tir/tir_13_04_3_horwitz.pdf, accessed 5/8/15.

68   For example, Ford and Bridgestone/Firestone's response to the Explorer rollover problem. Ford officials discussed the problem even as far back as May 1, 1987, while the Explorer was still in the design phase. The story reached the US press in a report by CBS affiliate KHOU, of Houston—long after Ford had already recalled tires in Malaysia, Saudi Arabia, and elsewhere. Public Citizen, a watchdog group founded by Ralph Nader, prepared a detailed chronology at http://www.fordexplorerrollover.com/history/Default.cfm, verified 4/5/15.

69   J.J. Levine, "Maala index indicates a revolution in Israel's corporate philosophy," http://www.jpost.com/Business/Business-Features/Maala-index-indicates-a-revolution-in-Israels-corporate-philosophy, verified 4/5/15.

In the US, companies are also becoming more strategic in their corporate giving. Consultant Kellie A. McElhaney chides Ford Motor Company for its large contribution to Susan G. Komen for the Cure, a well-known cancer charity because she doesn't feel alignment with Ford's core mission.[70] The company would be better served, she says, supporting alternative fuels and global environmental/transportation issues.

She praises companies whose charity efforts complement their core mission, such as dog food company Pedigree. Partnering with the American Humane Association on a big public dog adoption campaign, the company brands itself as animal loving, highlights the problem of unadopted dogs being killed, helps abandoned dogs find new homes—and positions itself as a choice for dog lovers.[71] As of March 11, 2015, the company website's main navigation bar offers only five choices. One of those, "help dogs," is about dog rescue and adoption, and the "all things dog" page also includes information on this. A footer on every page of the site notes, "At PEDIGREE® Brand, everything we do is for the love of dogs, from the dog food we make to the dog adoption drive we support."

Christopher Bauer, author of *Better Ethics Now*, points out that corporate responsibility should reward individual responsibility:

> Once you show employees that doing the right thing is a tool for their personal success and not just the success of your company—then it will be much easier to keep ethics problems from developing.[72]

THE MAGIC TRIANGLE: QUALITY, INTEGRITY, HONESTY

Ready for the big principle of this book? It's not a secret at all, just a simple truth. But it's crucial. Here it is:

Create value for others in everything that you do

---

70 McElhaney, Kellie A. *Just Good Business: The Strategic Guide to Aligning Corporate Responsibility and Brand* (San Francisco: Berrett-Koehler, 2008, p. 20.

71 Ibid., pp. 53-55.

72 Bauer, Christopher, "Taking Responsibility For Taking Responsibility—Part 2," Weekly Ethics Thought email newsletter, September 1, 2008.

That's the magic formula. You help yourself best when you're helping others. And the way you do that is by basing your business on a solid foundation of three principles:

Quality, Integrity, Honesty

Quality: Provide the best value you can. This is especially crucial for green businesses—because if you produce crap you not only lose a customer, you create an enemy of going green. The last thing we need is people going around saying, "I tried to use some green products and they were terrible."

Yet some companies rushed the stuff to market long before it was ready, turning their products into evangelists against green. Example: The early, leaky, biodegradable disposable diapers converted users right back to Pampers and Huggies—and made them much less likely to try better green products such as LED light bulbs.

Integrity: Run your business in alignment with your core values; don't try to be something you're not.

Honesty: Value the truth and be eager to share it with your prospects and customers—even if it means that your solution is not the best for them right now—in other words, that it is not appropriate for a particular prospect to become a customer at this time.

Who Wins When You Market with Quality, Integrity, and Honesty?

Your customers or clients realize you're not trying to cheat them. And they will so value the experience of being treated well that they will come back again and again—and tell others.

Your suppliers will relate to your honesty and integrity, to your understanding that you're partners who both benefit by helping each other.

Your competitors benefit, too, when they see how your ethical behavior lets them improve their own operating standards. As you make space in the market for quality, integrity, and honesty, you begin to see each other less as rivals and more as collaborative partners who can help each other in many ways.

Here's how Shel puts these core ideas to work in his own business:

Because I try to deliver extremely high quality while keeping my prices affordable, the value of my work to my clients is very high. My clients become my "marketing evangelists," excited and delighted by my impact on their business. Integrity keeps me close to my core values: making the world a better place, creating meaningful work, and enjoying a great life. Out of honesty, I've turned down work projects because another person might be better equipped to do the job; out of integrity, I've refused work assignments that clashed with my values.

I work because I enjoy what I do—I take great satisfaction in consulting, writing, and speaking—and do these quite well. And the world becomes better and more interesting if I inspire businesses to incorporate profitable solutions to hunger, poverty, war, and climate change into their DNA.

As for honesty—it's the right thing, and also good for business. For instance, two of my books on marketing covered similar ground. When someone ordered both books, I always explained that they only needed one—and why. People are invariably shocked that I actually tell my customers that they should reduce the amount of my sale. I want a long-term customer relationship—and word-of-mouth buzz—more than the short-sighted short-term profit of selling customers a book they don't need.

HOW THE MAGIC TRIANGLE POSITIONS YOU BETTER IN A TOUGH ECONOMY

When the economy contracts, businesses that use the Magic Triangle are better positioned to survive and thrive. You retain more customers—who help you acquire new business—and the lower price sensitivity of your loyalist customers means you enjoy higher profits. Thus, you have more surplus capital to invest in marketing, while your competitors pull back and retrench, focusing only on survival and not on growth or retention.

In fact, many experts pin a good part of the blame for the 2008 recession on unethical behavior. Clemson University's Rutland Center for Ethics 2008 survey of 302 CEOs with $10 million+ in annual revenues pointed out that many of these CEOs suffered from an advanced case of greed.[73] The Center's Director, Professor Dan Wueste, claims that poor business ethics and practices directly led to the economic downturn, because when there's no trust, there's no confidence in the stock market:

> The current crisis has everything to do with the failure to act in a way that would count as ethically acceptable. We start with the assumption that people will be acting rightly and not take unfair advantage of us. Then people do things to prove that we can't trust them (risky mortgages, frivolous spending). It's irrational to believe that trust will remain.[74]

As the economy spiraled down, poor choices by executives with their hands out for a government rescue caused public relations disasters. The lavish post-bailout parties thrown by AIG[75] and the decisions by auto company CEOs to fly to Washington on separate private jets[76] added to the perception that these business leaders are completely clueless about economic responsibility, and that their lavish lifestyles and vast compensation packages are the first places to look for cuts.[77]

Green economist/ethicist Hazel Henderson, author of *Ethical Markets: Growing The Green Economy*, calls the ultraleveraged economy a "global casino," and noted that historically, overpumped economies have a tendency to "metastasize," as happened in 1929 and 2008, among other recessions. She sees reforming the energy sector as critical:

> Taxing carbon emissions, pollution, waste, planned obsolescence and resource-depletion while reducing income and payroll taxes. Shifting

73 "Ethics plays major role in business collapse," http://archive.upstatetoday.com/?p=35275, verified 4/5/15.

74 Ibid.

75 http://www.azcentral.com/arizonarepublic/business/articles/2008/11/11/20081111biz-aigresort1111.html, verified 4/5/15.

76 Josh Levs, "Big Three auto CEOs flew private jets to ask for taxpayer money, http://www.cnn.com/2008/US/11/19/autos.ceo.jets/, verified 4/5/15.

77 Heather Landy, "Growing Sense of Outrage Over Executive Pay," http://www.washingtonpost.com/wp-dyn/content/article/2008/11/14/AR2008111403789_pf.html, verified 4/5/15.

the still-massive subsidies showered on the oil, coal, gas and nuclear industries to production tax credits can accelerate the growth of renewable energy. Solar, wind, geothermal, tidal, fuel cells, hydrogen, mass transit, smart DC electric grids as well as capturing the 40% of energy currently wasted in the US fossil fuel economy can shift human societies to the Solar Age.

Henderson saw the 2008 crisis as a fabulous opportunity to change the whole definition of a successful economy:

And as we change the financial games and fix accounting errors in the global casino, we can also change the obsolete scorecards. There is widespread public recognition in global surveys of the errors of money-measured GDP growth, and correcting its omissions of social and environmental costs has begun (http://www.beyond-gdp.eu). Including all these factors and indicators of health, education, poverty gaps, environment and quality of life can help shrink the global casino and restore finance to its proper function.[78]

HOW THE MAGIC TRIANGLE TURNS
PROBLEMS INTO SALES OPPORTUNITIES

The Magic Triangle is a doorway into new ways of thinking about how to help your market. By anticipating their needs and greeting them with honesty, integrity, and quality, you create new opportunities.

Alexander Hiam, author of *The Portable MBA* and many other books, offers this example. if you sell photocopiers with a five-year lifespan, don't wait until the customers start to complain in the fifth year about high repair costs. After four years, send a mailing to your customers, noting that their machines are aging—and you want them to know about your Borrow-a-Photocopier plan, in which they can sign up to use a brand-new loaner while their own machine is down for repairs. Instead of an angry customer,

---

78   Henderson, Hazel, "Changing Games in the Global Casino," email newsletter from www. ethicalmarkets.com, June 25, 2008.

frustrated that the equipment is down, you've created a loyalist who is aware that you'll go the extra mile, alerting your customers to an issue that hasn't even surfaced yet, and providing an easy solution. Better still, there's a good likelihood that they'll like the modern machine so much better, they'll purchase one.

With problem resolution, Hiam says it's not enough to simply address the customer's grievance. Use language that accepts responsibility and moves the customer's agenda forward. For instance, instead of responding in a sentence that begins, "We would…," take personal responsibility for the outcome by starting your answer, "I will…" This immediate, direct language tells the aggrieved customer you've accepted the challenge to make it right.[79]

In Shel's consulting and copywriting business, the Magic Triangle provides many chances for a gentle upsell that has turned many clients from a small one-time job into an ongoing relationship. In researching the initial small assignment, Shel will notice other areas that need attention, and communicate them politely to the client with an offer to help or provide a referral.

WHEN THE MAGIC TRIANGLE TELLS YOU TO SAY NO TO A SALE

Ethics sometimes demands that we turn from *selling* to *not selling*.

When would you need to refuse an order? Here are several situations, and they all come back to our Magic Triangle:

- You don't have the appropriate solution; someone else is better equipped to solve the client's problem (honesty)
- There isn't enough time to do the job well (quality)
- You could do the job, but it's an area you're trying to get away from (honesty—to yourself)
- The client will obviously be so high-maintenance and/or so demanding that the job isn't worth the price you can charge (quality—of the client)
- The client asks you to engage in unethical behavior (integrity)

---

79 Shel Horowitz, " Employee/Customer Skills are Key to Business Growth, *Related Matters*, UMass Amherst Family Business Center, Fall 1998, p. 7, http://www.umass.edu/fambiz/articles/just_business/marketing_business.html, verified 5/9/15.

- The product is too shoddy and you don't feel good about working on it (integrity/quality)
- You find the job itself morally distasteful (integrity)

As an example of that last bullet, Shel was developing a relationship with a local PR firm that wanted to subcontract some copywriting assignments. The very first job he got was so clearly wrapped up in a cause that he has spent his life working against that it actually made him ill to look at the client's publicity fliers. Shel's only hesitation was knowing that the PR shop was overextended and needed materials on a short deadline; he didn't want to strand the woman who was subcontracting.

After spending an hour agonizing about it, he picked up the phone and explained that while he didn't want to leave her hanging, he couldn't in good conscience take the job—but he could still help her manage her overload by taking on a different client.

He was fully expecting that she'd be furious—but actually, she told him she respected his stance. She took back the problem assignment and gave him one that he felt totally comfortable handling. Now, when a client contacts Shel about doing some work, there's a clause in the return email that allows Shel the right to back out of a project if it's not a good fit.

All marketers are asked to take on poor-quality projects. When you're in that situation, just say no. If you think the product is shoddy, or a terrible value, or just unable to capture your interest, you can't write decent copy or plan good strategy for it anyway—and the client will hate what you turn in. You need to feel good about the product in order to take on the job.

Interestingly enough, Arthur Andersen (the person—founder of the accounting firm that was driven out of business after ignoring major audit flags at Enron) turned down a major account after refusing the company's request to engage in exactly the sort of unethical accounting that brought down his company almost 70 years later—at a very early stage in his career, when he wasn't sure he could meet his next payroll. He told the company president that there was "not enough money in the city of Chicago" to change his mind.[80]

LESSONS

- Success in business is about providing value to others—the Magic Triangle is your success formula
- When values and value align, your chances of success are greater
- All things otherwise equal, stakeholders prefer to do business with companies they perceive as ethical
- Successful selling is about relationships...and relationships are about really listening
- Sometimes, saying no to a sale makes more sense than saying yes

ACTIONS

- Develop five to ten deep, probing but not-too-personal *business* questions you can ask prospects about the situation they're trying to solve.
- Practice asking these in ways that feel natural and unscripted.
- Create different responses depending on the responses you might get
- Identify three steps can your business take to increase trust from all stakeholders?

---

80   This story is widely quoted; see, for instance, the *Chicago Tribune* of September 1, 2002 http://www.chicagotribune.com/news/chi-0209010315sep01,0,538751.story (verified 4/6/15). We first found it in a book called *Reclaiming the Ethical High Ground,* by John Di Frances (Wales, WI: Reliance Books, 2002).

PART II

THE NEW GREEN, SOCIALLY CONSCIOUS MARKETING MINDSET

CHAPTER 4

THE NEW MARKETING MATRIX

ost marketers say you need more than one impression to move someone up the ladder from unaware to aware to prospect to customer to evangelist. Some use the figure of seven impressions within 18 months (though, as the bombardment of ads increases, many would say that those seven impressions need to be much closer together, or that even seven isn't enough).

So, in the traditional view, the more you rain down messages upon the head of any particular individual, the more you push that person toward being first a prospect, and then a client. This idea leads to saturation advertising—the sort of thing that Coca-Cola or McDonald's calls a marketing strategy. There is a certain amount of truth in the theory of repetition, but it's only part of the picture.

The saturation "strategy" only works if you have essentially unlimited resources. Coke and McD's can afford to throw away millions of dollars in advertising in order to assure that everyone hears their marketing messages— because some percentage of people actually do respond to the constant bombardment. But as small business owners and managers, we cannot afford to buy that kind of saturation, nor should we want to. It's so much better to figure out who our real prospects are, and talk to them as colleagues in a mutually beneficial partnership.

And then, under the right conditions, even a single marketing message may be enough to move someone from totally unaware to writing the check.

Here's our twist on the formula:

The effectiveness of your marketing depends on three variables:

1. Relevance of your message to your prospect's immediate wants and needs
2. Message quality
3. Number of positive exposures to your messages

Message quality consists of:

- Your offer's perceived value
- Its sense of trust and reliability
- Perceived quality of the product or service
- The user's experience of your marketing message—the interplay of your message's copy, visuals, audio, and/or usability

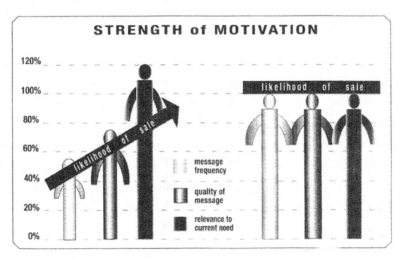

Graphic by Robin MacRostie, Choreographic Designs

As you see, you're very likely to make the sale when all three of these variables are toward the top of the scale—but if any one variable—especially relevance—is very high, a sale is possible even if the other variables are low. When they work in harmony or in sync, your chances are much greater.

In other words, if someone's looking for exactly what you offer, and you connect with a beautifully crafted message that touches all the hot buttons, your prospect might be ready to buy immediately, on the first contact. And if the desire is strong enough, that person will take action, right then and there. If the desire is not yet strong enough, it may take several more messages—different messages, not an exact repeat—to convince your prospect to become a customer.

The frequency axis is particularly tricky. In general, more *unique* messages move the prospect forward toward making the purchase—in part because, over time, increased frequency artificially increases desire, so that eventually, the perceived need to act on the desire moves up the ladder of the consumer's consciousness. However, repeating the exact same message in too close proximity will not be effective; it will start getting annoying very quickly. Think about watching a one-hour television show. If you hear the same commercial at the beginning and end of the show, you're likely to be pretty tolerant of it. But if you hear the same commercial at every single break, you might feel like throwing something at the TV after the third or fourth time it appears.

Yet if instead of the same commercial, the advertiser ran a series of six commercials, each of which stressed a different benefit, you'd probably still be listening by the end of the show, even if you felt the advertiser was overdoing it a bit.

On the other hand, 20—or 200—messages won't move a non-prospect, but will annoy.

PULL VERSUS PUSH

Most traditional marketing is built on push. Focused heavily on advertising, push marketers shoves their marketing at prospects. Push marketing is interruptive, sometimes even in-your-face. It shrieks, "you need to know about this, and you need to buy it! Now! Don't delay!" It wants to intrude, wants you to stop what you're doing and process this "important" information, all the way to the store.

Some would say that a marketer's job is to artificially create desire for a product—but we don't think that's following the Golden Rule. If a consumer is already in the market—for a breakfast cereal, a car, a computer, whatever—it's totally appropriate to create interest in your particular product. But to push a consumer with no previous interest toward a product that doesn't address that consumer's real needs and wants is dishonest—and not conducive to that all-important long-term relationship.

Pull marketing, on the other hand, allows the consumer to be in charge of the process. Someone decides to solve a problem, answer a need, or gratify a desire, and that consumer self-selects into a prospect. The prospect begins a research process to find the right solution, and the prospect chooses how to find messages that help refine the search. The research process could take just a few seconds...or several years. It might involve such activities as:

- Entering a search phrase into Google or one of its competitors
- Looking up information in the Yellow Pages or in the classified pages of a trade magazine
- Asking friends or social media contacts for recommendations, or following recommendations from experts
- Consulting trusted sources such as Consumer Reports or Trip Advisor
- Reading product reviews on magazines or websites—including customer-written reviews on e-commerce sites
- Examining vendors' websites, publications, and printed sales materials
- Initiating or following vendor-specific ("Does anyone have experience working with...") and general ("Who would you recommend to do...") discussions on Internet discussion groups and social networking websites
- Searching social media for positive or negative experiences with particular vendors
- Participating in a focus group or beta test

In short, pull marketing is never intrusive. It's driven by your own customers. You can influence it, but you can't control it. And pull can even open up new ways of thinking, leading to solutions that would have been ignored if presented through push.

And it works a whole lot better in our information-overloaded world. When people get hit with as many as 3000 marketing messages every day, smart consumers have learned to filter out this barrage. They use technological tools, such as web browser pop-up blockers, TiVo, the mute button, or simply taping a TV show and fast-forwarding the commercials—and they also use psychological filtering: mental cues that say, *this is an ad, ignore it.*

Unfortunately, the response of most marketers has been to up the volume, push harder, increase the frequency, and turn formerly ad-free spaces into commercial zones: to beat us into submission with even more, and more aggressive, push marketing.

So those who understand and use pull marketing have a huge advantage; you win in marketing by reaching the exact people who are ready to buy—with a message they can't resist, because it appeals directly to their current wants and needs.

Think about it. Say you're moderately interested in new technology and how computers continue to make our lives easier. Right now, it's a mild, purely academic interest. Marketing messages about the latest technologies catch some small part of your attention and you file them deep in the back of your mind. Then suddenly you try to boot your computer and nothing happens; it's dead. Now, when you see an ad or an article about the latest technology, you pay very close attention. Since you need to replace the computer, you think carefully about which of those new capabilities or customer service qualities are important to you—and very quickly, you research the available choices and place an order. If a marketer happens to send you a mailing about a special sale on exactly the computer you need, you'll order it. But if you'd gotten the same mailing a week earlier, you'd have tossed it in the recycle bin.

The change in circumstances—your computer breakdown—moved you instantly three rungs up the ladder—from vaguely aware, right past prospect, and all the way up to *hot* customer, ready to move immediately.

The problem for marketers, of course, is knowing how to be there exactly when changed circumstances convert someone from a non-prospect to a buyer.

How can you be in the customer's mind at that magical moment, without having been a pest before the buyer made that transition? Here's where pull media, such as World Wide Web and social media search engines, classified ads, and—for the few people still consulting them—Yellow Pages, can have a huge impact. Pull media are customer-driven. They wait for a user to approach and pull the marketing information into their consciousness, unlike push media, which thrust messages into the audience's awareness without being invited in. When the customer is finally ready and turns to such a medium, where he or she is in control of the selection process, then a previous build-up of positive, nonintrusive messages over time can provide immediate advantage to the savvy marketer.

Writing in *Sustainable Brands*, Lukas Snelling points out that marketers need to separate their approaches to pull and push marketing. Push marketing engages fantasies, seeking to woo the consumer into becoming a customer. But in prospect-driven pull marketing, the prospect doesn't need to be sold on the idea—just on which solution and vendor. So pull marketing provides facts.[81]

Snelling's statement makes tangible all the abstract talk about content marketing. We've long known that consumers buy on a mixture of facts and emotions; Snelling's key insight is that we use these different parts of our buying brain in different circumstances.

Thus, getting into the mind of the prospect *when that person starts being a prospect* is a tricky business that requires a long buildup. If you wait until that person has a need, someone else may be top of mind already.

A real-life example: Some years ago, Shel had a kidney stone, which caused extreme pain. He remembered that a former participant on a publisher's discussion list had written a book about kidney stone treatment—and that she had always been helpful and intelligent, not just about medical issues but about publishing topics as well.

Shel first tried entering her business name as a .com domain name; it didn't come up. So then he went to a search engine and searched for her

---

81   Lukas Snelling, "Why Green Consumers are Leading the Inbound Marketing Revolution," http://www.sustainablebrands.com/news_and_views/june2012/why-green-consumers-are-leading-inbound-marketing-revolution, accessed 3/2/15.

business name plus the phrase "kidney stone." Instantly, he had her website and ordered the book. Because she had, over a period of years, established herself as the authority Shel would trust if he knew someone with a kidney stone problem, he didn't want or need to sort through all the results for kidney stone treatment; her prior participation had created confidence that she could help. Even though Shel used a pull medium, he'd already chosen the vendor; only if he'd been unable to locate her would he have explored other options.

Other writers also point out the holes in the standard formula of seven impressions. For example, Roy Williams's *Secret Formulas of the Wizard of Ads* refers to the APE, or Advertising Performance Equation. In his view, the effectiveness of your advertising is directly tied to other variables beyond frequency, including the prospect's personal experience with your firm. He says that if you multiply your "Share of Voice"—the percentage of advertising in your category that comes from you—by the ad's power to convince ("Impact Quotient"), you get "Share of Mind," and then, when you multiply the result by the prospect's "Personal Experience Factor"—direct experience of your company by the prospect—you can determine your market share. Multiply the Share of Market by the Market Potential (the number of customers actually out there) and you can determine your sales volume.

Expressed as a formula, it looks like this:

$$\text{Sales Volume} = \text{SoV} \times \text{IQ} \times \text{PEF} \times \text{MPo}$$

So customers who have positive previous experiences with a company are *far more likely* to respond to that company's ads than those with a history of bad experiences.[82]

Williams is on to something, but he misses one crucial point: advertising is only one part of marketing (often, the most expensive and least effective part). You can get to that share of mind and market without having to pay for it.

---

82   Roy Williams, *Secret Formulas of the Wizard of Ads*. (Austin: Wizard Academy Press, 1998), Ch. 47.

PRACTICAL PULLS

The secret to effective pull marketing is two-fold. 1) Be found when your prospect searches. 2) Position yourself so that your prospect decides to trust you with those hard-earned bank notes.

As you begin to explore this new and different world, you'll find dozens if not hundreds of ways to do that, most of which involve providing useful content that positions you as the expert who can help. A few ideas:

- Articles and book excerpts to distribute to your own customer and prospect base and seed to other websites, newsletters, etc.
- A book or ebook
- Helpful and engaging participation on Internet discussion groups and social media
- Speaking and coaching
- Introductory teleseminars, webinars, white papers, special reports, and other "content marketing"
- Trivia quizzes or other contests related to the problem you solve
- Do-it-yourself assessment tools that lead your prospect inexorably conclusion to hire you

Amplifying that last example, consultant David Wood writes,

Assessments are a fantastic way to attract visitors. Assessments are quizzes and questionnaires that create an interactive experience for your prospects. "How Successful Are You?" "Are You Ready for a Relationship?" "Are You Stressed?" People love to fill them out and better yet, they like to pass them on to their friends… Once you have a visitor's email, you can contact them more to build the relationship you started with the give away. And you get a chance to show them what else you can offer them (i.e. coaching, an information product, a teleclass, etc.).[83]

One of Wood's clients…

---

83   David Wood, "Pricing and Negotiating Fees," Solution Box e-newsletter, January 7, 2009.

...has a great system for following up with potential clients who take the quizzes. He asks for their name and email address before they hit the score button. He tells them where they are based on their score, and then follows up 6 times via an autoresponder specific to that quiz! The autoresponder messages are to upsell to his coaching.

Why aren't discount offers on that list? Putting something on sale brings traffic and business—but also reduces your margin and sets you in a commoditized no-win downward spiral. Some inexperienced vendor in a developing country can always underbid. Certainly, there are times to discount—e.g., to incent early response, help a charity partner, or reward your own list. But usually, you're much better off marketing on value, not price.

A COPYWRITING/MARKETING CHECKLIST

Although we don't have the space for a full discussion of practical marketing here we can give at least a brief summary. If you want more, please check out *Grassroots Marketing: Getting Noticed in a Noisy World*, Shel's comprehensive book on how to market effectively for maximum impact at minimum cost—as well as Jay's numerous books, especially *Guerrilla Marketing for Free*.

Not surprisingly, many of those techniques are totally suited to green, people-centered marketing.

These strategies are cheaper, more effective, and easier to implement than the typical win–lose strategies.

Here's a checklist; if your next proposed marketing or customer service initiative meets these criteria, the chances are good that it's in harmony with the abundance mentality, and that your prospects will see your message as beneficial:

1. Incorporate top-quality customer service into every aspect of your business. Providing a terrific experience is the very best marketing you can do—while failing to do so will undermine all your other marketing.
2. Always present information from the perspective of the benefit to the prospect: problems solved or avoided, goals achieved

3. Target your marketing to your exact audience—and, as much as possible, *only* your exact audience. Don't waste your money annoying people who are not your prospects.

4. Treat your prospects as intelligent, thinking, feeling people. Create marketing materials and campaigns that engage your prospect both intellectually and emotionally; those that only involve emotions and ignore rational thinking too often come across as patronizing, or just plain poorly thought out—while those that ignore the emotions come across as limp and boring. Conventional marketing says "sell the sizzle, not the steak." We beg to differ. In our vegetarian version, we say, "sell the sizzle, *and* the seitan." You want to attract both the left and right halves of the brain. Provide the emotional hooks, of course, but be sure to include the facts to justify them.

5. Be scrupulously honest in every headline, claim, or offer—but still use copy that makes your audience sit up and take notice. Every product and service should be strong enough to sell on merit, without tricking the buyer.

6. Be sensitive to the cultural nuances of your target audience. Know the demographics and psychographics, use the right media to reach your particular set of prospects, and creating marketing that "sings" to the people you most want as customers.

7. Build your reputation. Turn your customers, your employees, and your competitors into evangelists for your business.

8. Understand your customers' personas:
   - When they shop for clothes, are they status-conscious Fashionistas or price-conscious Bargain Hunters?
   - Do they listen to Bach, the Beatles, or Justin Bieber?
   - What kinds of communities do they live in: urban, suburban, or rural? How do they go to work—or do they work from home?
   - How old are they? From what ethnic background? Do they have kids at home? Do those kids attend mainstream public schools, charter schools, private schools, or are they homeschooled?

- Are they shopping for personal use, or for their workplace? What's their typical decision-making cycle—and their budget?
- Do they prefer tofu, granola, and kale...champagne, caviar, and brie...or burgers, fries, and chips?
- What are their political beliefs? Do they vote? What news media influence their thinking?

The more you know these demographic and psychographic details, the better you can sell your products and services. You could brainstorm a list of hundreds of these kinds of questions, and the more of them you can answer, the more your marketing messages will resonate with the exact people you'd like to turn into customers. For more on personas, look into the many books by Jeffrey and Bryan Eisenberg.

You might want bring in a professional copywriter like Shel, who is clued in about writing copy that's gripping and action-oriented, but not hype or overselling.

POWERFUL PRODUCT CREATION

By now, you understand that marketing is a conversation: a two-way dialogue between you and your customers, clients, prospects, and followers. So incorporate that attitude into every new product you develop. Find out what your market is looking for, and only then go out and fill the need.

In other words, find—and fill—customers' desires and needs, assuage their pain points, and further their goals.

This is an important lesson whether your product launch is enormous or tiny. Coca-Cola and Ford forgot this lesson when they introduced New Coke and the Edsel: utter failures that consumed millions of dollars. New Coke was actually focus-grouped, and the company did a lot of research prior to launch—but didn't know how to correctly evaluate the information it was receiving.

Ford learned from its expensive mistake; the original Taurus, one of the company's top sellers in history, was carefully crafted to reflect feedback from potential users, covering every conceivable detail and yet somehow avoiding the committee-think mentality that can kill a product.

On a much smaller scale, Spanish language and culture entrepreneur Myelita Melton of SpeakEasySpanish.com used client feedback to broaden her product offerings:

> I began interviewing people in the classes. Each told me about their jobs, their goals, and more importantly, exactly what they wanted to learn…Communication is more important than conjugation, and what you learn must be relevant to what you do. If you don't use it, you'll lose it!

One of her students, an ER nurse, suggested bringing her programs to the hospital.

> I thought her idea was the best thing since salsa…Offering customized Spanish courses at business locations where it would be convenient for small groups of employees made perfect sense to me.
>
> Quickly calls started coming in from across the region, and professionals in every job you can imagine began submitting vocabulary they wanted to learn.[84]

Similarly, Shel wrote his seventh book, *Grassroots Marketing for Authors and Publishers*, because for ten years, people had been asking him to do a marketing book just about books. When he finally decided to write it, he did a two-question survey to a group of independent publishers: what would you most like to see covered in a book about book marketing, and what's your greatest book marketing success story? The final book includes two chapters Shel hadn't intended to write, but were of keen interest to his market. And it also includes some 40 success stories from other authors and publishers, all of whom feel some sense of ownership in the book and become voices in the choir of its support.

To figure out what to offer, ask yourself five simple questions:

---

84 Myelita Melton, "Muchas Gracias to All of You!," Email newsletter, November 20, 2008

1. What problem can you solve, or desire can you facilitate?
2. How is your method different from and better than existing solutions (what are the advantages, in other words)?
3. Who needs this problem solved strongly enough that they're willing to pay (who is the market)?
4. How do you reach those people?
5. How do you convince them to buy?

Also keep your eyes and ears open for ways to redeploy other people's ideas in new industries. Remember:

- Drive-through service didn't start at restaurants; banks had them first (in 1930), and car washes were next
- Shopping carts were invented when an inventor studied folding chairs
- Sticky notes were a repackaging of a failed adhesive; it wasn't strong enough for a permanent hold, but a bright person (Art Fry) created a need for temporary adhesives
- Velcro was used in the space program years before it was redeployed to households and businesses[85]—where it became, among many other uses, an empowerment device for people with fine-motor disabilities and kids who haven't learned to tie shoes

And don't forget about improving the process or experience. Chip Bell, author of *Sprinkles: Creating Awesome Experiences Through Innovative Service*, discusses a medical practice that didn't eliminate the long wait to see a doctor, but got rid of patient frustration by providing not just a pager but a coffee shop gift card.[86] See Chapter 15, "Give the People What they Want," for more creativity-starters.

---

85 Claire Suddath, "A Brief History of Velcro," Time Magazine, June 15, 2010, http://content.time.com/time/nation/article/0,8599,1996883,00.html, accessed 3/26/15.
86 https://www.youtube.com/watch?v=0hFfMLuB10w&feature=youtu.be, starting at 32 minutes, accessed 2/11/15

THE LEARNING POSSIBILITIES OF FAILURE

Don't be afraid to fail. Have a good laugh whenever you hear that famous phrase, "failure is not an option." It shows not only enormous ignorance of the real world and the human brain, but also enormous hubris.

Let's get real. Failure is *always* an option—with sufficient bad luck or timing, loss of motivation, key player defections, or inadequate funding.

This doesn't mean the task is impossible; Shel even uses the theme, "Impossible is not a fact...It's a dare" as the theme for his speeches on how business can transform hunger, poverty, war and catastrophic climate change, as you'll see later in the book.

But just because something is possible doesn't mean the conditions are ripe for success. It's At that moment, for whatever reason, it doesn't seem worth marshaling the necessary resources to finish the task.

Sometimes, we can minimize the impact of choosing failure. Almost always, we can embrace it as a learning opportunity.

The trick is to fail cheaply and early—and maybe often. Make your mistakes...and move on. See what can be salvaged, what can be reinvented, and what should be thrown in the trash. Thomas Edison took 10,000 steps to invent the light bulb. Most people would say he failed 9999 times. He saw it not as a failure but as a 10,000-step process. In other words, our failures teach us enough to achieve our successes.

LESSONS

- The purpose of business is to create value—by addressing customers' dreams, needs, goals, and pain points—and we can do this in life-affirming, planet-healing ways
- The effectiveness of marketing messages depends not only on frequency but also on the relevance and quality of that message
- Too much repetition actually weakens the message
- Customer-driven "pull" marketing is better positioned to succeed than company-driven "push" marketing
- Sell the sizzle *and* the seitan
- Problem-solving is a better strategy than discounting

- Effective marketing encompasses multiple integrated streams of conversation, and much of that conversation flows from your stakeholders (customers, prospects, suppliers, resellers, neighbors, and regulators) back to you—listen to the feedback you get!
- Gain perspectives from other industries and weave them into your new product strategy
- Treat failure as a learning opportunity

ACTIONS

- Pick two informational channels where prospects can pull themselves to you, and begin implementing a strategy to draw them in (if you need help, please get in touch).
- Once you've let your prospects pull themselves toward you, provide something substantial and useful enough to begin to cement their perception that you're the answer to their prayers.
- Consider developing an assessment tool that prospects can fill out on your website, and set it up so both you and the client get the results— you now have great data to use when you follow up (which you should do within 48 hours).
- Answer the five questions about product creation.
- List three or more requests you've gotten from customers or prospects for new features or capabilities. Pick one to implement and work it into your offerings. Notify the people who made the suggestion that you've done what they requested.
- Jot down three or more successful practices from completely different industries and think about how you might make them a part of your business.

CHAPTER 5

ABUNDANCE VERSUS SCARCITY

THE OLD SCARCITY PARADIGM

The pie, you've always heard, is finite. If you win, someone else has to lose. There's not enough to go around. If you believe this, you're forced to spend lots of time and energy competing, striving to win and defeat the others.

But the whole premise of this book is that it's simply not true. There *is* enough to go around. Perhaps the distribution system needs some readjustment, but the pie keeps expanding. The eighteenth-century economist Malthus was wrong; the world, so far, produces enough for its growing population. And businesses can thrive and prosper without trying to drive their competitors out of business.

One analyst, Ramez Naam, argues that the reason Malthus was wrong is that innovation is exponential, while resource use has been linear; we are able (as one among many examples) to grow more food on less land.[87] Let's hope that still holds as the earth passes 7 billion people.

THE "PROSPERITY CONSCIOUSNESS" PARADIGM—AND ITS PROBLEMS

Some years ago, it seemed that all the buzz was about prosperity consciousness; if you tapped into the right vein of the universe, you'd prosper. Of course, the stock market was zooming. When the market tanked in 2008, nobody was talking about prosperity consciousness anymore—they were too busy surviving.

For marketing heretics like us, the idea never held much water in the first place. While we enjoy material wealth, we recognize that money is not an end in itself, but a means. Money enables us to trade it for purchases that make our life better, or the world better. This ability to trade it for other things is what gives money value; otherwise, even a million-dollar bill would be just another piece of paper. While you don't *need* a lot of money in order to embrace abundance, it is nice to have, and does make a whole lot of things easier—including the kind of social and environmental change we'll discuss in the last few chapters.

In other words, money is one more tool, a lever, to convert brain power and work into bettering conditions for yourself, your loved ones, and the world. Think of money—and time—as forms of energy, just like solar or wind.

So, rather than Prosperity Consciousness, let's think in terms of Abundance Consciousness.

Rather than working toward material wealth, Shel started focusing on the blessings in his life:

- Good health
- A loving family
- A beautiful house in the country with wonderful friends and neighbors
- Enjoyable work that actually improves the world
- Community involvements that also make the world better
- The chance to travel

---

87 Ramez Naam, The Infinite Resource: The Power of Ideas on a Finite Planet, by Ramez Naam (University Press of New England, 2013). Read Shel's review at http://thecleanandgreenclub.com/the-clean-and-green-club-october-2013/

- An average of six weeks of vacation per year
- A house full of books, art, and music
- Schools that stimulate his children's creativity
- Nearby colleges and cultural centers that bring amazing performances and lectures
- Closeness to nature, with terrific places to hike, bird-watch, bike ride, cross-country ski, and swim—either within walking distance or a very short drive away
- The pleasures of farm-fresh food and home-cooked gourmet meals, as well as the pleasures of sophisticated gourmet restaurant fare

He writes,

My life is one of great fortune and privilege, but not one that revolves around material wealth. I've learned to be a good shopper for what I want, and I've discovered that I can live a very comfortable, dare I say pampered, lifestyle. Many people I know who have a higher income actually seem less happy than I am. They seem desperate to go out and make more and more money, while I make a comfortable living but leave lots of time in my life to walk in the woods, explore foreign cities, enjoy family time, attend concerts, and so forth.

The amazing thing is that when I opened my life up to the idea of Abundance Consciousness, the already-abundant blessings in my life increased manyfold.

Jay, too, is an abundance thinker. As one of the best-known marketing authors in the world, he has no obvious need to cooperate with others. Some in his position would just think they 'no longer need to be nice to others, and wouldn't see any gain from helping them. But Jay discovered years ago that when he helps others, good things come back to him. He has a long history of giving support to younger, lesser-known marketing writers—and as a result of his willingness to collaborate, he has co-created far more books than he could do on his own, and his information empire is much more lucrative.

THE NEW VISION: NOT SCARCITY,
NOT PROSPERITY, BUT ABUNDANCE

Here's another way to express that radical, heretical idea:

> Your life can be abundant and full of blessings,
> with or without material wealth

Abundance is fundamentally different from prosperity. Prosperity still works on the idea that you have to conquer others, that you have to strive for more money, and that the pie is finite; your gain is someone else's loss. Abundance says that the pie is infinite, and that helping others is one way to help yourself—the more you help, the more the whole pie expands. And this is key as we, the business community, develop profitable ways to turn hunger and poverty into sufficiency, war and violence into peace, and catastrophic climate change into planetary balance and regeneration.

If you think and act from a scarcity model, you will find scarcity. If the energy you put into the universe comes from the mindset that you can easily get what you need and more, that's what you're likely to find.

We've been talking about this idea long before it was popularized as the Law of Attraction, in the movie, "The Secret." As we've already seen, abundance and attraction thinking attracts clients and customers who seek you out; you're not chasing them down and competing with others.

The Abundance Model in Business

Lots of things change once you start looking at business through the abundance filter. The biggest difference is that your competitors don't threaten you. Because there's enough for everyone, you can cooperate. Form powerful alliances; they're far better than scrambling like mice to beat one other to the cheese—never realizing that the cheese is inside a mousetrap.

Most importantly, you benefit yourself. Your business thrives, you feel good about what you do, you build warm relationships based on the best human qualities. You walk the streets with a light heart and your head held high.

Internet marketing consultant B.L. Ochman of http://www.whatsnextblog. com says:

> I used to be afraid to put news about my competitors' ebooks, newsletters and teleconferences in my newsletter. But I've completely changed my mind. I have begun to promote my competitors' works and to include them in the affiliate program for my ebooks. I do teleseminars with them.
>
> Why? There is plenty of work to go around. People looking for Internet marketing are going to shop around anyway so why deny that fact? We can refer work to each other and we can enjoy the halo effect of being associated with smart, accomplished people. Try it, you'll benefit.

Huh—what just happened here? As copywriters and marketing strategists—why on earth would we give you the name and contact info of one of our competitors?

Maybe, just maybe, it's because we really do believe in abundance thinking.

And B.L. believes in abundance too; when Shel wrote for permission to use her story in his earlier book, *Principled Profit: Marketing That Puts People First*, she not only reviewed it in her newsletter, but even connected him with a very well-known author who blurbed the book.

Yes, this philosophy really does pay back. B.L. had been living just blocks from the World Trade Center in New York City until 9/11; she'd had to move when her apartment became uninhabitable after the attacks, and her ex-landlord was trying to retain many thousands of dollars that she would have paid in rent. She turned to her allies online, and within weeks, the pressure campaign she created accomplished the desired effect.

We think the reason B.L. was able to get so much help from some of the world's heavy hitters in sales and marketing is because she had long ago established herself as a person who doesn't just take, but gives—again, operating out of that abundance mentality. If B.L. had been a cutthroat, if she had tried to steal business from her competitors or turn in useless work to her clients, would there have been a mass movement to come to her rescue? We strongly doubt it.

Scottie Claiborne is another entrepreneur who succeeded by embracing the abundance paradigm: Recognizing that she was getting national and international traffic to her website for a local service, she turned her site into a directory to find the nearest vendor—then asked other companies to list on her site. In other words, she drove traffic to competitors. She believes her listing of other sites was directly responsible for her Number 1 rank at Google, which in turn generated lots and lots of traffic directly. The site was successful very quickly, and she started selling equipment to other companies—all of whom knew her company because she'd been funneling inquiries to them.[88]

She eventually sold that business and turned her new expertise in search engine marketing into a new career.

Abundance and Going Green/Addressing Social Change

We've been told for decades that going green means sacrifice—that we have to choose between doing the right thing and our quality of life. Fortunately, this is a bunch of nonsense.

Of course, it's possible to make unwise choices that reduce your energy and resource use. But there's no need. Embracing green from an abundance mindset is a lot more comfortable. We know literally thousands of ways to lower energy and materials costs *and usage* by going green. (111 of those ways are in one of the free gifts you get for reading this book: Shel's ebook, Painless Green.) A green mindset in business will save money, make money, and *increase* quality of life.

Similarly, in the past, many companies have chosen to address the world's deepest problems through philanthropy. That's fine and good, but why not make it better? The solutions to problems like hunger, poverty, war, and catastrophic climate change can actually become profit centers, rather than a giving program strapped onto (and sapping money from) more conventional products and services.

We'll explore many pieces of the green/social change abundance mindset throughout this book. Here are two great thinkers who use the Abundance Principle in business; it's not a coincidence that the first of them uses a biological (in other words, green and natural) key metaphor:

---

88   Scottie Claiborne, "Links Are Good for Business," *High Rankings Advisor*, Nov. 20, 2002.

JOHN KREMER AND BIOLOGICAL MARKETING

John Kremer, author of *1001 Ways to Market Your Books* and one of the foremost authorities on book marketing in the US, says marketing is making friends and creating a "word-of-mouth army" that will sing your praises. [89]

Kremer suggests turning your customer into a participant, letting that customer become emotionally attached. So, for example, let your customers vote among different packaging alternatives or product names. Or package the same information in a free report with several different titles. A clear reader preference helps you pick the right name.

He's developed a new paradigm called *biological marketing*, and with his permission, we'll share it with you:

Farmers have incredible ROI [return on investment]. They plant one seed of corn and get back 900. Nature does not follow physics. Instead of an equal and opposite reaction, there's an incredible multifold giving back. It follows biological laws, and when you give and share, it comes back to you in abundance. Physics says that the ultimate end of the universe is entropy. Biology says the opposite, that everything multiplies and becomes incredibly rich and diverse. That's the law of life. Physics is the law of non-life. And it's the laws of life that determine marketing.

When you understand that, you know it's OK to give. The authors [or business owners] who are generous with their time get it back, they build legions of fans. That kind of relationship makes marketing fun and successful. You cannot replace it with mechanical rules, but once you learn it and take it to heart, that becomes the basis for success in anything you do. If you treat people right, it comes back over and over again. If you build a network of relationships, it's only three degrees of separation [versus the classic six to reach anyone in the world]. Another part of the law of nature is that you have to break out of your shell, just as birds and reptiles do. You can do it one person to one person.

---

89   Kremer's quotes are from his speech at the 3rd Annual Infinity Publishing "Express Yourself" Conference, Valley Forge, PA, October 3, 2002.

BOB BURG AND WINNING WITHOUT INTIMIDATION

Bob Burg gets what he wants almost every time, and his "opponents" are happy to hand over victory—because he believes in "positive persuasion" or "winning without intimidation":

When you're not getting your needs met, find the best way to de-escalate potential conflict *and* get the results you want. Treat even angry people with kindness, phrase your requests with language like "I totally understand if you can't"—and work little miracles in every interaction.

One of Burg's books, *Endless Referrals,* applies this concept directly to sales. This book was published by McGraw Hill and sold over 100,000 copies. His self-published *Winning Without Intimidation* also sold about that many, so clearly, Bob takes his own principles seriously. (Most business books sell 10,000 copies or less; typical self-published books sell far fewer.)

When things could get heated, we take a deep breath and a step back, and think, "How would Bob handle this?" And a lot of the time, we're able to access that smarter brain that can figure out what Bob would do, defuse the conflict, and achieve our goal. For instance, if two people are publicly escalating inappropriately on an email discussion list, instead of writing a nasty public post to shame the offenders into better behavior, we might ask the two offenders in a polite private note, as a personal favor, to change their behavior. The response from both is usually extremely positive.

As an ex-Chicagoan (Jay) and an ex- New Yorker (Shel), raised in loud, in-your-face cultures, we've also found Bob's approach helpful in talking to people from a different, quieter cultural background—such as the New England Yankee farm community where Shel now lives.

Burg's principles work not only in customer service situations but elsewhere—like employee relations. Rewarding positive behavior outperforms negative consequences for inappropriate behavior pretty much every time Workplace ethicist Christopher Bauer devoted a whole newsletter to reinforcing positive behavior from employees when you "catch them being good."[90]

---

90   September 22, 2008. Bauer's Weekly Ethics Thought is available by email subscription at www.bauerethicsseminars.com

Burg's Networking Formula

Ever go to a business networking function and watch some idiot pressing business cards into other people's hands, grinning insincerely, giving the elevator pitch, and moving on to the next victim? Eeeew!

Fortunately, Bob Burg also happens to be an expert on networking the right way. His audio program, "Endless Referrals," describes a far superior approach:

- Observe the group and identify a few well-connected people you'd like to meet
- Focus on the quality and depth of the contacts, not on quantity
- Make contact, remember their name, and listen much more than you talk
- Find ways to do something nice for them right then and there—such as introducing someone else who could help
- Follow up rapidly with a hand-written thank you that doesn't hawk your products and services, and continue to follow up with nice little touches over time (for instance, sending news clippings that mention your new contact)

Eventually, that other person will begin to see you as a person who adds value in his or her life, demand to know what you do and how to help you, and refer prospects to you. Wow.

If that kind of approach feels scary, get a copy of Bob's program. He breaks down every step and role plays it out.[91]

You can also take a more structured approach, such as joining a local chapter of Business Networking International (BNI), which gathers a team of non-competing businesses together to serve as referral agents for each other. BNI is a commitment, with required attendance at weekly meetings, reports back on how many referrals you gave and received, and their results. But for many people with a primarily local market, it's possible to build an entire business around referrals from the network, and there's a lot of safety built into the rigid structure. Most

---

91 All of Burg's programs as well as his current blog articles are available directly from him, at http://www.burg.com

chapters will let you attend as a guest or substitute to check it out and see if it's right: http://www.bni.com.

And as a purchaser of this book, you're entitled to a bonus package that includes Shel's 1-hour interview with BNI founder Ivan Misner as part of the Business and Marketing For a Better World Telesummit (25 calls altogether).

Here's a great relationship-building tool that combines the power of online technology with the appeal of hand-written notes: SendOutCards can digitize your handwriting, create either a completely original and personal card or one from a template, and send the card or even a gift through physical mail, for not much more money and a lot more convenience than the old-fashioned method: http://www.BusinessByReferrals.net.

ICELAND'S RENEWABLE ENERGY SYSTEM: APPLYING THE ABUNDANCE MODEL TO A WHOLE COUNTRY

Iceland runs almost all its buildings almost entirely on renewable energy: hydro and geothermal. You can't travel in Iceland without encountering the power of geothermal energy, and many Icelanders brag about their geothermal systems. You'll even find several museum exhibits highlighting volcanic and geothermal activity.

In Massachusetts, where Shel lives, temperatures typically range from -5°F/-20.5°C on a cold winter night to around 95°F/35°C on a sunny, hot summer afternoon. Harnessing geothermal typically involves drilling below the earth to a layer with year-round consistent temperature at about 50°F/10°C, and tapping into that layer to boost heating in the winter, and cooling in the summer, right at the saource. Most geothermal installations in the US use the thermal power directly, to heat and cool water.

Actively volcanic Iceland also heats water geothermally. But temperatures in many of the hot springs are hot enough to kill a person quickly, approaching the boiling point of water (212°F/100°C). Water coming out of the hot tap is as hot as the solar-heated water in Shel's home—generally hotter than fossil-heated tap water. Much of its geothermal power is harnessed to create steam, spin turbines, and generate electricity—sometimes transported across significant distances.

Geothermal is ubiquitous in Iceland. Municipalities harness and pipe it into virtually every house and building, as well as the geothermally heated municipal swimming pools and hot tubs (up to 111°F/44°C) that were in literally every town we visited. And because it's municipal, individual property owners don't have to invest tens of thousands of dollars, as they do in the US.

In other words, Iceland's ultra-green energy grid embodies the Abundance Principle. In a country with only 323,002 inhabitants,[92] this tiny country has the capacity to supply much of Europe's energy needs. Plans are afoot to build deep-sea cables that will export as much as 5 billion kilowatt-hours of clean, renewable electricity to the rest of Europe—enough to power 1.25 million homes.[93] Those of you based in Europe, especially, should be on the lookout for opportunities to profit from this coming industrial shift. And those in other seismically active parts of the world might want to think about how to get your country into massive geothermal.

There is, however, a down-side. We were shocked that saving water or electricity didn't seem to be a value. People just ran the water or left lights on. Their attitude was that they had plenty, it was really cheap, and they didn't have to worry about running out. Even in an abundant world, we think resources should be conserved, not squandered.

LESSONS

- Abundance is different from—and more powerful than—scarcity, or even prosperity
- Givers, who act from abundance, create a reservoir of goodwill that they can draw on in times of need
- "Biological marketing" can create large results from small inputs
- "Winning without intimidation" turns adversaries into allies
- Networking the right way turns contacts into streams of referral
- Understand the true meaning of money

---

92 Google search for Iceland population, 1/27/15.
93 Diane Pham, "Iceland Harnesses Geothermal Sources Able to Power Over 1.2 Million Homes," http://inhabitat.com/iceland-harnesses-geothermal-sources-able-to-power-over-1-2-million-homes/, verified 5/9/15.

ACTIONS

- Make a "gratitude list" of the abundant blessings in your life. Read that list at least once a week, perhaps daily. Keep adding to it.
- Name three instances where you benefitted from abundance thinking.
- Analyze a heated situation—how would Bob Burg calm it down?
- Observe five people carefully at your next networking function. Note whom you'd like to emulate, and who turns you off—and why.

CHAPTER 6

BUILD POWERFUL ALLIANCES—
WITH COMPETITORS, TOO

he word *"guerrilla"* traditionally implies an armed struggle. In war, the usual way to neutralize an enemy is to render that enemy impotent through dramatic losses of personnel and resources; you drive out the oppressor by making the cost of an invasion or occupation too high.

But Guerrilla Marketing has never been about shooting your opponent. Marketing guerrillas outflank the competition by moving swiftly, nimbly, and unexpectedly. We find and exploit new markets before the big, slow-moving household names even know they exist. And sometimes we're out again before they even come in.

Another way to disarm your competition is to *turn those companies into part of your marketing team.* By working together, you leverage the strengths your former opponent already has; you tap into the markets your so-called adversary already created.

Yes, we're talking about cooperating with your toughest competitors. This is a strategy that...

- Gives you access to an existing and proven market
- Lets you take a privileged position in the customer's mind, because you have the powerful endorsement of a company s/he already trusts
- Allows you both to be stronger by enabling initiatives that would be too big or expensive for either of you to do alone
- Eliminates the wasted energy you previously spent fighting each other, putting each other down, or battling negative perceptions of you caused by their other marketing

In many cases, the cooperation is going to be some kind of *"joint venture"* (JV)—a fancy phrase that simply means working together with another business. JVs might range from a simple co-marketing deal like stuffing fliers for each other in outbound orders or giving a purchase link in an e-zine, all the way up to a full-scale corporate merger. In between, there are many steps on the ladder: forming project-specific partnerships, bundling products from different companies to add value, handing out a freebie from another business as an incentive award, and on and on it goes.

Since, for many people, the idea of working with a competitor feels peculiar, we'll start with some examples that show how very easy it actually is to work with people in the same field. Then we'll look at some more Guerrilla JVs for businesses that don't compete directly.

TURN YOUR COMPETITORS INTO ALLIES

Get to Know the Other People in Your Niche

When you notice a new arrival in the marketplace—or if you enter a market new to you—pick up the phone and get acquainted. Become active in business associations for your industry and your geographic. Participate in Internet discussion groups with others in your own or closely related fields. Talk shop, discuss approaches to problems, let each other know about events or opportunities of interest. Know each company's Unique Selling Proposition (USP)—the key reason why it makes sense to do business with that company—and that way, you'll know when and where to refer accounts that aren't quite right for you.

Key Guerrilla Principle:

> Find out how you can provide assistance to the other person—before you bring up your own wants and needs.

Market Together, Cooperatively

Here's a wonderful newspaper co-op ad from eleven local florists, who teamed up just before Mother's Day:

When 11 competitors join together, they can afford a big, dramatic ad.

By joining forces, the consortium could afford a big, noticeable ad. An ad one-eleventh the size would have been easy to ignore, but this one filled a quarter-page (in a large-format broadsheet newspaper) and demanded to be noticed.

Another example: in publishing, many small presses will include a flier for a complementary book from another publisher as they ship out orders. For the very low cost of printing and mailing the fliers, participating publishers get to reach an entirely new audience. Sometimes, publishers will even sell a bundle consisting of their own and other firms' books, gathered together at a value price.

It's not just small companies doing this, either. Some of the largest and most fiercely competitive corporations in the world engage in joint ventures regularly. The first car Shel ever bought new was a 1988 Chevrolet Nova, which was essentially identical to the Toyota Corolla. Built by Chevrolet to Toyota's specification, it was a marvelous car, and cost about $2000 less than the same car with the Toyota nameplate. Similarly, the popular Ford Escort wagon was really a Mazda, etc., etc.

FedEx and the United States Postal Service have a very interesting arrangement; the USPS subcontracts intercity air transportation of Express Mail and Priority Mail to FedEx, which gets a substantial new revenue stream and utilizes otherwise wasted air freight capacity. And meanwhile, FedEx has installed thousands of drop boxes at post offices around the country, thus helping its consumers avoid pick-up charges and making shipping with the company incredibly convenient.[94]

For service businesses, sometimes your biggest competitor is not another company, but the idea of doing it yourself. Certainly, this is true in the writing and consulting that Jay and Shel both do for a living. Professional writers compete not only with homegrown do-it-yourselfers but with software tools. Most people believe they can write well; few of them understand the difference between putting sentences together on paper to convey information— something most people can actually do themselves—and writing materials with a sharply defined focus and a powerful call to action, or a news hook. Only a very small percentage of businesses ever hire outside professional copywriters. Large firms hire this skill internally, and many small firms use their own (untrained) marketing departments, never seeing the opportunity costs. Not

---

94 William Pride and O. C. Ferrell, *Marketing Concepts and Strategies,* 12th ed. (Boston: Houghton Mifflin, 2003), p. 56. This contract was renewed for seven years in 2013: http://www.bloomberg.com/news/articles/2013-04-23/fedex-to-flyEmail-for-postal-service-for-10-5-billion, accessed 3/12/15.

surprisingly, many writers and editors attempt to stem the tide by forming professional organizations, setting standards, and marketing together, just as those florists did in their cooperative ad.

Refer Business to Each Other

Typically, you will each have areas of specialization that you do better than others. So if you get an inquiry from someone best served by your competitor, you help the customer by playing matchmaker. And your competitors will do the same for you. With both competitors and complementary businesses, you may choose to pay or charge a referral commission, or simply pass appropriate clients to each other.[95]

Very early in his business, which he started in 1981, Shel discovered the power of this kind of marketing:

> My business started primarily as a typing service, but very quickly, I branched out into writing résumés and marketing materials. I joined a local association of secretarial services, and because people knew my specialties, I got a lot of résumé work through referrals.
>
> At the same time, after my first two tape-transcription assignments, I decided I really disliked that part of the business and began referring those jobs out to other services.

This kind of cooperation always has three winners: the client, of course, who gets the best providers for the services s/he needs—but also both the referring and the receiving businesses: you don't let the things you dislike get in the way of doing what you enjoy and excel at, yet you're able to keep your clients happy when they need those services.

Wendy Shill Kurtz, MBA, APR, CPRC, president of the PR firm Elizabeth Charles & Associates, LLC, http://www.elizabethcharles.com, has a similar outlook:

---

95 Assuming, of course, that paying for referrals is legal in your industry, within in its code of ethics, and is properly disclosed.

Some of my best referrals have come from vendors and those competitors with whom I maintain a sense of "we're in this together," rather than "we're out to beat each other to the top." [96]

Subcontract, Joint Venture, or Even Merge

If one of you has too much work and the other has too little, doesn't it make sense to work with a professional that you trust and even it all out? After all, if fierce competitors like Apple and IBM could join together (with Motorola as a third partner) to develop the Power PC chip architecture, surely you and your competitors can put aside your differences.

In some cases, if you work so well together, and enjoy advantages of scale, increased buying power, and so forth—and your corporate cultures harmonize well with each other—a permanent merger or acquisition may even make sense.

Be There if Your Competitors Fold

If you've maintained strong positive relations, if you've cooperated on several projects, if your competitor leaves the business, *you* will get the referrals.

In the earliest days of Shel's business, he formed a strong working relationship with one of his competitors. When that competitor later moved out of the area, he was one of several who sent all their clients to Shel when they closed their shops. He got those referrals because they were on friendly terms and had often sent each other clients.

The above examples are only a small slice of what's possible. Dave Pollard lists six different large categories of JV possibilities (there are others, too):

- Collaboration on large projects that either need extra horsepower or complementary skills
- Cooperative purchasing
- Research and development, including new products
- Marketing
- Cross-industry licensing
- Leveraging skills [97]

---

96 *I-PR Digest*, Oct. 22, 2002.
97 Dave Pollard, *Finding the Sweet Spot*, op. cit., p. 184.

YOU'VE DONE THE HARDEST PART—
NOW, NETWORK WITH COMPLEMENTARY BUSINESSES

Psychologically, it may be pretty hard, at first, to accept the idea that your competitors can be extremely powerful allies in growing your business. That's why we put it first in this section. We wanted you to see that these techniques work even with the people you might have thought you were least likely to develop partnerships with. The next subsections will seem really easy after you've already started thinking about how you and your competitors can help each other.

Online Joint Ventures

Partnering with established businesses can completely reinvent your business model. Consider the way Amazon.com birthed the modern affiliate program by syndicating the ability to have a bookstore without needing inventory to thousands of website partners. All of a sudden, those sites and newsletters had a way to offer their members relevant, highly targeted titles from the convenience of home, with no need to carry inventory, no need to worry about selection, and even a small income stream.

It was a brilliant move, and it took Amazon from a relatively small startup to the most well-branded bookseller online—because it seemed back then that if you visited ten sites, five or six would have an Amazon store.

Amazon's strategy is a case study in what marketing legend Alex Mandossian calls "the paradox of syndication"[98]—that restricting your presence to your own website is counterproductive; the more channels offer a company's message (or products), the faster it grows. This is true both online and off. Consider how the power of syndication built such brands as Dear Abby, the Peanuts comic strip, and every chain store franchise you can think of.

Mandossian developed this theory after years as an active promoter of Internet-based JVs. These are extremely common in the Internet-marketing superstar world, where you find the same gurus speaking at each other's conferences and endorsing each other's products. We believe that one of the

---

98 http://www.alexmandossian.com/2008/11/13/the-3-marketing-paradoxes-explained-part-3/, verified 4/7/15.

reasons this small group has generated so much wealth is this strong cooperation. Rather than make all the sales on the basis of your own client and prospect list, get others to reach their lists and cut them in on the profits. You can reach a far larger audience and make many more sales.

But there are special considerations in setting up Internet JVs. Master copywriter and commercial writing coach Bob Bly outlines some of the concerns he has when he's approached. Recognizing that if you over-email, your readers start unsubscribing, Bly figures he has 100 slots a year to promote other people's products, and each one should be worth at least $4000 to him if he wants this aspect of his business to bring in $400,000—which means a 20 percent commission on a $20 book isn't going to cut it. He suggests you answer four questions when approaching "gurus" about partnering with you:

1. Who are you?
2. How do you know the guru: Are you a subscriber? Have you bought product? Attended a workshop?
3. How will your product directly benefit the guru's subscribers
4. What payout terms are you suggesting? (Bly looks for 50 percent on a product price of $20 or more, though a lower percentage is acceptable if the price is above $1000).

Send this information and offer or provide a free review copy of the product; the good gurus will want to kick the tires and make sure they can see the value in the product, so they can honestly enthuse about it to their audience.[99]

Geographic Alliances

If your business uses a retail model—you have a storefront or office where your customers and clients come to you—geographically based partnerships make a lot of sense. It's in everyone's interest to draw people into the area where your business is located. And that area can be as small as a single office building, strip mall, city block—or as large as an entire state or country. This is why Chambers

---

99 Bly, Bob, "Playing the Slots," Early To Rise e-zine, July 30, 2008, http://www.earlytorise.com/2008/07/30/playing-the-slots.html, verified 4/7/15.

of Commerce and neighborhood business associations get organized, why economic development offices and tourism departments promote their region as a place to locate or visit.

Here are some ideas for promoting based on geographic proximity:

- Organize and promote a special event that draws traffic. It could be as simple as a group promotion with 20 percent off any one item, or as complex as a street fair with live concerts, children's activities, dignitaries, and so forth.

- Market the neighborhood or region as a destination. In Minneapolis, the many restaurant owners along Nicollet Avenue banded together and dubbed it "Eat Street," and got the destination promoted by local tourism officesa.

- Seek partnerships with complementary businesses in the neighborhood: Cooperative Life Leader magazine reports that a food co-op in Durham, New Hampshire invited the weekly farmers' market to set up shop outside the store.[100] The existing storefront provided a natural base for the farm stands, and customers seeking fresh produce were drawn into the store to buy other natural foods.

- Join with your neighbors to advertise the neighborhood. There are many ways to do this: list several businesses in one ad; give more space to one business at a time, rotating through all the members; create and distribute a group flier, website, ad-supported map, catalog, or discount coupon book...

- Organize together under an association banner for neighborhood-improvement projects—anything from a group litter-pick up to creating public pressure to close down health and safety hazards—and tell the media what you're doing.

- If there's a major attraction nearby, work with the local tourism bureau to develop a brochure about other nearby attractions (including yours) that the large attraction can distribute; the participants can reciprocate, of course.

---

100 Electronic edition, Sept. 2002. Published by the Cooperative Development Institute, Greenfield, Mass. http://www.cdi.coop/.

Bundle Complementary Products and/or Services Together

Pull all the pieces of the right solution from different vendors. Combine complementary products that add value, for less money than buying them all separately. And of course, share the marketing costs and reach each other's customers.

To compete with integrated software, four different software companies bundled together a word processor, spreadsheet, database, and graphics package. One company coordinated marketing.

Using the same principles, a carpenter, plumber, electrician, and painter could offer a one-stop home repair clearinghouse...rental car, airline, and hotel chains could join forces to offer a great one-stop deal for business travelers...a used-car dealer could team up with a car wash and an oil changer...In short, the possibilities are limitless.

Other JVs

Sharing a neighborhood is only one possible bridge to collaboration. Consider a tiny startup that joined forces with the largest and most powerful player in the entire computer industry back in 1981, in order to supply operating systems for the giant's new line of microcomputers, If you guessed Microsoft's partnership with IBM, you get the gold star.

If you're in a service business, especially, you may be able to partner with complementary services. For instance, wedding planners, caterers, banquet halls, photographers, florists, and musicians can cooperate to provide a one-stop wedding service. And if your business is not local, your partnerships can spread out around the world.

The partnership can be active or passive—and sometimes can lead to whole new opportunities. A marketing-savvy graphic artist brought Shel and a local web designer into a three-way pitch meeting to produce some collateral and a website for their local Board of Realtors.

The organization had asked the web designer to register a very obscure, hard-to-remember domain name. Although they hadn't been hired yet, Shel and the graphic artist started telling the organization why the domain would be a marketing disaster. They told the executive director to imagine giving out that name on the radio, and asked the group to find a name that would reinforce the group's identity and message. The whole room brainstormed a bunch of better domain names

Years later, Shel got a call from the president of the largest real estate firm in the service area. He'd been impressed at that meeting and came to Shel to rewrite the firm's entire collection of a dozen or so brochures—a very juicy assignment. By advising the prospect that its course was strewn with obstacles, Shel had put himself in the position to receive a much, much larger assignment: one for which he was not competing against any other copywriters.

Most of our JV relationships are far less formal. We often recommend vendors who provide complementary services: graphic design, search engine optimization, website coding, press release distribution, etc. Other professionals who offer complementary services send us referrals, using one of three models:

1. Informal referrals (no money changes hands)
2. Formal referrals, earning a commission
3. Subcontracting

CO-SOLVE: BEYOND SILOS, BEYOND SINGLE-PURPOSE

Imagine that you've developed a product or service that helps to fix poverty or war at the same time it makes a difference on climate change. Imagine that this product is cheap enough to reach the poorest of the poor, yet profitable enough to build a business.

In nature, and in our bodies, many things have more than one purpose, and nothing is wasted. When we start thinking beyond the simplistic economics of profit and loss that only count some factors, our eyes open to the wider world of "geonomics" or "planetnomics." As an example, think about a tree. Trees provide a number of "ecoservices":

- Food for people and other animals (fruits, acorns, nuts, leaves, maple or birch syrup)
- Oxygen for us to breathe
- Shade to make us more comfortable in summer

- Carbon sequestration
- Light modulation, allowing more light to reach the forest floor at the times of year when it's most needed
- Habitat for a large assortment of birds, bugs, fungi, and mammals
- Temperature modulation, making summer and winter more bearable
- Emergency shelter
- Construction material (wood)
- Heat energy (when burned)
- Paper
- Soil rehabilitation (as leaves drop in the fall or rotten branches fall off and are composted)
- Rainwater and groundwater management

That's 13 different functions, and there are others. Ten of these happen with no need for human intervention, and with no need to remove the tree.

As Janine Benyus, inventor of the term, "biomimicry," puts it,

Nature has already solved many of the problems we are grappling with: energy, food production, climate control, benign chemistry, transportation, packaging, and more. Mimicking these earth-savvy designs can help humans leapfrog to technologies that sip energy, shave material use, reject toxins, and work as a system to create conditions conducive to life.[101]

We'll visit with Benyus and the whole concept of biomimicry in some depth in Chapter 20.

How can we emulate nature in co-solving several problems at once? Many companies and organizations have come up with wonderful ideas, as you'll read later. Here's one to get started: Urban food projects that...

---

101 Janine Benyus, "A Biomimicry Primer," available for download at http://biomimicry.net/about/biomimicry/a-biomimicry-primer/, accessed 3/26/15.

- Turn abandoned or empty spaces such as rooftops, vacant lots, traffic islands, median strips into attractive, living spaces (benefits: quality of life, and eventually attracting economic development)
- Bring fresh, local food into poor communities (benefits: health, quality of life)
- Create pollution-absorbing buffer zones, reducing asthma, emphysema, etc. (benefits: environment, health)
- Train local urban youth in food production, providing marketable skills, positive experience with collaborative problem solving, and a respect for the land (benefits: economic: job skills training, job creation; quality of life: reduction in vandalism, sense of purpose and of ability to change unhealthy/undesirable situations)
- Decrease CO_2 and other greenhouse gas emissions (benefit: environment)

Another kind of co-solving involves bringing people together from different disciplines to work on a problem or group of problems. The corporate world talks about "getting people out of their silos" so Marketing, Sales, and Engineering can all brainstorm together. Academics gather in "interdisciplinary teams" to study phenomena that might include astrophysics, biology, and sociology. Nonprofits and government agencies understand "partnerships" such as public-private collaborations and cause-related marketing. Online marketing masters organize "joint ventures" (JVs) for massively successful product launches. Community organizers "build coalitions" with other groups, coming together on the issues where they agree, and separating when they diverge.

Just as co-solving itself brings people from different spheres together to solve one set of problems or address one set of issues, these different but overlapping perspectives all teach us something. We can create win-win syntheses of the best of all this thinking, and use that power and synergy to address—and solve—even the most intractable problems.

Let's take our thinking even bigger. Could this kind of collaboration end war? Organizations such as Neve Shalom/Wahat al-Salam, a mixed community of Israelis and Palestinians with a peace agenda, work actively to:

- Expose both cultures to the humanness of their "enemy" and debunk myths/stereotypes (benefit: peace)
- Share best practices in desert agriculture and architecture (benefit: environment)
- Increase fluency in the other's language (benefit: economic: more employable
- Form a constituency for long-term solution (benefit: peace)
- Spread the benefits and knowledge through public outreach—speaking, performing, media, etc. (benefit: peace)

SOCIAL PROOF—TURN YOUR CUSTOMERS AND SUPPLIERS INTO EVANGELISTS

If mutual-success cooperative approaches work so well horizontally, with competitors, won't they also work vertically? The people who choose to do business with you, and the people with whom you choose to do business, are natural allies. Both Jay and Shel are ardent believers in the marketing power of social proof: convincing people to take a certain action because a critical mass of the populace, or of people they respect and trust, have told them to do so. Testimonials, endorsements, referrals and other social proof techniques allow your customers, others in your networks, and perhaps even celebrities, to do your marketing for you. Note: disclose any kind of money exchange in securing the endorsement, including affiliate relationships. To keep the focus on the message, we've chosen not to include affiliate links in this book.

Here are a few ideas:

Use Testimonials in Your Advertising, and Submit Testimonials to Other Businesses

If you're delighted with a product or service, offer a testimonial for that company's ads. Jim McCann's wildly successful 800-FLOWERS was plugged in national TV and print ads by AT&T—because McCann praised the telecommunications giant's toll-free service. It would have cost him millions of dollars to get the exposure if he'd paid for it himself.

On a much smaller scale, years ago, Shel offered a local telephone book publisher a plug, noting that this directory outpulled three others combined.

The company ran his testimonial in local papers—and upgraded Shel's own ads in its book. Meanwhile, he got his name, company, and then-current book plastered all over the three-county circulation area.

If you advertise anyway, ask your clients' permission to quote their testimonials in your ads If the ad is on radio or TV (or your own website), ask if they'll let you tape them reading the quote. (For ideas on how to get really great testimonials, please see Shel's earlier book, *Grassroots Marketing: Getting Noticed in a Noisy World*).

But even if you don't advertise, you can grow through referrals. It could be as simple as handing each client a business card and saying, "If you have friends or colleagues who need this service, please spread the word." And sometimes, the client will turn to you and say, "I actually know several people. May I have a few more cards?"

And this works online, too. If you participate in any online groups (and you most definitely should), leverage the enthusiasm of your clients who participate. Make it a practice to ask people who've used and been enchanted by your services to mention their delight to the list. So over a period of years, participants in this community will hear dozens of people exclaim about your skills and expertise.

Shel's participation in these online communities brings in thousands of dollars a year *with a marketing cost of zero*, in part because happy clients post to the lists. One of his clients was initially somewhat skeptical, so he ran a test. He sent out a press release Shel had written to one group of journalists, and one of his own press releases to another set. He reported back to the entire list that Shel's release had pulled six times as many responses as his own effort, and hired Shel for several subsequent projects.

Sometimes, the buzz goes viral and you may actually get referrals from listmates who haven't hired you—and industry gurus might list you as a resource.

Much-published marketing author Marcia Yudkin, citing a booklet by sales consultant Paul Johnson called "Let Your Customer Sell You," talks about the art of asking for small favors: once someone gives you a testimonial, there's an emotional commitment to you and your product. And the person who did the small favor may be more willing to do a larger one.[102]

If the favor is a testimonial, your clients not only publicly state their commitment, but also cement the reasons why they felt so good about you in their own minds. They may provide more projects and referrals.

And that relationship can be easily rekindled, even after an absence. For instance, you could send a quick note—perhaps accompanied by a small gift or a discount coupon for a future order—that says, "I just wanted to thank you again for your beautiful testimonial, below. For six months, it's helped me turn prospects into clients. I'm honored and gratified by your continued faith in my work."

David Frey, author of *Marketing Best Practices*, notes that you can use your clients and customers as case studies, and write articles or white papers about them. If you publish articles in magazines, you're not paying for advertising; with some publications, you even get paid. Again, they get exposure, you get exposure, and you show how you've solved a problem for them. (Get their written permission ahead of time, of course.)

Frey also suggests giving out an award to a big customer or supplier; by so doing, you can build brand awareness, customer retention, and the opportunity for quite a bit of publicity and marketing oomph.

Explore Co-op Advertising Programs

In co-op programs, a supplier partially subsidizes the cost of a retailer's ads and in-store displays. Many manufacturers will provide logos, sales aids, and actual dollars to help you tell the world that you carry their products. You can sometimes also get this kind of help from credit card companies, retail co-ops, professional associations, and so on.

If you're the manufacturer or distributor, consider sponsoring a co-op program. And it doesn't have to be just advertising, either; for instance, offer co-op dollars toward your retailers' direct-mail and Web campaigns, too—but insist on approving the copy before you put your name on the marketing piece

---

102 Reported in Yudkin's email newsletter, "The Marketing Minute," Sept. 25, 2002.

or provide any funds. In fact, because so few businesses understand effective marketing, you may want to offer co-op dollars only if you supply the creative elements (copy and design).

Institute Cooperative Loyalty, Referral, And Incentive Programs

Design loyalty programs that not only keep your customers coming back, but have your partner businesses actively recruiting new customers for you. These programs offer wonderful opportunities to partner with other merchants. Find complementary businesses whose offerings will resonate with your customers; you offer a reward from the other store, which in turn rewards its own customers with something from you. This is something even some of the country's largest corporations do. For instance, a cereal box may have a coupon good for a bottle of juice from a different company, or a fill-up at a gas station gets you a deep discount on a car wash. Use goods and services from other businesses as rewards in each other's loyalty and incentive programs, and then you have the benefit of reaching their customers as well as your own.

You can operate similar programs, not only to reward your own customers for frequency and amount of purchase, but also to actively solicit referrals. If a customer sends you a customer, it's nice to say thank you. This could just be a quick note (handwritten and postally mailed, if you want maximum impact). But if someone sends a whole bunch of clients, a small gift is probably appropriate.

And unlike the frequency reward, where it makes the most sense to bring in other businesses, here's a perfect time to use your own offerings as a reward, so that your own client comes back to you again. We might give one of our books as a thank-you to a marketing client who has sent a large amount of business, for instance.

Larger companies have been known to be very creative with this, too. Intercontinental Hotels, one of the largest hospitality chains in the world, offered triple reward points for a three-night stay, and provided codes to share the offer with three friends. Every single person who received the initial mailing shared the offer, and the promotion went viral, with an unheard of 1,766% response.

In other words, the company *got responses from almost 18 times more people than they sent the offer to.* [103]

Talk about a triple-win. Intercontinental added substantial immediate revenues with all those three-night stays, paying only in slightly decreased revenues much later, when the new guests qualified for a free stay or other reward. The elite customers felt special, honored for their patronage. And the new guests started their guest careers with a big head start toward free lodging.

Of course, you can also incent your own employees. Set up a standardized system of performance awards. Partnering with other businesses once again expands the market for everyone. Ask a restaurant owner to donate a monthly free dinner for two as a sales achievement award, in exchange for publicity in your company newsletter and on your website. (Use this strategy in your outbound marketing, too. Donate a door prize to your local Chamber networking event, for example.)

Network with Organizations That Service Your Customers

Become a preferred or endorsed supplier. When you provide products or services through an association, several wonderful things happen:

- You reach the organization's membership at no cost, through its newsletters, website, and other promotional materials—and sometimes, this could be tens or hundreds of thousands of members
- You receive the organization's implied endorsement, and thus, the members are predisposed to choose you (and even recommend you to their own networks)
- The members benefit from a better price, while the organization can receive a donation or a sales commission—and because you had no marketing cost, this is an easy benefit to offer

---

103 Marketing Sherpa, "Viral Email Nets 100% Response from Brand Champs: 3 Simple Steps," http://www.marketingsherpa.com/article.php?ident=30752&pop=no, August 5, 2008. Verified 4/10/15.

Enlist Your Customers' Help For Programs That Benefit Both Of You

Cause-related marketing offers all sorts of possibilities for environmental or charity initiatives, fundraising for independent stores, etc.

Since at least 2007, Florence Bank, a local bank in Shel's community has divided an annual pot of money among a number of local charities—and the bank's customers get to vote on how the money will be divided, by nominating their favorite organizations. The bank apportions the grants according to the number of votes, above a very low minimum number. But only customers can vote. Of course, if you don't already happen to have an account there, the bank will be glad to set one up—and needless to say, this bank gains a lot of new accounts as people sign up to support their choices. This program has been so successful that the bank started with $50,000, raised it to $75,000 and then to $100,000.

Speaking of getting new accounts, in 2015, this same bank offers $25 each to the favorite charity of a referring customer and the new account customer.[104]

And don't be afraid to embrace more controversial causes, if your markets support it. Sure, everyone loves to help charities working on curing various diseases or solving poverty problems. But there's definitely a place for being willing to walk your values talk, even if your position is not universally popular. If there's strong alignment between your market and your chosen cause, doing so will build your reputation as a firm of integrity and courage—while allowing you to benefit from the exposure you get.

Framing and Social Proof

Social proof can be a two-edged sword. It's very easy for a crowd to convince itself that bad behavior is socially acceptable. In a must-read article, Brian Clark points out the danger: a negatively phrased message might actually *encourage* the behavior it tries to prevent, by planting the idea that so many people do it, it must be okay. He sites a fossil park that put up signs to prevent vandalism and theft, but because the signage focused on the problem, the number of

---

104 https://www.florencebank.com/resources/help-a-friend, accessed 3/12/15.

incidents went up. A sign phrased positively about protecting the common heritage reduced the incidence.[105]

Framing is an extremely powerful technique in business, nonprofit/NGO, and politics. It's a matter of creating the imagery, in words, sights, smells, sounds, tastes, and touches, to move your audience's thought and emotions where you want them to be. And framing is especially valuable when it hooks into core values. Thus, the anti-abortion movement gained traction when it stopped describing itself as *"anti-abortion"* and began calling itself *"pro-life."* It's really hard to be perceived as "against life," and "pro-choice" doesn't have the same oomph. When the pro-choice position finds a metaphor as powerful and values-laden as the anti-choice, that pendulum will swing—just as it did when advocates were able to shift the discussion of same-sex marriage from "attacking the traditional family" (a frame that never held up to close examination) to "marriage equality."

Similarly, the 2008 Barack Obama presidential campaign, with its uplifting framing and messages of "yes we can" and "change," its elegant use of social media to empower volunteers, supporters, and contributors in two-way communication, its soaring oratory, its transparency, and its focus on core values like bringing people out of poverty and achieving peace, was a powerful message to an American public that had been battered by physical, economic and social storms, watched its leaders get caught in a web of secrets and lies, and seen its standing in the world, its budget surplus, and its considerable post-9/11 political capital depleted.

We suspect Obama's advisors had read George Lakoff's *Don't Think of an Elephant,* which lays out in very clear terms exactly how the Republican Party was framing divisive social issues as recruitment tools, and discussed how the Democrats could recapture the American mindset.

However, once in office, the Obama administration seemed to ignore the very lessons that led to victory. The White House let its opponents do the framing, forgot to keep its ready-to-keep-acting constituency mobilized, backed away from the deep-seated change it was elected to accomplish, and found itself tangled up in deadlocks on issue after issue.

---

105 Clark, Brian, "How to Change the World Using Social Media," November 6, 2008, http://www.copyblogger.com/social-media-change/, verified 4/10/15.

In the green world, just as in the political world, framing is crucial. For example, you will not catch Shel using the phrase, "global warming." Instead, he talks about "catastrophic climate change." Others have used the term, "global roasting."[106]

Why?

- Warming" is a joyous word, with happy connotations. Think about "warm-hearted" friends or a "warm lead" in sales—but climate change is nothing to be joyous about

- "Warming" implies a gradual shift, nothing to be very concerned about, just a natural evolution—rather than the reality of intense and cataclysmic storms

- Shifting weather patterns are not all heat-related; recent winters have often contained patterns of extreme cold, as "global warming" deniers are quick to point out"—and other climate issues have to do with increasing intensity of hurricanes, typhoons, and tsunamis, drought, and other once-unusual events

- It's hard for many people to make the connections between rising temperatures and the major weather events they influence—such as the human engineering interventions that turned Hurricane Katrina from a "normal" hurricane into one of the most destructive storms up to that point

Please remember this discussion of framing in Chapters 12, 13, and 14, when we talk about the need for different language and messaging for deep green, lazy green, and nongreen audiences.

---

106 Shel Horowitz, "John Holdren: The "Roasted World" of Unchecked Climate Change: What the Numbers Actually Mean," included in Shel's report on the 2005 Bioneers-by-the-Bay conference, http://www.frugalmarketing.com/dtb/bioneers-by-the-bay2.shtml, verified 3/17/15.

IT'S NOT ABOUT TRANSACTIONS...IT'S ABOUT RELATIONSHIPS

So far, we've talked about ethics and values...charity partnerships...green initiatives...customer retention-to-loyalty-to-evangelism programs... What do all these strategies have in common?

Each of these approaches shifts the customer interaction from a one-time transaction to an ongoing relationship.

And customers crave that relationship. Roy Williams cites an MIT study that watched buyer behavior on a best-deals website. Although the study authors fully expected that nearly 100 percent would choose the lowest price, Williams wasn't surprised that "51 percent scrolled down from the lowest prices at the top of the list to buy from a better-known retailer down below, voluntarily paying several dollars more."[107] According to Williams, many businesses draw about equally from both transactional (price-sensitive, looking to squeeze out all they can from you, support-intensive but not necessarily appreciative) and relational (appreciative, long-term, repeat, loyal) customers.

Relationship-oriented customers account for far more profitability, create far less hassle, and are much more likely to refer others. So those are the customers you want to reach out to, and nurture. Some businesses go so far as to deliberately disincent the bottom 10 or 20 percent of their market: to drive these transaction-based, high-maintenance, low-profit customers elsewhere.[108] However, since relational customers often start as transactional, we prefer converting transactional customers to relational ones.

LESSONS

- Neutralize your enemies not by disabling them, but by befriending them or even joining forces on projects
- Gain access to their existing complementary markets, and work together to build new markets—increase the pie for everyone

---

107 "Monday Morning Memo from the Wizard of Ads," December 12, 2004, http://www.mondaymorningmemo.com/?ShowMe=ThisMemo&MemoID=1534.
108 Ibid.

- Compete effectively together against do-it-yourselfism or deep-discount non-specialists
- Incorporate social proof such as powerful testimonials
- Frame your discussions to emphasize positive rather than negative steps and harness core values
- Understand and harness the difference between transaction- and relationship-oriented customers—move people from encounter to prospect to customer to fan

ACTIONS

- Identify between one and three competitors and approach them from the abundance perspective with a win-win way to cooperate.
- Build additional alliances with not only competitors but customers, suppliers, nonprofits, and at least one business in a completely different market.

CHAPTER 7

WHY THE ABUNDANCE PARADIGM ELIMINATES THE NEED TO WORRY ABOUT MARKET SHARE

nce you get rid of *I win = you lose*, many new horizons open up. Including the understanding that market share might not even matter.

THE DEATH OF "MARKET SHARE"

You hear it constantly: "We need to gain market share."

Our question: Why?

If your business has enough, why would it possibly be a problem if others have enough as well? In fact, a rising tide is more likely to lift other boats; more for them may very well mean more for you as well.

Consider a famous case: PC operating systems. In the beginning, believe it or not, Apple pretty much owned the market. The Apple II, which ran the first PC spreadsheet, dominated. IBM, with its tremendous brand equity, introduced its PC in 1981 and changed the equation. Because IBM actively courted business software developers, the business community migrated to IBM's platform. But the Apple Mac (introduced in 1984) quickly made inroads in graphic design, education, publishing, advertising, music, and video—where the much faster learning curve, better graphics, and full visual display were more important than the ability to crunch data.

Then IBM opened its architecture, and cheap clones drove a vast expansion of the overall market. IBM's market share went down—but its sales went up, because a smaller piece of a much larger number turned out to be larger than the largest piece of a smaller number. By creating an entire new class of competitors, IBM helped itself.

Yet, despite a tiny 6.89 percent market share,[109] Apple Computer was highly profitable even during the downturn—and during the recovery, it's been on fire. In the last three months of 2008, Apple took in a record $10.17 billion (up over a billion dollars from the previous year). $1.61 billion was profit[110] Apple's growth has been quite rapid; in 2001, the quarterly numbers were just $1.5 billion in revenue, of which $40 million was profit.[111] Seven years later, the quarterly profit was greater than the overall revenue had been. And by the fourth quarter of 2014, Apple was raking in revenue of $42.1 billion and net profit of $8.5 billion.[112]

On January 29, 2015, the New York Times devoted an entire article to analyzing why Apple's $683 billion market cap was more than double Microsoft's.[113] Less than a month later, on February 24, 2015, Apple's market

109 Obtained by adding up the numbers for the different Windows and Apple operating system versions at NetMarketShare.com, "Realtime Analytics With no Sampling: Desktop Operating System Market Share," http://www.netmarketshare.com/operating-system-market-share.aspx?qprid=10&qpcustomd=0 , accessed 3/29/15.

110 Dalrymple, Jim, Jonathan Seff, and Philip Michaels"Apple reports record profit for first quarter," Macworld, January 21, 2009, http://www.macworld.com/article/138362/2009/01/earnings.html, verified 4/11/15.

111 Fried, Ian, "New iMacs lift Apple's quarter," CNet, April 17, 2002, http://news.cnet.com/2100-1040-885301.html, verified 4/11/15.

112 "Apple Reports Fourth Quarter Results: Strong iPhone, Mac & App Store Sales Drive Record September Quarter Revenue & Earnings, http://www.apple.com/pr/library/2014/10/20Apple-Reports-Fourth-Quarter-Results.html, accessed 3/13/15.

113 James B. Stewart, "How, and Why, Apple Overtook Microsoft," New York Times, January 29, 2015, http://www.nytimes.com/2015/01/30/business/how-and-why-apple-overtook-microsoft.html?_r=0, accessed March 29, 2015.

capitalization hit USD $769.86 billion, up from $637 billion at the beginning of the year.[114] That day, General Motors' market cap was $61.02 billion;[115] General Electric's, $254.97 billion;[116] Walmart's, $272.59 billion.[117] And IBMs was $162.92 billion. In other words, with less than 7 percent of the market, Apple was worth more to investors on that day than the largest car maker, the largest purveyor of electrical goods, the largest retailer, and the computer company that used to own the market—combined!

Could you make a comfortable living on those numbers? With an installed base of tens of millions of users, the Apple OS could be a big, promising, market for software developers. In fact, even when its installed base was far smaller, Apple often was first to get popular business software out there: PageMaker, Quark XPress, Adobe Illustrator and Photoshop, and even Microsoft Excel were first piloted on the Mac platform and then rolled out to the admittedly much larger DOS/Windows world. Even AOL (then called AppleLink) was available for Mac long before Windows.

Also, rather than buy its way into PC dominance, Apple brings superior products to vast untapped or poorly tapped markets and understands that the innovation has to provide practical utility. An iPod is much easier to carry and offers more music choice than a Sony Walkman; an iPhone has a lot more functionality and user-friendliness than an early Blackberry or ordinary cell phone; there were no successful tablets at all before the iPad. And all three products created and owned their category for a few years until the competition could duplicate their functionality.

In a service business, market share is even less relevant than it is in manufacturing. In a product-based environment involving manufacturing or high-volume retail, there are economies of scale that allow a market leader to command more favorable terms than smaller competitors. But these simply don't apply in most service businesses.

Every service business offers a USP. For a green and social change profitability consulting and copywriting shop like Shel's, it might be the ability to bring laser

---

114 http://ycharts.com/companies/AAPL/market_cap, accessed 3/13/15.
115 http://ycharts.com/companies/GMM.U.TO/market_cap, accessed 3/13/15.
116 http://ycharts.com/companies/GE/market_cap, accessed 3/13/15.
117 http://ycharts.com/companies/WMT/market_cap, accessed 3/13/15.

focus into the possibilities to make more money doing the right thing. For a baker, it might be the luscious chocolate filling that only this one shop offers. For a lawn-care business, it's simply the time and trouble the homeowner saves by farming the work out to someone who will show up every two weeks and never need a reminder. And if a community has 50,000 lawns, and 200 lawn-care businesses each service 25 households a week, that still only serves one-fifth of the potential base. Even though the market may appear saturated, there's plenty of room to grow. Those 25 companies can also spread to other product lines. Homeowners would happily hire the lawn-care person they already know and trust to prune trees, remove leaves, set up a composting system, perhaps even plow snow in the winter.

This idea works in the real world, even with much larger entities. Which was the only US airline to show a profit in the aftermath of the World Trade Center attack? Southwest Airlines. In their history of the company written some years earlier, Kevin and Jackie Freiberg quote founding CEO Herb Kelleher:

> Market share has nothing to do with profitability. Market share says we just want to be big; we don't care if we make money doing it…To get an additional 5 percent of the market, some companies increased their costs by 25 percent. That's really incongruous if profitability is your purpose.[118]

Does this mean market share is *never* a consideration? Or that you can't attempt to grow your market share without being predatory? No, in both cases. When you enter a new market, you need to calculate whether it will be worthwhile for you—and that means figuring out how much you'll sell. If you're entering a market that already exists, you need to calculate what percentage of the market will shift to you, how you'll attract them, how you'll draw in new customers who hadn't yet seen a need for what you offer—in short, you'll need to have some idea of how large a piece of the market will become your customers. However, ultimately, the number you really need to

---

118 Kevin and Jackie Freiberg, *Nuts! Southwest Airlines' Crazy Recipe for Business and Personal Success* (New York: Broadway Books, 1998).

look at is how much money you will make, and not how that number relates to your competitors' performance.

Just so you can make up your own mind, some people think market share matters a great deal. Shel's friend Eric Anderson says market share

- Has little to do with your competitors, and everything to do with your customers
- Monitors how well your company serves its market, and provides early warning when something goes wrong
- Brings down the cost per sale of innovation (because fixed costs are spread over more units sold)
- Provides a key metric to funders

CREATE EVEN MORE ABUNDANCE

Whether the market is small or large, you can influence people to choose you. You can even do this with price shoppers, even if you're not competing on price.

How to Handle the Price Question

When someone asks prices, provide the information, and then follow immediately with, for example, "The other question you should be asking is, 'What are your qualifications?'" [for a service business] or "The other question you should be asking is, 'What makes yours better?'" [for products]. You might close many extra sales then and there after responding to a question they hadn't even asked.

Diversify Your Products and Services

Three times in the first 15 years of Shel's business—first with term-paper typing, then with his wife's writing workshops, and finally with résumé writing—he found that a service line was very strong for a few years, but because of technology, saturation, or other factors, that market largely disappeared. In all three cases, by the time the market dried up, his company had already shifted, and was actually able to increase both revenue and profitability in those new areas.

Would he go back to typing term papers, even if the market were still there? Definitely not. Every time his previous largest market dried up, he was already in a new, better, more enjoyable, more lucrative market—and developing in-demand new skill sets.

In the years since then, Shel has continued to diversify as his interests and skills expanded. Starting around 2001, he has…

- Shifted his business model from primarily one-shot copywriting to a mix of 1) deeper, long-term consulting (on green profitability, harnessing business to achieve deep social change, and successful book publishing); 2) speaking nationally and internationally; 3) continuing the short-term copywriting, but in many cases converting those clients to a longer, mutually profitable business relationship
- Created stand-alone products to sell or give away
- Developed relationships with other consultants, so he can offer one-stop service

Tightly Define Your Niche

Niching is an excellent strategy when you're facing changing technology, or you're feeling pressed by a deep-pockets competitor. You can't serve *everybody* effectively. Even Coca-Cola and McDonald's flagship products can't serve everybody. Diabetics don't drink Classic Coke; vegetarians or those who keep kosher or halal won't be buying burgers under the golden arches. And these big companies understand niching and diversification; Coca-Cola not only provides sugar-free and other alternative sodas but owns several juice and water brands, including some that appeal directly to conscious, green-thinking consumers (including Odwalla juice and Honest Tea).[119] McDonald's owns the gourmet coffee brand Lavazza.

In 1900, many companies made horse-carriages and buggy whips. Still, even now, tourist carriages roam through New York's Central Park and New Orleans's French Quarter. Mass manufacturers can't profitably serve this market. But for a few companies, it will still be a nice, profitable niche.

---

119 Ocean Robbins, "Coca-Cola Now Owns Zico Coconut Water, Honest Tea, Odwalla, and Vitamin Water: The Dark Side of Coke's 'Healthy' Brands," http://www.alternet.org/food/dark-side-coca-colas-healthy-brands, accessed 3/14/15.

We have known a hand-bookbinder. Although most books are bound by high-speed machines, our friend never lacks for work: he restores old books for libraries and private collectors, and creates works of art out of new books. His industry couldn't support thousands of hand-bookbinders, but it does support dozens.

Beginning in 2002, Shel branded himself as a go-to person in two niches: marketing and profitability for green, ethical, and socially conscious business—and book shepherding/book marketing for authors and publishers. Along with the concurrent process of diversification described a few paragraphs ago, this shift has been key to his success.

LESSONS

- Why market share is often the wrong thing to measure
- How opening up the PC architecture to competitors and giving up market share saved IBM
- How Apple's reinvention of itself in new categories revitalized the company and made it the darling of Wall Street
- How existing market penetration positions you to sell new products and services to your existing customers
- How diversification and niching can help

ACTIONS

- Use Apple's ability to create new markets by satisfying desires their customers never knew they had to sketch out one or more products or services that address hunger, poverty, war, and/or catastrophic climate change? (Shel can help you with this process.)
- Draw up a marketing plan that treats market share as irrelevant. What new products and services become possible? How can you open new markets?
- Choose two niches to specialize in, and plan an approach to each

Chapter 8

EXCEPTIONS: ARE THERE ZERO-SUM, WIN-LOSE SITUATIONS?

hile, in many cases, the concept of market share actually gets in the way of success, sometimes there really are winners and losers.

In these four situations, you may have to modify the mutual success approach. But even here, you can win the race through ethical, green, socially conscious behavior that leaves your opponent standing and your conscience intact. Ruthlessness poisons your own well. Be the best, get the prize—and look at yourself proudly in the mirror afterwards.

MAJOR MEDIA

Media coverage would seem to be a zero–sum game. Although anyone can get into local newspapers or on small radio shows, the most coveted slots are quite a bit tougher. A newspaper or broadcast station has a finite amount of space; if you get in, someone else doesn't.

Still, over time, that finite space is actually quite expansive. If a TV show uses two guests per show, five shows per week, that's over 500 guests a year. Each newspaper feature writer might profile four people in a week; that's more than 200 a year—and the paper might employ a dozen feature writers, so you have 2400 chances each year in that paper. And of course, many print publications offer extra content on their websites, where space is essentially unlimited. You still get bragging rights if you're quoted on a major media website. Your media contact materials must make obvious what readers, listeners, or viewers will learn.

You'd expect someone of Jay's stature to get quoted frequently in the media, and he does. But Shel, who is far less of a celebrity, also usually scores 30 to 50 media interviews a year. You can also get major media, if you're interesting, informative, and entertaining, with relevant talking points.

What if a competitor gets the coverage? *Don't* call up the editor and complain; that would just get you blacklisted.

Here's one among many more effective strategies: write a letter to the editor, thanking the publication for the good story about your subject area and volunteering some new angle. You get the exposure, you're noticed as someone with something to contribute, and you may well get the call the next time that topic is covered.

And that helps you be perceived as a *thought leader*, worthy of media coverage. Rachel Meranus, writing in *Entrepreneur*,[120] offers other strategies to build that. Once you identify a few key publications that you'd like to feature you, tilt the odds in your favor:

- Study the publication's editorial calendar, and pitch articles that align with the featured topics (either as a writer or a source)—well in advance of the issue's closing date
- Tie your pitch to larger social trends, and give the big-picture broad-based view of your company's role
- Follow news closely, and contact the press instantly when a relevant story shows up

---

120 http://www.entrepreneur.com/marketing/publicrelations/prcolumnist/article172276.html

- Conduct surveys (and release the results to the media) that "suggest a course of action, particularly one that supports your company and its business strategy"

(Shel's book, *Grassroots Marketing: Getting Noticed in a Noisy World*, goes into extensive detail on how to gain media publicity—and how to turn that publicity to your advantage as you market your products and services.)

EXTREMELY LIMITED OR SATURATED MARKETS

What if there aren't very many customers, and a sale to you means that someone else doesn't get one? If there are only ten customers in the world for what you do, you probably want all ten.

Has the abundance paradigm finally failed us?

Even here, there are many ways to achieve your agenda and keep within your principles.

You can be like Google, Amazon, Microsoft or General Motors and buy out your competitors or those with complementary technologies and offerings—that's certainly a win–win if you've made a fair offer.

A more affordable strategy is to demonstrate your advantages, e.g., better service, more thorough understanding, favorable financing. Without putting your competitors down, you provide the information necessary for your prospects to choose you. The benefit extends to your customers, and you're not trashing your competitors, even if you're not actively working with them.

And still, if a competitor is obviously better qualified, you serve these clients best by referring them to that other business. It doesn't take many referrals before those competitors realize that you always have the *prospect's* interests at heart.

PREDATORS

So, we can hear you thinking, people-centered marketing is all well and good if you have competitors that think the same way. But what if your competitor is a cut-throat trying to drive you out of business? You can nicey-nice yourself right into bankruptcy.[121]

If a big, scary company, with vast purchasing power and potentially predatory practices, moves into your territory striving for market domination, how do you deal with that?

Interestingly enough, independent hardware stores and lumberyards continue to exist, despite pressure from homeowner superstores. Often, their survival stems from developing cooperative approaches, such as purchasing co-ops. For a single hardware store, it might actually be cheaper for the store's purchasing manager to go to Lowe's or Home Depot and buy at retail. But by joining co-ops like Service Star or Tru-Value, they create enough volume to buy cheaply—*and* get the benefits of a bigger brand.

When competing with superstores, the local stores that thrive avoid the price-cutting game. Lacking the ability to purchase warehouse quantities, they compete on value, not price.

Of course, if you've created a brand new market, your calculations need to be figured differently: how many people will you convince of the desirability of your new approach, and how long will you have before other companies move into the territory you've created?

We've already discussed some ways to survive and thrive when a large, well-financed competitor enters the market. But sometimes, with someone who is actively trying to own the entire market, you need a tougher approach. If a competitor comes in determined to drive you out, and brings a huge amount of firepower to bear, you certainly need a response. And in all likelihood, you won't have the budget to fight fire with fire. When you face massive ad campaigns across multiple media, you're not going to be able to spend your way out, because the other business may have deeper pockets— or a willingness to lose money until it can drive competitors out and own the market.

---

121 This section owes much to Patrick and Jennifer Bishop's *Money Tree Marketing*, which has numerous ideas on mutual-benefit marketing scenarios. However, not all their strategies are in the mutual success/mutual assistance mode; we strongly disagree with some.

So what's a small-business owner to do? How can you survive an onslaught by a well-funded competitor who doesn't understand that there's enough to go around?

Here are two excellent approaches:

1. Identify and *use* your strengths.

You have your customer list—so do some postal or electronic direct mail. *You* have carefully built up local contacts in the press. Explain to these contacts how you'll meet this new challenge—and what it would mean to the community if you can't. *You* have the benefit of your existing store traffic while the new competitor is under construction; how can you create allies out of those visitors? *You* have access to nimble, innovative marketing methods that nonlocal chain superstores simply cannot use, because they have to spend months learning about them and then seeking approval from headquarters. *You* can compete as an equal, perhaps a superior, in cyberspace—because *you* can spend the time to optimize your pages for your own local area, for your own special product mix and USP, and for the value that you add.

The brilliant marketing visionary Seth Godin talked about this:

> What's being rewarded now is insight, authenticity, and innovation, and speed, and alacrity, and flexibility ...organizations that can bring smart, connected, motived people straight to the client... that can change quickly...that can synthesize lots of ideas all at once, those organizations are busier than ever...the opportunity you have when you're small is ... to say, "If you need this, we are the single best choice"...If you're a small business, change is your friend. If you're the Chrysler Corporation, it's the enemy.[122]

2. Try a little marketing jujitsu. In jujitsu, you redirect your opponent's greater strength so that your opponent, and not you, feels the brunt of the blow. In jujitsu, you can flip someone much larger than you over your shoulder

---

122 http://www.ducttapemarketing.com/sethgodin.pdf, accessed February 17, 2009.

and onto the mat. So, if your competitor insists on a winner and a loser, be the winner.

Here's where the "political capital" you've built up over time can really help. If you've been in business several years, filling a unique niche…if you consistently support local artists by exhibiting their art on the walls or giving them space to perform…if the community turns to you to sponsor a Little League team, chair a civic improvement committee, or raise money for the local hospital—it's time to harness some of that good karma.

Write your customers and explain that you've tried to show the new store there's enough to go around, but they're not playing; they want to drive you out, and you need community support to stay in business. Ask not only for people to patronize you, but ask for other kinds of help: testimonials, buying scrip to generate extra cash, even outright donations. Flood the market with testimonials that not only show what you've done for them as customers, but what you've meant to the entire community. Approach reporters on your beat to do a story on you. Expose the competitor's predatory policies and show how they're selling below your wholesale cost (if that's true). Bring in your existing, nonpredatory competitors for a joint effort. And most of all, show how you're different—and better. Show where the dollars go—how dollars spent in your store continue to circulate locally, while dollars spent in a big chain are sucked away to a distant corporate headquarters—and what that means for the local economy.

All this information is out there. Books by Al Norman, Bill Quinn and Don Taylor and Jeanne Smalling Archer will give you plenty of reasons why big box chains hurt local communities.

If someone comes in and starts undercutting your price, it won't take much to find the weakness. One service business owner faced down a deep discounter by offering to fix the competitor's bad jobs. A little creativity can go a long way against a predatory competitor.

Consider the strategies of Dave Ratner, owner of three pet food stores. His flagship store shares a parking lot with a Walmart—and Dave is making a new career speaking about innovative success strategies that surpass the category killers. For instance, he displayed a cheap Walmart fish tank along with a sign about why he'd never sell that model because he wouldn't want to be responsible for dead fish. See more at <http://www.DaveRatner.com>.

By forcing a win–lose model on you, the competitor takes a loss—but you and your customers win, and your community wins because this approach strengthens local businesses that keep dollars circulating in the community.

CROOKS

There are two kinds of people who engage in fraudulent behavior. One kind is naïve. As writers, we run up against this frequently: we discover an article that one of us wrote, reprinted without credit, negotiation for reuse, or payment—but when we investigate, we find that the violator is simply ignorant. He or she does not realize that this is our property, our livelihood, and that we have the right to get paid for it. By treating them nicely, we convert nearly all of these into paying customers, and everybody wins.

But then there are the real crooks: the ones who write piracy software that steals affiliate commissions or banner impressions…who try to steal millions of dollars through fraudulent chain letters…who simply refuse to pay their bills or deliver the goods and services their customers paid for…who break into a store with guns pointed and demand the money…who steal identities and credit card numbers to run up big bills before they get another card number and start all over again…

If someone is deliberately trying to cheat you, there's no point in being nice. Bringing your competitors along on the success train does not extend to thieves. But the rest of you, the honest ones, who are already working together in all these other ways, can get rid of the problem faster by banding together. You can lobby, organize suppliers, inform the public, and press for action through the police and courts much more easily than you could if working alone.

LESSONS
- Initiate people-centered strategies for working in saturated or limited markets
- Be an ally to the media
- Put predatory competitors and crooks in their place

- Survive and thrive in rapidly changing markets

ACTIONS

- Refer one project to a competitor who's better suited—and let that competitor know
- If you're facing competition from do-it-yourselfers or superstores, join with your competitors and start a campaign to reclaim those customers

PART III

GREEN BUSINESS, GREEN MARKETING

CHAPTER 9

BECOMING A GREEN COMPANY

efore you can market effectively to the green world, you need to be in alignment with the values of people who seek green products and services—in other words, to have your green "chops" in place. While the largest corporations can simply open—or buy—a green division, most smaller businesses can't afford to do that. You need to present a value-affirming commitment to being green—ideally, one that permeates every aspect of your business.

DEFINING GREEN

You can find hundreds of definitions for green. Here's ours:

> Creating the best result with the most efficiency,
> the least use of resources, and the greatest possible
> positive impact on the environment.

Note that we go well beyond the least negative impact. That's a start, and it takes us *greener*, but not *green*. While none of us always see the best way to achieve it, the goal is to create businesses and lives that leave the planet *better* than we found it. We'll share lots of ways to do this as we explore this fascinating, economically and spiritually rewarding territory.

THE ECONOMIC *AND* ETHICAL IMPERATIVE

Going green is not just a need; it also should be a desire. Not only will you feel better when you produce goods and services that are in harmony with your values, and those of your market., but—as you'll see in the next chapters—you'll also have an easier time attracting clients.

Economic Imperatives

Fortunately, the economic arguments for going green are utterly convincing, and will give you lots of help convincing Boards of Directors, stockholders and other vested interests. After all, it's hard to argue with numbers like these:

- General Electric created $25 billion in new revenue from $2 billion invested in sustainability innovation research—a 1250 percent return on investment (ROI)[123]

- New York City chose not to build an $8 billion water filtration plant and protect its water instead through buying $1.5 billion worth of conservation land in the Catskill Mountain watershed—saving $6.5 billion[124]

- Walmart not only saves and makes hundreds of millions of dollars a year by greening its operations—just one of its many sustainability initiatives, diverting waste from landfills, was already saving the company $231 million a year by 2012[125]—but also making an

---

123 http://www.livingprinciples.org/19295/, accessed 2/12/15

124 "Seeing the Full Value of Ecosystems," in *Dream of a Nation: Inspiring Ideas for a Better America,* edited by Tyson Miller, See Innovation, 2011, p. 289.

125 http://www.triplepundit.com/2012/10/walmart-save-150-million-sustainability-programs/, accessed 2/12/15

estimated $15.44 billion per year by 2011 selling green products to its retail customers[126] (expanding the overall market for green products, as Walmart's customers for the most part are not the people who shop at places like Whole Foods)

- General Motors also started selling materials that used to be thrown away, creating $1 billion a year in revenue. And its sustainability director, David Tulauskas, says going green "is a long-term concern that creates stakeholder value…Globally, customers have become much more focused on the environmental and social impact"[127]

- Marks and Spencer, a large British department store chain, began to measure 100 different sustainability metrics and share its results very publicly as "Plan A." Using that information to change its practices saved the company so much money that it now measures 200 sustainability metrics.[128]

- Cruiseship operator Carnival's many brands incorporate numerous environmental programs that far exceed government requirements: separating waste streams, refilling ink cartridges with soy ink, breaking down biological waste in an aerobic digester, switching some lighting to LED…but few passengers are aware of any of this.[129]

- Microsoft, listening to employee feedback, made a conscious choice to reduce cafeteria waste, including switching from landfill-

126 Extrapolated from information found at these sources: Walmart controlled 54% of organic food market, as of 2009: "The Big Boys and Organic Food Marketing," The "Friendly Grocer, September 15, 2009. http://grocery.wordpress.com/2010/09/15/the-big-boys-and-organic-food-marketing/, verified 4/11/15. That market was $28.6 billion in 2011 according to Jennifer Chait of About.com, "6 Largest Organic Retailers in North America 2011," http://organic.about.com/od/marketingpromotion/tp/6-Largest-Organic-Retailers-In-North-America-2011.htm, verified 4/11/15.
127 Mark Phelan, "Automakers learn green is the color of money," Detroit Free Press, April 25, 2015, accessed 5/2/15.
128 Bob Willard, *The New Sustainability Advantage*, New Society Publishers, 2012, p. 159.
129 Van Dam, Martijn, Ship Environmental Officer, "Custodians of the Sea," lecture aboard the Holland America MS Veendam, January 17, 2009. For a much more in-depth discussion of best practices for cruise ship waste management, please visit http://www.sustainablecruise.eu/wp-content/uploads/D-4.1.1-Preliminary-Report.pdf (accessed 3/15/15).

clogging polystyrene hot cups to compostable cups—and plates and cutlery, too.[130]

Even as massive and diverse a company as Cox Enterprises, with 83,000 employees across multiple industries (newspaper, radio, TV, automotive, and Internet advertising) saw enormous changes after instituting a corporate-wide environmental awareness program: In the first eight years, the company kept 37.7 tons of obsolete electronics out of landfills…saved more than 2 million gallons of water per year by switching to waterless urinals…switched 98 percent of its fleet to low-emission vehicles (among many other initiatives).[131]

Ethical Imperatives

Because we write about green, ethical, socially conscious business, we get asked whether these can stand alone. Can you be an ethical business that isn't going green? Is there such a thing as a green company that has poor ethics? Does social change really need to be baked in?

And we respond:

In today's world, ethics has to mean something beyond treating humans well. Care for other species, and for Earth, has to be part of business ethics. A planet-raping or polluting company with great employee policies still could not be called ethical.

While it's possible to run a business that's very pro-environment but with poor ethics in other areas, why would you want to? Yes, there are some famous examples of companies that have greened their operations enormously, but still treat workers, suppliers, host communities or other stakeholders very badly. We choose not to knowingly shop at those sorts of companies, and we hope you see the wisdom in running your business more holistically—for both ethical and practical reasons; we've already seen that ethical businesses outperform unethical ones.

---

130 Fister Gale, Sarah,"Eat, Drink and Be Greener," GreenBiz, December 8, 2008, http://www.greenbiz.com/feature/2008/12/08/eat-drink-and-get-greener, verified 4/12/15.

131 "8 Steps to Roll Out a Successful Employee Relations Campaign + 2 Pitfalls to Avoid," MarketingSherpa.com, December 5, 2008, https://www.marketingsherpa.com/barrier.html?ident=30952#, verified 4/12/15.

The answer to the third question is also yes. Running a green and ethical business is certainly possible without a wider social agenda. But there are so many practical benefits to incorporating a higher cause that we think any business that can align with a higher calling will gain enormously. You'll see dozens of examples throughout the book.

Becoming a Green Company

Becoming a green company has three primary components, all of which are essential if you want to be seen as a company that "walks your talk":

- Changing your entire company to a green mindset
- Greening your operations
- Offering green products and services

CHANGING YOUR ENTIRE COMPANY TO
A GREEN/SOCIAL CHANGE MINDSET

This might be one of the coolest parts of this entire book: if you structure it correctly, you get multiple benefits from the initiative. Organize the initiative so it actively encourages employee engagement. Once they're happily contributing their own ideas, time, and resources, they'll feel a sense of ownership in the process. And your commitment to become a green business can empower and motivate your entire workforce. Your employees will feel valued, and increasing retention, productivity, and employee happiness. You may even find that hiring is much easier, because your employees happily recruit their friends and family.

Adding a serious commitment to address one or more of those deep-rooted social and environmental problems exponentially increases these advantages. Most people really want to feel that they're making a difference.

Of course, at the same time you're inspiring your employees, you're inspiring others. Your offerings become much more attractive to your customers and prospects—not just to the LOHAS (Lifestyles Of Health And Sustainability) or Cultural Creative[132] consumer, but also to the "Lazy Green" consumers who would like to do more but won't go out on a limb for it (more about them in

---

132 Defined at https://en.wikipedia.org/wiki/The_Cultural_Creatives, accessed 4/11/15.

Chapter 13). These initiatives could also raise your standing among all the other stakeholders—vendors, abutters, government regulators, sales channels, etc.—as well as the media

How? By *making the whole green/social change-mindset project a collaborative, employee-led activity with the full support of the C-suite.*

GREENING YOUR OPERATIONS

It's an exciting time to be a green business advocate. In the last few years, the whole business world has made huge leaps in awareness not just of the need for more sustainability, but of the ease with which we can often achieve it. Many companies have already achieved massive reductions in energy, materials, water, carbon footprint, transportation miles, and many other metrics. Wasteful practices we used to accept as a necessary cost of doing business have been replaced by healthier, better-engineered workarounds.

You may even find that you've created a new tourist attraction, as Ford has with its truck plant in Dearborn, Michigan, featuring a green, living roof and a host of technologies that highlight waste-free, energy-efficient manufacturing.[133]

And the wonderful part is that we don't have to reinvent the wheel. So much of the groundwork has been done! Books, magazines, and even videos show us exactly how to slash our resource use—and our costs. (See specific recommendations in the Resources listing.)

But there's plenty more to be done! It's not enough to maintain the status quo. We need to start reclaiming some of what we've lost in the past 200 years or so. Thus, in the coming years, the business world will move from mere sustainability to regeneration and thriving.

Expect to see buildings and vehicles that put more energy back into the grid than they take out...farming practices that leave the soil richer than it started, without chemiculture...reclamation of materials from landfills, meaning less needs to be mined...and a whole new way of thinking about recycling, creating new products every bit as good as the originals, with no waste—just as nature does. (Today, most recycling produces lower-quality products than the originals—but that will change.)

---

133 Mark Phelan, "Automakers learn green is the color of money," op. cit.

And expect to see manufacturing processes that can used mixed recycled materials instead of requiring pure, virgin ones. Mikhail Davis of the global flooring company Interface (one of the world's leading green companies) sees this as one of the next frontiers—because as pure, untapped raw materials become less abundant, these mixes can take up the slack. He says we have to stop designing production processes that require large quantities of pure raw materials, and start designing to use mixed streams, including from landfills.[134]

Let's stay with Interface for a moment. The firm is widely recognized as a leader in bringing innovative, green, sustainable approaches to the floor covering industry—as well as one of the largest commercial carpet manufacturers in the world. Its founder, the late Ray Anderson, "got religion" about the need for business to take the lead in solving the environmental crisis it did much to cause, after reading Paul Hawken's book, *The Ecology of Commerce*, back in 1994.

Interface has integrated many green innovations into manufacturing, distribution, sale, reclaiming, and disposal. It was the first company to do modular carpet tiles, so that if a section wears out, only that section needs to be replaced. The company even has a process to recycle both the nylon face and the vinyl backing of the tiles—whether manufactured by Interface or by one of its competitors! Interface has become enormously successful as it climbs "Mount Sustainability" (as Anderson called the struggle to take the business world green).

Anderson's vision was to "become the first sustainable corporation in the world, and, following that, the first restorative company…to spend the rest of our days harvesting yesteryear's carpets, recycling old petrochemicals into new materials, and converting sunlight into energy. There will be zero crap going into landfills and zero emissions into the biosphere. Literally, our company will grow by cleaning up the world, not by polluting or degrading it."[135]

With a goal of zero environmental footprint by 2020, Interface had achieved a 94 percent net reduction in greenhouse gasses and lowered water consumption

---

134 http://www.greenbiz.com/blog/2012/10/19/rage-against-machines-revolutionizing-industrial-design?page=full, verified 2/14/15.

135 As quoted in Dave Pollard, *Finding the Sweet Spot*, op. cit., p. 148.

by 83 percent by the time Anderson died in 2011. All the costs of this effort were more than paid for out of the $433 million saving in waste costs.[136]

OFFERING GREEN PRODUCTS AND SERVICES

As you begin to explore eco-friendly possibilities to serve your market, keep in mind these four categories—think of them as a ladder of possibilities:

Green Versions of Traditional Products and Services

Pretty much every industry now has greener ways to do what they've been doing all along. Eco-friendly real estate brokers offer green or bike-friendly properties...organic goods supplant conventional in food, personal care, and apparel...electricity-sipping LED lights replace their inefficient incandescent cousins...Even a fitness center that collects the energy of its members as they pedal their bikes.[137]

To show how this works, let's look at one industry in a bit more depth—in this case, printing:

Putting words onto paper has all sorts of environmental issues: logging forests, chemicals in the waste water, paper going into landfills after it's read, carbon impact of powering all those presses (to name a few).

However, you have lots of leeway to choose a printer who's working hard to minimize negative environmental impacts. Things to look for include

- Forest Stewardship Council or other reputable certification that monitors chain-of-custody from the time the wood is harvested until the paper is used (note: there are several different levels of FSC certification, so make sure you know what you're getting)
- Recycled paper, processed without chlorine bleach, with a high post-consumer waste (PCW) percentage
- Renewable energy used for all or most of the printing plant's energy needs (a net-zero or net-positive building is even better)

---

136 Ray C. Anderson, "Good Greed," *Green Money Journal*, December 2014, http://www.greenmoneyjournal.com/december-2014/good-greed/, accessed 4/14/15.

137 http://energiastudios.com/going-green/, accessed 2/17/15.

- Short-run and on-demand printing options, allowing customers to use just-in-time inventory management instead of warehousing large quantities of printed materials.
- Recycling of paper-roll ends and other usable scrap
- Biodegradable, vegetable-based inks
- Zero contamination of water sources through waste discharge

Most printing companies offer at least a selection of recycled paper these days (and often at prices comparable to non-recycled). But as an aware consumer, you can go much further, and seek out printers who proudly offer these sorts of green add-ons.

And not just for small-format printing like brochures and books. Carmen Rad, a California printer, worked with Hewlett-Packard to develop an eco-friendly banner printing process that produces zero waste—and the banners themselves are compostable.[138]

Swedish entrepreneur Mehrdad Mahdjoubi thought about how little water astronauts use in space and how much of their water gets recycled; he wondered why we couldn't adapt that water use pattern to our own households.

The result? The OrbSys: A shower that uses only 3 percent of the water and 20 percent of the energy of a typical shower, while claiming to produce higher comfort and better sanitation (note the appeal on multiple benefits). Mahdjoubi claims typical users could save $1000 per year.

By recycling most of the water, much less is needed. But the extra benefit was that much less energy is required as well, *because the water going back into the showerhead is already hot from its first pass.* If you've ever stood to the side as a whole lot of cold water came out of the showerhead before it was warm enough to step under, you know exactly why this is important. (Read more about Mahdjoubi and the OrbSys at http://www.ibtimes.com/eco-shower-orbsys-inspired-astronauts-recycles-90-percent-water-used-1466878[139] and many other places; he's good at getting publicity.)

---

138 http://www.environmentalleader.com/2010/03/04/american-latinos-greening-the-nation/, accessed 2/15/15.
139 Verified 2/11/15

Green Alternatives to Traditional Products and Services

Pedal Power

In many parts of the world, when people think about transporting people, animals, or products, they think first about gasoline-powered motor vehicles: cars, trucks, and buses. Yet, we've all seen those pictures of human-powered contrivances cobbled together from old parts and carrying enormous loads, often through traffic-choked streets where they can make better time than a motor vehicle.

Even in the early 1970s when Shel was a high school student in New York City, he learned that bicycling the five hilly miles to his school on his 3-speed was generally faster than taking the bus the long way around, and almost always much more enjoyable.

And local grocers often used delivery bikes: industrial, heavy-duty one-speed bikes with a big storage compartment on the front.

Modernizing that concept, we discover that bikes with trailers can haul enormous loads. In Northampton, Massachusetts, for example, Pedal People, a bicycle-powered trash hauling and produce delivery service, has been operating many years. Its small fleet of trailer-equipped bikes prices its services fairly close to truck-powered trash haulers, and has picked up contracts from many local stores and offices.

But let's not stop there. The bicycle world has been full of innovation lately.

Want examples? How about the Copenhagen Wheel, a nonmotorized device that stores a bicyclist's kinetic energy and releases it when that rider needs extra power (like going uphill)?[140] Or the ELF, a pedal vehicle with solar assist, an enclosed cab, disc brakes, enough lockable storage for 12 bags of groceries, infinitely variable gearshifting, and enough other cool features that Jerry Seinfeld bought one.[141] With a 14-mile range on just battery power (much farther if you're pedaling some of the time), this can actually replace a commuter car. It

---

140 http://sharepowered.com/copenhagen-wheel-mit-bike-invention/, verified 2/11/15.

141 http://www.usatoday.com/story/news/nation-now/2014/03/31/elf-bike-car-ends-first-year-of-production/6961901/, accessed 2/11/15.

comes in one-, two-, and three-passenger configurations, with prices starting in the $5000 range.[142] A similar venture, the Virtue Pedalist, raising capital via Kickstarter at press time, offers similar features in a smaller footprint at a comparable price.[143] Not only are these practical commuting vehicles for people who work up to 20 miles from home, they're also being marketed to people with mobility disabilities, some of whom can now ride a bike again for the first time in years.

Of course, switching to bikes creates immediate health and fitness benefits for the riders. But here's something interesting: a paper published in the scientific journal *Environmental Health Perspectives* found that the combination of cleaner air and lower medical bills provided a huge economic boost as well: switching half the trips of five miles and under from car to bike would create a $7.1 billion boost to the economy in the 11 cities studied.[144] Wow!

Diaper Doings

Sometimes, the eco-friendly alternative is nothing more than a return to—or refiguring of—the way things used to be through much of history. Consider diapers (nappies, if you're in the UK). When Jay and Shel were toddlers in the 1930s and 1950s, our parents used cloth diapers; there were no such things as disposable diapers. Today's earth-conscious parents will use cloth diapers—perhaps organic cotton—unless they live in a water-shortage area (in which case they may choose biodegradable disposables). But now, they can buy natural-fiber wraps with Velcro closers that slip on over the diaper and keep things a lot neater (and more comfortable for the toddler) than the horrible plastic undies and sharp pins of yore, and get their dirty-diaper hamper picked up in a hybrid or a bicycle by a cleaning service that uses non-chlorine bleach and gentle, hypoallergenic, all-natural fair-trade soaps.

---

142 http://organictransit.com/base-elf/, accessed 2/11/15.
143 http://www.pedalistcycles.com/
144 "How Biking Can Save Cities Billions of Dollars in Health Expenses" by Zak Stone, Good Magazine, http://magazine.good.is/articles/how-biking-can-save-cities-billions-of-dollars-in-health-expenses, accessed 2/18/15.

Green Funerals

It's ironic: you can live a fully green lifestyle, bicycling or walking everywhere, living in a zero-net-energy, zero-waste renovated house, growing your own organic food—and then when you die, your body gets filled with toxic preservatives and you're laid to rest in a carbon-intensive vault that isolates your body from the earth—or turned to ashes in a fossil-fueled 1270-degree crematorium that generates 110 pounds of carbon waste in the process.[145]

But there are some exciting green alternatives that allow you to be a friend to the environment in death as well as life. Some green cemeteries are actually nature preserves. You can now quietly and peacefully decompose in an organic landscape where your body will nurture plants and trees and animals as it becomes part of the soil. This industry is nascent, with lots of opportunities for entrepreneurs to get in on the ground floor, from biodegradable caskets to organic forest cemetery maintenance. And whether or not it's where you want to plant your business flag, it's worth making sure your death is in keeping with the values you lived. For a fabulous introduction to this world, read the 15-page handbook at http://d3n8a8pro7vhmx.cloudfront.net/bullfrogfilms/pages/873/attachments/original/1401990491/will_greenburialQA.pdf?1401990491.[146]

Thousands of Other Opportunities

In pretty much every sector, there's room to replace eco-nasty products with eco-friendly ones.

Consider the once-ubiquitous foam packing peanut. 20 years ago they were in pretty much everything. Now, they're often replaced by shredded used office paper, or even all-natural versions made from mushrooms or other organic matter; computer giant Dell is one major company that's gone down that path.[147]

Or think about bricks. Conventional bricks spend days in a high-heat, high-intensity kiln, creating as much CO_2 worldwide as Germany.[148] Can you see an opportunity in doing that differently?

145 http://d3n8a8pro7vhmx.cloudfront.net/bullfrogfilms/pages/873/attachments/original/1401990491/will_greenburialQA.pdf?1401990491, accessed 2/26/15.
146 Accessed 2/26/15.
147 http://www.dell.com/learn/us/en/vn/corp-comm/mushroom-packaging, accessed 2/9/15.
148 http://www.fastcoexist.com/3040740/3-amazing-bio-materials-that-are-growing-a-more-sustainable-world, accessed 2/12/15.

There are even people talking about returning to wind-powered cargo ships.[149]

Green can be about the process as well as the product. For instance, if you own a restaurant and can source fresh organic vegetables grown on the roofs and vacant lots of your own city, you lower the food miles and the carbon footprint of the meals you serve. Urban rooftop farming, which Shel has advocated since 1980, is now cropping up (pun intended) in cities all over the world, sometimes in conjunction with the Green Roof movement that uses grasses and other plants to add oxygen and reduce heat.

Even the most densely populated urban areas in the world can produce quite a bit of their own food. Consider Shanghai, China, the fifth-most-populous city in the world.[150] With 14.35 million inhabitants, Shanghai grows an astonishing 85 percent of its vegetables.[151]

Here's a five-minute video interview Shel conducted with a farm manager who grows hydroponic vegetables eight stories up in another densely populated urban area: the South Bronx in New York City: <https://www.youtube.com/watch?v=YwJ-eHYdRlA>.

How about a charging station smaller than a Frisbee and weighing under a pound that uses running water from any stream to power up mobile phones, cameras and other USB devices—no need for a wall plug? Think about how this could be used not just by outdoor enthusiasts, but in the construction industry, in rural electrification projects, for communities without electricity in the developing world, and more.[152]

Can you find entrepreneurial opportunities in statistics like these?

- The average European Union resident creates 10 metric tons of carbon each year, but the average resident of the United States creates 20—yet, the average for Vaxjo, Sweden (a place that needs a lot of heat in the winter) is just 3.5 metric tons

---

149 http://GreenAndProfitable.com/carrotmob-support-fair-trade-coffee-transported-by-wind/.
150 http://www.worldatlas.com/citypops.htm, accessed 2/26/15.
151 Review in Shel's newsletter of *Farm City: The Education of an Urban Farmer* by Novella Carpenter, http://thecleanandgreenclub.com/the-clean-and-green-club-february-2014/
152 http://blue-freedom.net/, accessed 4/12/15.

- Similarly, Europe uses far less energy per person than the United States—in some countries, less than half as much.[153]

- Following a "deep energy retrofit," the Empire State Building slashed its energy costs by $4.4 million dollars a year on a $13.2 million investment—achieving a 33 percent annual return on investment (ROI)[154]

- Springfield, Massachusetts's Materials Recycling Facility purchases collected recyclables from area cities and towns, paying $24 per ton—and selling the sorted waste for anywhere from $53 per ton for paper up to $1570 per ton for aluminum—five of the streams obtaining prices above $100 per ton[155]

- Enough solar energy lands on the earth every day to power the planet for 27 years[156]

- While the US coal industry lost 49,530 jobs between 2008-2012, solar and wind combined to add more than 79,000 new jobs in the same period, creating more than three jobs for every two lost by coal[157]

- Solar's astounding 139,000 percent US growth from 2005-2015 is only the beginning, according to a remarkable article by ecojournalist Debra Atlas. Efficiencies have jumped from 14 percent in the early days to 25 percent in 2015's commercial panels, to new technologies that promise 40-46 percent. Prices have plummeted 70 percent since 1998. And demand continues to skyrocket with the creation of new funding models (e.g., lease-back programs) that eliminate big capital outlays. And new technologies allow big, clunky solar panels to be replaced by spray films that turn any surface, even windows, into solar collectors. These factors could combine to boost solar from its current

153 https://en.wikipedia.org/wiki/List_of_countries_by_energy_consumption_per_capita, accessed 3/1/15.
154 http://www.esbnyc.com/esb-sustainability/project, accessed 2/26/15.
155 "Beyond the Bin: A Behind the Scenes Look at Household Recycling," *Reduce Reuse Recycle*, supplement to the *Daily Hampshire Gazette* newspaper, April 21, 2015, pp. 3 and 6.
156 http://www.txses.org/solar/content/solar-energy-facts-you-should-know, accessed 3/1/15.
157 Sean Cockerham, "Green energy job growth outpaces losses in coal industry," McClatchy Washington Bureau, http://www.mcclatchydc.com/2015/04/21/263915/green-energy-job-growth-outpaces.html, accessed 4/22/15

fraction of one percent of total energy to the world's dominant energy source by 2050.[158]

- Contaminated water, which causes about 80 percent of diseases, can be fixed for just $20 per person, according to Charity: Water[159]
- Producing a single ream of paper using standard practices consumes an astonishing 60 liters of water[160]
- GE's Ecomagination line of earth-friendly products brought in $18 billion in 2009, up from $10.1 billion in 2005. This was roughly 10 percent of total revenue, and was expected to grow at twice GE's overall rate in the following five years[161]
- IBM turned a $1.5 mm cost into a $1.5 mm revenue stream by selling something it used to throw away, adding $3 mm to profit each year; the US Postal Service turned a $9.1 mm annual disposal cost into $13 mm annual income, or $20 mm in profit (page 72)[162]

Products and Services Made Possible by Green Thinking

Another way to come up with offerings for the green market is to think about market niches that are created by green thinking—products or services that would not exist without the green consumer.

Remember the five questions we suggested in Chapter 4 in developing your new product? Let's put that into practice with a real product.

Problem/Desire:

Thousands of gallons of water per household are wasted flushing small amounts of urine. An entrepreneur would like to help people save this water.

---

158 Debra Atlas, "A Bright Future? Yes, With These Solar Power Technologies," http://www. earth911.com/eco-tech/a-bright-future-yes-with-these-solar-power-technologies/, accessed 5/2/15.

159 Scott Harrison of Charity: Water, cited in *Billions Rising: Empowering Self-Reliance*, by Anita Casalina with Warren Whitlock and Heather Vale Goss, and in Shel's review, http://thecleanandgreenclub.com/the-clean-and-green-club-january-2014/

160 Bob Willard, *The New Sustainability Advantage*, Op. Cit., p. 88.

161 *Ibid.*, p. 42.

162 *Ibid.*, p. 72.

Possible Solutions:

There are several possible ways to fix this, such as composting toilets, graywater recycling (so that the water for flushing has already been used once, in a sink, dishwasher, shower, bath, or washing machine), and European-style two-way toilet switches that allow you to select a large flow for solids or a smaller flow for liquids. But this particular entrepreneur chose a different route: Why Flush?, an enzyme compound that reduces the odor and stain, allowing the urine to remain in the bowl with no ill effects.

Advantages:

Most of the other solutions involve extensive hardware modifications, and that's expensive. Why Flush?, by comparison, is cheap to buy and easy to implement (a couple of squirts on a standard hand-operated spray pump such as you'd use for window cleaner).

Possible Markets:

Green consumers who care about saving water are an obvious market—and because of its low price and intuitive use, the product appeals not only to homeowners but also to renters. But there are several other markets, too.

Large consumers of water have economic reasons to save. Think about how much water is consumed in the bathrooms of sports stadiums, concert halls, schools, transportation terminals, and so forth. However, to reach this market, there would have to be a way to control the flush schedule and add the product remotely, which might be difficult in most circumstances (other than public urinals, some of which already use a timer instead of individual flush handles). So this would be a back-burner market, to pursue later once the technology catches up or the social expectations around flushing have shifted enough to create a space in the market within the society as a whole.

But there are at least two other huge markets that are much easier to approach: First, homeowners who live with septic systems and private water supplies (their own or a neighborhood well). Unlike the owners of large public bathrooms, this group has no technological or sociological challenges in implementing Why Flush?, and has a strong interest in conserving water. These homeowners extend their infrastructure's lifespan while decreasing the number (and thus the cost) of septic tank pumpouts.

The second large market consists of people who live in places that face drought frequently, and where the culture has shifted in favor of flushing less—as it has in many parts of California, for example. Those folks are already letting the yellow stuff sit, and they would welcome such a simple solution to the problem of odors and stains.

Getting the Sale:

Target your appeals to each of these audiences. For green homeowners and tenants, saving water is enough of a reason. For the industrial bathroom owners as well as the well and septic crowd, a purely economic argument will work better. And for those already not flushing because of drought, an appeal based on a clean, germ-free house and a toilet that is once again easy to clean should close the sale.

These four different markets are going to congregate in different places—and be attracted to different message points.

To reach green consumers, exhibit at green festivals…demo products in stores…do radio interviews…advertise in demographically/psychographically appropriate publications and radio shows…seek out product reviews in green publications and websites.

Articles in trade magazines and targeted direct mail would effectively reach the industrial users. To reach homeowners with septic systems, rent customer lists from septic pumpout companies, and seek out print media interviews. And reach people in drought-centric cultures through mass-market media.

And of course, although the message points would be different, it's important to note that the marketing techniques can transcend the barriers and reach every group. With different audience-specific messages, the company could actively use social media, blogs, traditional media publicity, public speaking, product demonstrations, its own website…

Other products that only exist because
of the growing green customer base:

- Reusable portable water bottles with built-in filtering systems
- Small-space "vertical gardens" that let apartment-dwellers grow their own food in about one square meter/square yard
- Upcycled jewelry, clothing, and home décor options made of used printed circuit boards, vinyl records, tires, etc.
- Fine papers made from raw materials as diverse as beer waste[163] and elephant poop[164]
- Nature discovery programs for urban dwellers wanting to be in touch with the natural world
- Services that convert dog waste to biogas, and use the gas to power quaint streetlamps[165]
- Battery-swap businesses to get electric vehicles back on the road in minutes instead of waiting hours while the battery charges
- Tiny home composting bins for use on a kitchen counter

The building industry has been a particular hotbed of innovation, with thousands of new products that offer either a greener variation or brand new technology. A few examples:

- Roofing shingles and tiles with embedded photovoltaic solar electricity (even Dow, about as established a company as you could name, has gotten into this business[166])
- Smart sensors that allow HVAC, lighting, computers, and machinery to only go on when someone's in the room[167]

---

163 http://www.twistedlimbpaper.com/index.php/beer-paper, accessed 2/19/15.
164 http://mrelliepooh.com/, verified 2/18/15.
165 http://www.triplepundit.com/2012/05/streetkleen-starts-dog-waste-to-biogas-system/, verified 2/15/15.
166 http://www.dowpowerhouse.com/, accessed 2/9/15.
167 Gottfried, David, *Explosion Green: One Man's Journey to Green the World's Largest Industry* Morgan James Publishing, 2014, p. 254.

- Heat pumps—geothermal or above-ground—that replace furnaces and air conditioners with inexpensive, energy-efficient, and utterly proven technology (basically, this is how refrigerators work)
- A solar-powered movable LED lighting system that does not need to convert solar's DC into AC and can be set up without an electrician[168]

Green thinking has so infiltrated the building industry that some Realtor associations are demanding that the Multiple Listing Service database of homes for sale be updated to allow green rating criteria.[169]

What's possible is limited only by your imagination. Consider the brief (six-minute) video, "Solar Freakin Roadways,"[170] which went viral following its May, 2014 release. As of February, 2015, 19,183,035 people had seen it, and 23,727 had commented on it. And by November, 2014, someone had built a 70-meter (229-foot) demonstration project on a bikeway in the Netherlands.[171]

Lots of other promising new technologies will provide ground-floor business opportunities for entrepreneurs, and good green jobs for those who don't want to start a company. A few examples:

- The Bloom Box, a fuel cell that creates energy by oxidizing fuel, with no need to burn it—which has sold to such corporations as Google, Walmart, and eBay[172]
- Mushrooms that can clean up oil spills and then add to the food chain as they decompose and are eaten[173]

---

168 *Ibid.*, p. 255.
169 Charlotte (NC) Regional Realtor Association, "Greening the MLS," http://www.carolinarealtors.com/support/greenmls.aspx, accessed 2/20/15.
170 https://www.youtube.com/watch?v=qlTA3rnpgzU, accessed 2/9/15.
171 http://www.extremetech.com/extreme/194313-the-netherlands-has-laid-the-worlds-first-solar-road-we-go-eyes-on-to-investigate, accessed 2/9/15.
172 "World-Changing Innovations," in *Dream of a Nation: Inspiring Ideas for a Better America,* op. cit., p. 288.
173 Ibid.

- A magnetic-levitation wind turbine that requires no electricity, generates no friction, rotates on a vertical axis, and can successfully generate power for 750,000 homes at wind speeds as low as a third-of-a-mile per hour (compared with 13 mph for conventional horizontal-axis tower-based wind-farm turbines) and as high as 89 mph[174]

Wind power, incidentally, is an area where dozens of innovations are on the horizon that will likely make the technology quieter, more affordable, less environmentally intrusive, and safer for birds. The mag-lev system described just above claims a 500-year lifespan and requires just 1/960 of the land to generate as much wind power as a typical windfarm. There are even people working on utility-scale wind systems that have no turbines,[175] as well as smaller no-blade systems. The developers of the smaller system claim their Saphon Zero Blade offers 230 percent greater efficiency than conventional wind turbines, while reducing costs 45 percent.[176]

What niche will you create?

Products and Services that Address Deep Rooted Social Problems

Perhaps you've read the game-shifting book *The Fortune at the Bottom of the Pyramid*, by C.K. Prahalad (you can read Shel's review at http://www.principledprofit.com/subscribe-2#fortune) or the later book *The Business Solution to Poverty* by Paul Polak and Mal Warwick, reviewed at http://thecleanandgreenclub.com/the-clean-and-green-club-june-2014/ (scroll down). While of course, they are fundamentally motivated by a desire to help the world, these authors prove that the most economically disadvantaged people on the planet not only create a great market for social entrepreneurs brave enough to venture into that territory, but also that developing countries

---

174 http://inhabitat.com/super-powered-magnetic-wind-turbine-maglev/, accessed 3/6/15. Math calculated by Shel from numbers on that page.

175 "Accio Wind Energy Generation Overview," http://www.accioenergy.com/how-it-works/, accessed 3/22/15.

176 Derek Markham, "New Bladeless Wind Turbine Claimed to be Twice as Efficient as Conventional Designs," http://www.treehugger.com/wind-technology/new-bladeless-wind-turbine-claimed-be-twice-efficient-conventional-designs.html, accessed 4/20/15.

provide a terrific testing ground for innovation and cost control—and offer numerous examples of companies profiting handsomely by serving the poorest of the poor.

Their products and services become even more powerful through a lens of deep sustainability, co-solving multiple problems and incorporating multiple benefits. Here are two companies doing just that:

Let There Be Light

d.light—one of the companies Polak and Warwick mention—simultaneously addresses poverty, education, air pollution/toxic fumes/health risks, energy savings, carbon footprint, and more—and makes a huge difference in lives of those at the bottom of the economic pyramid. All with a simple three-item product line.

Headquartered in San Francisco with additional offices in China, India, and Kenya, d.light sells inexpensive freestanding bright-light LED lanterns with lifetime batteries powered by dual solar/plug-in electric chargers. The company's mission statement: "to create new freedoms for customers without access to reliable power so they can enjoy a brighter future."

And to accomplish this mission, the company employs a deeply holistic analysis of the problems faced by people at the bottom of the heap, and how a reliable and renewable source of good light can help solve them.

The lights go into two types of environments: places where light has been supplied by kerosene (or, conceivably, open fires)—and those with no pre-existing night-time light source.

If the lantern replaces an existing kerosene model, it accomplishes many desirable goals: It provides a better quality of light that needs no fuel, does not produce toxic fumes, has no risk of setting the house on fire, reduces pollution, and leaves considerably more money in the hands of the family using the lantern—because the savings over purchasing kerosene typically pays for the lantern in about two months.

Where the lantern provides light in a previously unlit area, the benefits are different, but just as significant: four more hours per day of productive time. Children can advance much further with their studies; cottage industries, farms, and microbusinesses can produce and sell more. In short, the lamp becomes a ladder out of poverty.

Using classic Prahalad-inspired design principles, the units are cheap, extremely durable, and designed for multiple environments. A company video shows the lamps dropped from a high balcony and run over by a car, and still working afterward. At least one of the three models can be mounted on a wall or ceiling. The top-line model can also charge mobile phones. In developing countries, payment plans can be arranged for less than the previous monthly cost of kerosene; in developed countries, 10 percent of the proceeds goes to fund lamps for children who could not buy them. Worldwide, they're sold with a two-year free-replacement warranty.

Operating 6000 retail outlets in 40 countries, d.light is very successful, both financially and in the social and environmental good it has created. As of February 28, 2013, the company claims:

- 13,638,438 "lives empowered"
- 3,409,610 school-aged children reached with solar lighting
- $275,817,462 saved in energy-related expenses
- 3,589,490,280 productive hours created for working and studying
- 656,952 tons of CO_2 offset
- 10,115,224 kWh generated from renewable energy

(You can find the latest update of these statistics at http://www.dlightdesign. com/impact-dashboard/ [177]).

These stats, confirmed by email discussion with company spokesperson Darin Kingston of the India office, were arrived at by looking at the maximum possible utilization for each category—and that means they may be overstating the benefits somewhat.

Shel asked Darin if he was double-counting—wasn't it true that if you max out the possible benefit, you can have either the $275 million in energy savings and the 657-ton CO_2 offset (replacing kerosene) OR the 3.6 billion newly productive hours (replacing darkness), but not both at once? But Darin assured him that no, they're not double-counting; the productivity benefit stems from the longer number of hours and better quality of light compared to kerosene. He did acknowledge that the stats assume a one-to-one relationship between the new lanterns and the kerosene lamps they replace.

Company executives hope to grow that user base from 13 million all the way to 100 million by the end of the decade—perhaps not an unrealistic estimate considering the company was only conceived of in 2004, following founder Sam Goldman's encounter as a Peace Corps volunteer in Africa with a neighbor child who had been badly burned in a kerosene fire.

Of course, other companies also replace kerosene with cleaner, safer solutions. For instance, the similar company WakaWaka has a mission "to end Energy Poverty by making the worlds best sustainable solar energy solutions available and affordable to the 1.2 billion people who lack access to electricity." Aiming at the market of people who make less than USD $2 per day, this company combines pay-as-you-go pricing and a buy-one/give-one campaign where customers in the developed countries fund a donated unit with every purchase. Customers pay roughly 75 cents to a dollar per week— and own the units free and clear within 12 to 16 months. The company also partners with major NGOs from the Red Cross and Save the Children to the International Rescue Committee and UN refugee camps.[178] As of March, 2015, WakaWaka had sold 134,958 solar lanterns and power packs throughout the developing world.[179]

"We Bake Brownies to Hire People"

Now, let's look at a completely different industry: wholesale food components and retail baking. Greyston Bakery, brownie baker to Ben & Jerry's since 1989, is known for its labor force of ex-addicts, ex-prisoners, and ex-mental patients. Its slogan: "We don't hire people to bake brownies. We bake brownies to hire people."

This is how the company describes its mission:

---

178 Audio interview with Camille Van Gestel, co-founder and co-CEO, conducted by Lorna Li of Changemaker Dojo, March 11, 2015.

179 From the map at http://us.waka-waka.com/impact/, accessed 3/12/15.

While baking 30,000 lbs of delicious brownies on a daily basis is no small task, Open Hiring is the hallmark of Greyston Bakery...offering employment opportunities regardless of educational attainment, work history, or past social barriers, such as incarceration, homelessness or drug use. We believe that employment is a first step in an individual's path toward success...

[A]nyone that comes to the front door of our bakery is given the chance to work, no questions asked. When a job becomes available we take the next person off our waiting list and give them a job. Once an individual starts at Greyston, they become a part of the apprenticeship program. Greyston provides them with resources, personal development tools and training in professional skills to give them the greatest chance for success in their new job. In 2012, Greyston Bakery provided employment opportunities and training to 181 residents within our community.[180]

Founded in 1982 by Bernie Glassman, who also founded the Zen Peacemaker order and several other undertakings that mix spirituality and social change, Greyston now does $3.5 million in annual revenues. It also sells its own line of baked goods at Whole Foods and through its website.[181] Located in economically depressed Yonkers, NY, just a few blocks over the line from New York City, the company was the first in New York State to achieve B Corp certification.

Hundreds of Similarly Conscious Ventures

How about a nearly-indestructible microscope made entirely out of paper, costing just fifty cents to manufacture, weighing nearly nothing, and fitting in a pocket? In this nine-minute TED talk, Manu Prakash demonstrates his amazing Foldscope and discusses its potential to eradicate disease in places where conventional microscopes are too expensive, heavy and bulky to be practical:

---

180 http://greyston.com/the-bakery-open-hiring/, accessed 2/8/15.
181 https://en.wikipedia.org/wiki/Tetsugen_Bernard_Glassman, accessed 2/8/15.

http://www.thebetterindia.com/19178/folding-microscope-made-single-sheet-paper-can-save-billion-lives/ [182]

Maybe you're more inspired to alleviate a water shortage affecting 12 million people using a simple, inexpensive device that collect rainwater—dripping through the ceilings of São Paulo's slum dwellings—for non-drinking purposes. [183]

These are just two of hundreds of other examples. It's good to see companies doing well by doing so much good—and combining environmental, social, and health benefits to serve the most needy.

LESSONS

- Going green can be affordable and easy
- Other businesses and even other countries can show us good paths to take
- You can develop profitable niches in green versions of existing products, greener alternatives, and even products that address deep-seated fundamental social problems

ACTIONS

- List and begin to implement three ways you could green your existing operation.
- List five potential projects that use your core capabilities to make a real difference on hunger, poverty, war, and/or catastrophic climate change. Working with your entire executive team, or even your whole workforce, pick the easiest one and explore feasibility. (If you have trouble with this, take Shel up on his offer of a 15-minute no-charge consultation.)

---

182 Accessed 2/10/15.
183 Andrea Garcia-Vargas, "She came up with an invention to save 12 million people. Genius? Kinda," http://www.upworthy.com/she-came-up-with-an-invention-to-save-12-million-people-genius-kinda?c=reconDFP, accessed 4/13/15.

CHAPTER 10

MARKETING GREEN

s we've already discussed, customers want to do business with companies who share their values—and these days, those values often include strong awareness of climate change and other environmental issues.

We live at a powerful moment: For the first time, the environment has penetrated our collective consciousness deeply enough to move a whole lot of people toward green lifestyle changes. At the same time, technology (especially the Internet) has made it possible to run a global business with little or no staff or resources, and without a big infrastructure.

This opens all sorts of opportunities for the green guerrilla who honestly fits into this market.

GREEN GOODS AND SERVICES ARE MUCH EASIER TO MARKET

When you look at all the advantages of running a green company, it's hard to understand why every company in the world hasn't shifted:

Worldwide, consumer consciousness on these issues is growing by orders of magnitude. The green market is growing faster than just about anything else; Green America reported that even during the 2008–2011 recession, the green building sector grew an astonishing 1700 percent, while the overall sector shrank by 17 percent; during approximately the same time, the organic food sector was up 238 percent, compared to just 33 percent growth in total food sales.[184]

Google searches for "climate change date:1990", climate change date:2004", and "climate change date:2014"[185] show the trend. Google found 1,810,000 results for articles published in 1990, 7,570,00 for 2004, and *58,200,000* for 2014—a 769 percent increase in those ten years.

Green products and services often command a premium price, and thus can be more profitable. A McKinsey study in 2012 found that close to 70 percent of consumers would pay a slight (5 percent) premium for a green product that performed just as well.[186] Here's something amazing: a worldwide study by Neilsen that surveyed over 29,000 people in 58 countries found a greater willingness to pay higher prices for green products in India (75 percent), Thailand, and the Philippines (both above 66 percent) than in countries we think of as both more socially aware and having more disposable income.[187]

Of course, green products are better for the environment: they use fewer resources, less energy, more organic and natural materials—and thus create less pollution, have a smaller carbon footprint, and are easier to dispose of

Against conventional wisdom, green products can actually be cheaper to produce—if properly designed (see the profiles of Amory Lovins and John Todd in chapter 20). Business leaders including Swiss banking giant HSBC, the Bank

---

184 "The Big Green Opportunity," special report from Green America, August 2013, accessed August, 2013. As of February, 2015, this appears to have been withdrawn from the Green America website pending the release of the updated 2015 version.

185 Conducted 5/12/15.

186 Mehdi Miremadi, Christopher Musso, and Ulrich Weihe, "How much will consumers pay to go green?" http://www.mckinsey.com/insights/manufacturing/how_much_will_consumers_pay_to_go_green, accessed 3/15/15.

187 Mike Hower, "50% of Global Consumers Willing to Pay More for Socially Responsible Products," http://www.sustainablebrands.com/news_and_views/behavior_change/50-global-consumers-willing-pay-more-socially-responsible-products, accessed 3/15/15.

of England, and Germany's largest utility, E.ON recognize the need to get our economy off fossil fuels.[188]

As far back as 2008, *Plenty* Magazine named "10 ideas that will change our world"—and six of those ten (turning waste into new inputs, green affordable housing, green media, green jobs, carbon labeling, and pay-as-you-go energy retrofits) are directly and explicitly rooted in green thinking. The other four all have a green component.[189]

Even the often-pessimistic Bill McKibben, author of the groundbreaking *The End of Nature* (widely recognized as the first book on climate change written for a mainstream, nonscientist audience, published way back in 1988) and founder of the climate-advocacy mass movement 350.org, sees that citizen action has turned the tide on public awareness of climate change.

Areas of living that we used to take for granted are now being re-examined under a green microscope. Suddenly, green is an issue in every single industry. We even found an article on choosing a green pediatrician. The doctor-author writes, "As you did when choosing an ob/gyn, you want to find a pediatrician who is top-notch medically. How much better if he or she is also on the journey to an environmentally sustainable perspective on pediatrics!"[190]

The more effectively a company can demonstrate commitment to environmental values, the easier it will be to convince those consumers to channel their business to that company. For instance...

- The hotel industry's change in towel washing policies—with essentially no consumer resistance because this cost-cutting move was successfully marketed as a green initiative

---

188 Bill McKibben, "Pressure is growing. A relentless climate movement is starting to win big, unprecedented victories around the world, victories which are quickly reshaping the consensus view," http://www.theguardian.com/environment/2015/mar/09/climate-fight-wont-wait-for-paris-vive-la-resistance, accessed 3/14/15.

189 http://www.mnn.com/earth-matters/wilderness-resources/stories/the-plenty-20-awards-for-2008-part-4, verified 4/20/15.

190 Alan Greene, MD, "When Your Baby Comes Home: Choosing a Green Pediatrician," November 12, 2008, http://www.healthywealthynwise.com/article.asp?Article=5565, verified 4/12/15.

- Moves among publishers to slash print inventories, shift many titles to on-demand printing, and eliminate the practice of allowing bookstores to return unsold books, citing both environmental and economic reasons[191]

Conveniently enough, many green initiatives not only make a company more attractive to consumers, but actually cut existing costs. And these will survive corporate restructuring. If they actually both save money and make money, they won't be on the chopping block when the company faces hard times or a new management team. As Joel Makower puts it in his book, *Strategies for the Green Economy…*

Companies that don't leverage their environmental achievements and commitment in a way that produces business value often find that green is the first thing to go when times get tough—when there's a change in leadership, when shareholders raise questions, or when your company otherwise finds that being seen as an environmental leader is no longer convenient. On the other hand, if you can say, "Our sustainability initiatives have reduced costs and boosted revenue by creating new markets, adding new products, and deepening loyalty with customers," this creates a long-term justification for a sustainability strategy and for environmental issues broadly.[192]

Reframing this discussion in line with the abundance mindset we discussed earlier, Melissa Chungfat advises companies to "move away from the language of

---

191 See, for example, this interview with Chelsea Green's publisher Margo Baldwin, which focuses on the environmental reasons, http://www.bookbusinessmag.com/article/working-toward-point-no-returns-chelsea-green-publisher-president-margo-baldwin-companys-green-partners-program-401270.html (verified 4/12/15), as well as this story in the Wall Street Journal about Harper Collins' imprint HarperStudio's nonreturnable deal with Borders: http://online.wsj.com/article/SB122939936289409805.html, verified 4/12/15

192 Makower, Joel, *Strategies for the green Economy* (New York: Macmillan, 2008). Excerpted at http://www.greenbiz.com/feature/2008/11/24/the-four-simple-steps-pitch-perfect-green-marketing, verified 4/12/15

sacrifice. Find ways to talk about how your product or service is easier, healthier, more convenient or lower maintenance. Be positive and solutions-focused." She also suggests pointing out actual achievements, rather than sometimes-vague commitments.[193]

TWO APPROACHES, ONE INDUSTRY

These two printing companies court the green customer very differently:

This ad from Webcom ran in a special online issue of *Book Business*—a book-industry trade magazine—previewing Book Expo America, the US publishing industry's largest trade event, and the clear call to action is to book an appointment at BEA. In short, the targeting is basically perfect. And amid all the

---

193 Chungfat, Melissa, "Junxion Strategy: green marketing grows up," http://ecopreneurist. com/2009/03/18/junxion-strategy-green-marketing-grows-up/, verified 4/12/15

ads from printers in that publication, this was one of the very few to have any point of differentiation related to the environment.

Forest Stewardship Council certification is a very big deal in the paper and printing industries. The FSC logo is there, and FSC certification is also mentioned in the color-screened text. The ad is attractively designed, although the daisy collage is kind of hard to figure out, in our opinion; another graphic element might have been better. And it's very much on-message: book publishers who care about the environment will want to know more. Of the two URLs, one is the home page and the other links to a request form for eco-friendly paper samples

This ad obviously was probably quite effective in bringing in new inquiries, but could have done even more. Webcom could have maximized its leverage of a display ad by driving traffic to not just to the book-a-meeting-at-the-trade show webpage, but also its existing set of webpages covering green printing issues with a nice, short URL that's hard to mess up when retyped. The ad could have included, "If you'd like to know more about green printing options, we've set up a special webpage with information, resources, links, and more, at http://www.webcomlink.com/environment/"—and then, from the sustainability section itself—currently lacking any call to action—insert links back to the paper-sample request form listed in the ad, and to more educational content.

Still, it's light-years ahead of what most companies are doing.

The second example is a very low cost, and very eco-friendly text-only electronic newsletter, from Fidlar-Doubleday:

Turn Green Into Gold

Following the first Earth Day in 1970, communities raced to introduce recycling programs and plant trees. Over time, interest in environmental issues waned, but now it has resurfaced in an almost over-the-top way. Companies promote everything from carrots to cars as organic, all-natural, recycled, biodegradable, ozone-friendly and carbon-neutral, with new terms introduced by marketing geniuses daily. This has created skepticism from consumers, leaving companies that are truly interested in eco-safe initiatives wondering how to rise above the vague and dubious assertions of their competitors.

There is no universal approach to going green, but there are a number of steps a business of any size can take to quickly reduce its environmental footprint and legitimize its environmental marketing efforts.

Green your operations. Whether your office is a factory or a penthouse, you can green your operations by using energy-efficient lighting, using local materials and supplies to reduce transportation emissions, and using recycled or reusable products. Set your office printers and copiers to print two-sided by default, create computer files instead of paper files and implement green and sustainable systems and policies.

Green your marketing. Make sure your message is rooted in a sincere effort to be socially responsible. Clearly define the eco-friendly qualities of your product or service, and publish supporting data in your marketing collateral and on your website. We can show you the least wasteful way to design and produce a project by introducing post-consumer recycled content, non-chlorine bleached papers, low-polluting inks and two-sided printing options. Include a reminder for the customer to recycle your printed materials.

Green your stakeholders. It is important to engage your employees, shareholders, suppliers, customers and community in your environmental efforts. These groups influence market and buying decisions, so the opportunity for gaining competitive advantage is greatest when you align your corporate strategy with stakeholder values. Consider producing an annual sustainability report as a tangible reminder of your long-term commitment to environmental stewardship.

At the end of the day, it is your actions, not your marketing claims that determine whether your company is green. By adopting a proactive approach to sustainability, you will effectively balance your financial objectives with social and environmental considerations, leading to higher sales, increased market share, happier employees and a better future for all

We can show you the least wasteful way to design and produce a project by introducing post-consumer recycled content, non-chlorine bleached papers, low-polluting inks and two-sided printing options. Include a reminder for the customer to recycle your printed materials.[194]

This is a classic example of marketing by supplying information. In the short space of 418 words, it provides a ton of useful and easily enacted tips. And that last paragraph provides a clear, specific reason to do business with this company. Phrased as an invitation to accept help, it's exactly the kind of hype-free, ultratargeted marketing we advocate (to an audience of existing customers and prospects)—delivered in total consistency with the green message. No four-color ink was spilled to create or deliver the message, no trees were cut down to print it. Yes, there could be a more explicit call to action, but the message is there, embedded in a solid and useful information piece.

PACKAGING AND VALUES

Like Fidlar-Doubleday, lots of other companies use low-cost/no-cost methods to spread the word about their ethical and environmental commitments. If you sell physical products, your packaging is a fabulous marketing tool for conveying values and benefits. Instead of paying for advertising, you let shoppers see your values message as they shop, and allow them to make the decision that you're worth buying.

The food industry is particularly good at this. Examples:

- Gary Hirshberg started Stonyfield Farm Yogurt (now the market leader in organic yogurt) without an advertising budget. Instead, he used his container lids to push for action on global warming, public transportation and so on—and boosted revenues by an astonishing 26%.[195]

---

194 Fidlar Doubleday E-Gram, September 18, 2008, prepared by Great Reach Communications.
195 Yudkin, Marcia, "Show Your Heart," Marketing Minute e-zine, August 13, 2008.

- Nature's Path, an organic cereal company in Canada, printed educational information about organic farming and nutrition on the normally-blank insides of its boxes
- Major food conglomerates like General Mills, Unilever, and Starbucks are sharing more and more information about their products' social, health, and economic benefits

Of course, many other industries do this, too. Some not only educate the consumer but actually turn that consumer into a green champion and educator. For example, Procter & Gamble's Tide Coldwater brand originally focused its entire marketing on the community benefits of saving energy as well as the savings to the consumer who's not paying to heat all that water. Tide partnered with the Alliance to Save Energy to publish energy saving tips (not just about laundry) on the product's page,[196] which on March 21, 2009 featured a TV ad that talked about powering a city with the energy saved by cold-water washing. This had been taken down by April 2015, but an article at http://tidecoldwater. com/en-US/article/coldwater-deep-clean.jspx noted,

> Every time you turn the water temperature dial on your washing machine to "warm," you might as well start writing a check to the energy company.
> When you wash in cold with Tide Coldwater, you can actually save up on your energy bill. And just think how good you'll feel knowing you've done your part to save precious energy.

We do wonder why the company has taken down the much more informative material that used to be there. Do they feel they've already convinced the entire public? We doubt it.

---

196 The energy tips were retained by archive.org on March 30, 2009, at https://web.archive. org/web/20090330020813/http://www1.tide.com/en US/tidecoldwater/energysavingstips. jsp, and the product page was archived on April 4, 2008 at https://web.archive.org/ web/20080404231335/http://www.tide.com/en_US/tidecoldwater/productinformation.jsp both accessed 4/14/15. Neither archive includes the video, however.

Marcal's packaging in 1965—not a word about recycling—and 2010
(1965 photo courtesy of Marcal; 2010 photo by Shel Horowitz)

Jacquelyn Ottman, author of *The New Rules of Green Marketing*, reports that Tide Coldwater's initial campaign in 2005 let consumers actually calculate how much energy they were saving, individually and in conjunction with everyone else who took the "Coldwater Challenge";[197] the campaign also included a number of viral elements, such as a tell-a-friend feature that actually drew a connecting line from the referring person's location to the friend's.[198]

Marcal, a Northeast US household paper products company that switched to recycled raw materials in 1950 and has been producing recycled paper towels,

---

197 Ottman, Jacquelyn. "The Five Simple Rules of Green Marketing," http://www.greenmarketing.com/files/5%20Simple%20DMI%20Nov%202008.pdf, verified 4/12/15.
198 Pamela Parker, "P&G Issues Tide ColdWater Challenge Online," http://www.clickz.com/clickz/news/1713460/p-g-issues-tide-coldwater-challenge-online, verified 4/12/15.

napkins, toilet paper, and tissues ever since, finally realized that long history of green behavior this was an enormous marketing asset. Launching its Small Steps™ brand only in 2009, with autumn-leaf themed packaging trumpeting "paper made from paper, not from trees,"™ it collects paper for recycling from a 300-mile radius. This new marketing initiative was a near-instant success, and within eight months, it was the #1 selling recycled household paper brand in the US, even though it was only available in one region.

Green messaging is showing up in every corner of society. In a news video, Autodesk, a computer-aided design software company, touted its software as a greener tool to design greener buildings.[199]

STUDYING THE ADS: WHAT'S WORKING IN GREEN MARKETING?

As a long-term marketer, media-watcher and journalist, I (Shel) learned long ago that you can tell a whole lot about market trends, as well as the thinking and feeling patterns of not just the overall culture but also the cultures of subgroups within niches—just by studying the ads aimed at them. And you can find out a great deal about people's hot buttons and how to persuade.

When large corporations pay good money to display an ad, it means their research shows their customers want to buy the sorts of products, services, or ideas described in those ads, and that at least a percentage of them will respond to the types of language, graphics, and offers that those ads encompass.

Here's an example directly related to the green world: a magazine called *GreenSource: The Magazine of Sustainable Design*, published in 2011 by McGraw-Hill. It's aimed at green architects, designers, and builders.

Firstly, it says a great deal that the green design and construction niche is big enough to get attention from a mainstream publisher like McGraw-Hill, and that this magazine apparently had no trouble finding advertisers, even in a down economy.

And secondly, looking at the ads, we see that the bar has gone sharply higher for sustainable design over the past few years. Going green, and being able to

---

199 "What Sustainable Design Means to the Bottom Line: Autodesk: Designing a Greener Future for Businesses," http://www.cbsnews.com/videos/what-sustainable-design-means-to-the-bottom-line/, verified 4/12/15.

convince a skeptical green consumer base that you've done so, is a lot more involved now than simply using recycled materials, driving a hybrid, or caulking all the drafty spaces. All sorts of new issues are coming into play.

Let's look at just the ads in the first eight pages:

The first is a two-page ad is for recycled ceiling panels. Joining the trend toward making claims believable by quantifying them, the ad claims 100 million pounds of old ceiling tiles were reclaimed, keeping 50,000 tons of them out of landfills. (These two numbers are equivalent.)

Turning the page—another two-page ad, for a "living wall": "biofilter technology [that] not only captures airborne pollutants, it breaks them down." The pictures show a standing forest on the left, a multistory building wall covered with plants on the right.

The outer half of the next page has a half-page vertical ad for "vertical landscaping". It shows plants growing thickly on the outside of a two-story townhouse. The inner half of the page is the magazine's masthead. Opposite, a full-page ad for "the only gypsum board that clears the air." This one claims to permanently remove Volatile Organic Compounds (VOCs) for up to 75 years.

On the next page, another half-page vertical for "drivable grass®"—a driveway paving replacement that allows storm water to drain through to the soil underneath. And opposite that, a full-page ad for a low-emissions certification agency.

The last ad before the contents page is for an aluminum building material with 70- to 80 percent post-consumer recycled content, and ISO certification to prove it.

Walls that filter rather than emit pollutants, and paving solutions that recycle the rainwater—were these the kinds of things you expected to be dealing with when you decided to take your company green? It all sounds so complicated!

But consider the positive side: if this level of awareness is becoming so common that these are the advertisers in the prized (and expensive) front-of-thebook pages at a major-publisher magazine, *that creates a huge opening for you to push for greater sustainability measures in your company.* You can use this kind of magazine to prove to the powers-that-be that the world isn't standing still, and that your organization needs to both be doing more on sustainability, and finding ways to convey that commitment to the public.

And that may turn out to be a very exciting task.

THRIVING AS THE BAR IS RAISED

Until fairly recently, it was still possible to draw on any green initiative as a positive point of differentiation, a way of moving consumers toward your brand. But that first-mover advantage is starting to fade. As sustainability becomes mainstream, expected, and even demanded, you must do better at heralding why your company, product, or service is special.

In 1995, it was enough to say, "we have a website." By 2000, you needed "visit our website to find these resources." In 2010, it was "visit our website so you can have real-time input into developing our next products…to have conversations with a community of product users…to get faster and better support." By 2015, many websites are offering real-time customization, such as designing or decorating your eco-friendly dream home.

Similarly, green messaging will have to get more specific and highlight advantages better. The old green messages are beginning to look a bit pale. Accusations of greenwashing are rife—and often, those charges have more than a little substance—does anyone really believe BP is a green company any more?

So does that mean green marketing is dead? What's a conscious marketer to do?

We don't for a moment believe that green is dying, let alone dead. But we green marketers need to take greater responsibility for our messaging. Like a toddler learning walking and talking and table manners and a whole bunch of other stuff all at once, we have to stand on our own feet, even if it feels a bit wobbly at first.

So here are a few reminders on your own wobble toward sustainable marketing:

1. Be clear and specific. Today's informed consumer doesn't just want to hear "we've gone green." They'll respond better to something like "by introducing this new, efficient packing machine, we've reduced solid waste by 18 percent and cut carbon emissions by 368 tons a year."

2. Make consumers understand what each of these accomplishments means to them: "That solid waste reduction means we don't have to bring nearly as much to the landfill, which means lower costs passed on to you, longer landfill life, and fewer non-degradable materials clogging up the landfill. Lower carbon means 68 fewer asthma cases in our county every year, as well as reducing catastrophic climate change."

Paragraph 1 stresses features—which are by themselves seldom enough to sell successfully—and paragraph 2 translates those features into direct benefits both to the consumer and to the world. Features let the gear-heads (who already understand what they mean) supply the benefits themselves; benefits speak to average consumers through their own emotional needs and wants, and are much more powerful. In many cases, you need both.

3. Raise the bar on your industry's standards for going green. Being not just the industry leader but the gadfly always pushing the industry to do more can be a powerful profitability proposition. When your competitors say something is too hard, and you go out and do it, you don't just prove them wrong. You get the first-mover advantage and show the public the value of buying from you.

Have you achieved zero waste in a facet of production? Have you not just switched to compostable plastics but actually compost them? Have you figured out a way to cut energy or water use by some huge percentage? Are you sourcing a larger percentage of materials from sustainable-practices vendors? Say so! You'll get the competitive advantage of doing this before others—and once your competitors start imitating, you can still get good marketing mileage out of having been first.

4. Involve your supply chain. Just as "no man is an island," neither is a corporation. You have vendors who sell to you, and customers who buy from you. You have ancillary services involved, such as transportation or security. And you have both carrot- and stick-flavored leverage you can exert to help these companies go green. The carrots: not only will they get more of your business, but you will promote them in your green marketing campaigns. The stick? If they fail your sustainability criteria, you'll choose another vendor who is more earth-centered.

We could name dozens of examples. Here are two of our favorites.

Dean's Beans Sends a Jolt of Espresso through the Coffee Industry

From the day it was founded in 1993, coffee roaster Dean's Beans, of Orange, Massachusetts, has managed not only to source 100 percent of its coffee and cocoa through organic, fair-trade farms, and to pay its suppliers well above the established fair-trade price, but also to fund very effective village-led community development programs covering such areas as access to water, economic development, and even educational programs to prevent domestic violence.

In the United States, the company chose to locate in an economically depressed community where the jobs it provides make an enormous difference—and to partner with hospitals and schools to raise funds through co-branded products such as "Way Cooley Coffee" for Cooley Dickinson Hospital in Northampton, Massachusetts. The beans are certified Kosher, too.

But company founder Dean Cycon does not stop with this ambitious social change agenda. He has been a voice of conscience in the entire coffee industry, assertively pushing companies like Starbucks and Green Mountain to increase their percentage of fair-trade coffee. He also co-founded two separate business associations for the few roasters who source 100% of their beans from organic fair-trade suppliers, and participates actively in a third. And he co-founded another organization doing charity work with coffee farmers who've been injured by landmines.[200]

The company does very little advertising and has benefited not only from a long string of positive publicity, but also from several major awards, among them the Oslo Business for Peace Award (considered the alternative Nobel Peace Prize) and a Best Practices Award from the United Nations Food and Agriculture Organization.[201]

Green Pioneering Helps Patagonia Climb More Mountains

Outdoor equipment retailer Patagonia has consistently broken new ground on environmental initiatives. Its founder, Yvon Chouinard, had read Muir and Thoreau, and was concerned about the environmental impact of thousands of pitons hammered permanently into mountains. So he developed a reusable

---

200 "Great Coffee Making the World a Better Place," https://deansbeans.com/mission, accessed 4/2/15.
201 Ibid.

Google search for "Patagonia take back program"

piton all the way back in 1957.[202] This was the product that launched him into business; he founded Patagonia in 1973.

The company was the first name-brand company we know of (in 2005) to offer to take back any product at the end of its useful life, to rehabilitate, remanufacture, or use as raw materials to make something else.[203] It's also still the only major company we're aware of that voluntarily tells people not to buy its products unless they really need them. You can see its famous "Don't Buy This Jacket" ad at http://www.patagonia.com/email/11/112811.html.[204]

These are just two among many pioneering Patagonia environmental initiatives. The company's website has a huge section devoted to the environment and the company's deep commitment. Its ads discuss them as well.

And it has received incredible amounts of publicity, not just in the outdoor equipment world, but throughout the business and environmental communities. A Google search for "patagonia don't buy our stuff" brings 836,000 results, with Bloomberg (financial and business wire service), *Huffington Post*, *Adweek* and *Treehugger* all on page 1. Searching for "patagonia don't buy this jacket"

202 As cited in Shel's July 2013 newsletter, http://thecleanandgreenclub.com/the-clean-and-green-club-july-2013/
203 http://www.patagonia.com/us/common-threads/recycle, accessed 2/28/15.
204 Verified 2/28/15.

brings 459,000 results. Searching for "patagonia take back program" (excluding patagonia.com from the results) yields 1,300,000 results, and the front page includes GreenBiz.com, Bloomberg again, *Sustainable Business*, and a trade magazine, *Textile World*.[205]

When was the last time one of your company's programs got more than a million results on Google?

LESSONS

- Green products and services can actually be easier to market
- Media that targets eco-conscious audiences can easily fill ad space
- Green claims are becoming much more specialized
- Smaller companies can often out-green their larger competitors, as Dean's Beans proves
- Patagonia's green messaging earned it enormous visibility on Google

ACTIONS

- Identify one or two areas where you can outgreen your big competitors.
- Understand what it would take to implement them.
- Create three message points about them for your marketing.

---

205 Search conducted 2/28/15.

CHAPTER 11

MAKING GREEN SEXY ACROSS ALL DEMOGRAPHICS AND INDUSTRIES

n essential part of green marketing, we believe, is eradicating the lingering perception that green has to be awful.

One of Shel's most popular speeches is "Making Green Sexy." He first gave it at a green buildings conference in Houston, Texas, back in 2012—and has given it many times since.

The interesting thing about that idea is that "sexy" is in the eye of the beholder—which is a good thing for those of us who don't look like supermodels yet have loving relationships. And that means we green marketers need to think about those "beholders," recognize their diversity, and craft messages that talk to the specific people with specific worldviews. One size definitely does not fit all.

Most people would consider the Tesla roadster sexy. Competing with brands like Porsche and Corvette, this super-sporty car screams speed, power, luxury, and high status (see pictures at http://my.teslamotors.com/roadster/gallery).[206]

---

206 Verified 4/21/15.

It was also the first ultra-high-performance fully electric car that's ever been out on the market.

In our view, living luxuriously while using far fewer resources is just as sexy. Yes, Shel shows a picture of the Tesla roadster in his talk. But he also shows pictures of Marcal's recycled toilet paper package and green buildings such as the Empire State Building or Amory Lovins' ultra-efficient house (built back in 1983 in the Colorado Rockies)—not what most people would define as sexy—at least until they look closely.

What makes Lovins' home sexy is not its looks—which are unusual, and even a bit jarring. It's sexy in several other ways, though:

- Despite the cold, snowy winters and hot, sunny summers in the Aspen, Colorado snowbelt (one of the downhill skiing capitals of the United States), this house has neither a furnace nor an air conditioner—because it doesn't need either one.

- The sunroom is warm enough, even during the winter, that Lovins actually grows bananas inside.

- At 4000 square feet/371.6 square meters, it's big enough to compare with the grand mansions that we popularly think of as sexy.

- Because expensive items like heating and cooling systems weren't purchased, the extra-cost green and sustainable energy features paid for themselves in just 10 months.

- As a passive solar home, much of the energy savings was achieved by thinking, designing, and building holistically, where a single component might achieve multiple goals; he referred to one arch in his house that accomplishes 12 different functions.

- Long before the terms "zero waste" and "cradle-to-cradle" came into use, this house was designed to close as many loops as possible, and to produce almost no waste.

- Even using 1983 technology, which we in the solar and green world would consider quite primitive by today's standards, the house makes nearly all of its own electricity

At a talk by Lovins several years ago, he said he averaged a USD $5 electric bill for the residential portion of his home/office. Even if higher energy prices have brought that up to, say, $25, that's still quite remarkable—and to our minds, sexy.

What's really sexy to Shel about the Lovins house is not even the individual features. It's the potential for world-wide planet-saving. Think about what kind of world we'd be living in right now if for the past 30+ years since Lovins proved it was feasible, most houses had been built for net-zero or net-positive waste, energy, and water:

- Atmospheric carbon would be greatly reduced—probably well below the 350 parts-per-million danger zone that we are now exceeding—and thus, global warming would not be a desperate situation.
- Pollution from burning fossil fuels (and from extracting them from the earth) would be a tiny fraction of what it is now, and this in turn would mean sharply reduced healthcare costs—because a lot fewer people would be getting sick.
- The world's largest economies would not chase after oil reserves, so foreign policy would have been reshaped—away from wars over energy resources and toward inspiring real democracy and economic self-sufficiency
- And finally, all that money that's been spent on buying energy would have been freed up to invest elsewhere causing a flowering of technology and the arts, and a massive rise in living standards around the world.

Fortunately, many designers besides Lovins have been building amazing passively heated and cooled buildings for decades. Manit Rastogi's large, elegant, and very beautiful Pearl Academy of Fashion in Jaipur, India, where temperatures of 113°F/45°C are common, combines several ancient passive cooling techniques to create comfortable temperatures in an industry where sweat is simply unacceptable.[207]

---

207 Lloyd Alter, "Architect Uses Ancient Techniques To Cool Modern Building in India," http://www.treehugger.com/green-architecture/architect-uses-ancient-techniques-cool-modern-building-india.html, verified 2/16/15.

And we don't have to stop at single buildings. Entire communities can be built around this kind of thinking. Masdar, just outside Abu Dhabi, United Arab Emirates, is a planned green community that uses systems thinking in every aspect, in the harsh Arabian desert.[208] Cars (tiny little things) have been moved underground, buildings are designed to let in light but not heat, and to shade the pedestrian areas below them. Opened in 2009 and already attracting major corporations, Masdar was built to accommodate 40,000 residents, 1000 businesses, and 50,000 commuting workers.

These principles work on the cold side of the climate spectrum, too—like the house in frigid Minnesota that doesn't need a furnace; Shel blogged about it at http://GreenAndProfitable.com/passive-solar-no-furnace-in-cold-minnesota/.

> This kind of world should have been our inheritance.
> Let's at least make it our legacy.

LOCAL AS GREEN

As the world becomes ever-more-conscious about environmental impact, opportunities abound for smart entrepreneurs. One huge opportunity is the Local Economy movement. As consumers become aware of the environmental and economic impact of transporting products across the country or around the world, many consciously seek out locally-based alternatives. Benefits include not only reducing carbon output but also keeping money and jobs in the consumer's own area while reinforcing local/regional identity. Some shoppers will even choose a local conventionally grown or processed product over an organic or all-natural one, to minimize their carbon footprint. Combine green engineering or organic agriculture with a local economic base, and you're golden.

In the next few years, we predict that entrepreneurs who create locally-based alternatives to faraway products will grow rapidly. The Schumacher Center For New Economics (formerly known as the E.F. Schumacher Society), a leader in sustainability thinking for decades, highlighted the tremendous possibilities of this trend:

---

208 "Why Masdar Matters," by Leon Kaye, http://www.triplepundit.com/2012/02/masdar-city-progress/, verified 2/17/15.

An independent regional economy calls for new regional economic institutions for land, labor…[that] cannot be government-driven… free associations of consumers and producers, working cooperatively, sharing the risk in creating an economy that reflects shared culture and shared values. Small in scale, transparent in structure, designed to profit the community rather than profit from the community, they can address our common concern for safe and fair working conditions; for production practices that keep our air and soil and waters clean, renewing our natural resources rather than depleting them; for innovation in the making and distribution of the basic necessities of food, clothing, shelter, and energy rather than luxury items; and for more equitable distribution of wealth.

Building of new economic institutions is hard work…fine beginnings are being made in the development of local currencies, community supported farms, regionally based equity and loan funds, worker-owned businesses, community land trusts, and business alliances for local living economies.

These initiatives are motivated by the affection that the citizens of a region have for their neighbors and neighborhoods; for the fields, forests, mountains, and rivers of their landscapes; for the local history and culture that binds these all together; and for their common future.[209]

Alternative Economies for the 21st Century

New models for human centered commerce are springing up all over the place. And the local economy goes a lot deeper than Main Street/High Street retail shops. Those are important, to be sure, and to live in thriving communities, we need to support those quirky little stores. But any marketing planning must also take into account the layers and layers of businesses hidden in the nooks and crannies of residential neighborhoods. It includes work-at-home consultants and health practitioners, as well as "sharing economy" micro-entrepreneurs with side businesses operating through networks like Airbnb and Uber. These tiny businesses build a level of resilience and community that national and

---

209 E.F. Schumacher Society, "Co-producers of Our Own Economies," email blast, September 1, 2008.

international chain stores can't match.[210] Small business experts Paul and Sarah Edwards call it the "Elm Street Economy":

> It's a local economy, composed of locally-owned and locally-financed enterprises, industries, and independent practitioners who are invested in bringing long-term well-being to all living there, including nature. Its focus is on working together to create a dependable, environmentally sustainable way of life that bring basic services, products, and resilience back to our local communities.[211]

Interestingly, while many well-established businesses have fought the sharing economy, others have embraced it. Patagonia has partnered with eBay to sell used clothing, GE is using Quirky for product idea generation and research, BMW has created its own car-sharing program similar to Zipcar, Walgreens contracts with Task Rabbit to deliver prescriptions, and UHaul has a portal to let its customers crowdfund their rentals.[212]

And the sharing economy is not a new idea. We've had barter for thousands of years, but today's technology opens many new models.

- The Grateful Dead may have been the first major music act (among many) to eagerly embrace bootleg recording at its concerts[213]
- Servas.org, an international homestay organization set up to foster world peace through cross-cultural exchange, predates Couchsurfing. org by decades (it was founded in the 1950s)

---

210 This is reportage, not endorsement. We are aware of these networks' negative impact on country inns/B&Bs and independent taxi services, and we are aware of the licensing issues. But the model holds promise, and these things can be worked out.

211 As reported in Shel's blog, "Is It Time for the Elm Street Economy?" January 5, 2010: http://GreenAndProfitable.com/is-it-time-for-the-elm-street-economy/

212 Jeremiah Owyang, Alexandra Samuel, and Andrew Grenville, Vision Critical whitepaper, "Sharing is the New Buying: How to Win in the Collaborative Economy," http://info.mkto. visioncritical.com/rs/visioncritical/images/sharing-new-buying-collaborative-economy.pdf, accessed 3/13/15.

213 https://en.wikipedia.org/wiki/Bootleg_recording, accessed 3/16/15.

- Residents of The Vale Community, founded in 1946 in rural Yellow Springs, Ohio,[214] chose to pitch in and buy a shared tractor instead of each household buying its own lawnmower[215]
- The Life Center, an intentional community of about 130 people in the far more urban setting of West Philadelphia, offered residents the option to borrow two cars, at a fixed cost per mile, at least as early as 1980[216]

The Schumacher Center has sponsored the research and development of an alternative local currency; BerkShares, usable in Berkshire County, Massachusetts, which has circulated more than $5 million as of March, 2015.[217] Many other local-economies groups around the world have local currencies, including local currency pioneer Ithaca Hours, in Ithaca, NY, founded in 1991 and now accepted by over 900 businesses.[218] Businesses that want to cultivate a local-first mentality gain a built-in marketing channel (plus community credibility) by accepting their local currency and participating in the meetings, business fairs, and other events.

Local currency is only one possible model. Another is timebanking, also called time trading, in which an hour of one person's time can be exchanged for an hour of someone else's time. A landscaper could trade with a neurosurgeon, and their time contributions would be valued equally.

Denise Rushing, active in the Lake County, California timebank,[219] says her organization

---

214 http://www.ic.org/directory/the-vale/, accessed 3/16/15.
215 As told to Shel by resident Ken Champney, around 1975.
216 Shel was a resident of this community and borrowed both vehicles on various occasions. Because the ethic of this community was on eco-friendly alternatives to private cars, most trips were done on foot, by bike, or using the trolley and bus lines serving the neighborhood. The cars were typically used to do things like getting a month's supply of drinking water for a household of six or eight people from a spring in an outlying town, and thus, two cars were enough to meet the needs of this community.
217 https://en.wikipedia.org/wiki/BerkShares, accessed 3/15/15.
218 http://www.ithacahours.info/, accessed 3/15/15.
219 "The time Bank of Thrive Lake County," http://www.thrivelakecounty.org/time-bank, accesse 5/14/15.

...Thrives because our economically poor residents are 'time millionaires' who easily understand and use time banking. Also, the ability to contribute to one another has raised our time bankers' self-worth in addition to getting physical needs met...timebanking builds community at the grass roots—people get to know each other and each timebanker feels valued as they share their gifts.

Rushing says timebanking software provider hOurworld is even using timebanking to reduce costs for health care delivery: by receiving timebanked services in their own home, health more patients can stay at home, with better outcomes—"a win-win for the agencies and for those in need of services."

A Champion for Local Foods

In the Pioneer Valley of Massachusetts, Communities Involved in Sustainable Agriculture (CISA) has been building consciousness about buying local for more than a decade. This trade organization for farmers started a "Local Hero" campaign back in 1999 that continues to involve farmers, retailers, and consumers; the region has experienced a huge shift in favor of buying local that extends well beyond food products.

People who want local foods seek them out, and buy from them. These farms willingly sell to a market that cuts out several of the middlemen and allows them to command a premium price. In an era when farms face huge challenges economically, the CISA member farms tend to be doing well. Consumers get fresh foods (often picked that day)—and the knowledge that they're building the *local* economy. The money they spend with these farmers and their retailers comes back to the community in a myriad of ways: from support for sports teams and community causes to preserving open space for farmland against encroaching suburban sprawl.

Farmers get ready markets—both wholesale and retail—of locals committed to the local economy, and of stores or food service establishments willing to facilitate that commitment by making the products available. Interestingly, some of the stores and restaurants that participate are not themselves locally based; a couple of very large chains are participating, selling local produce to local buyers even while they themselves are headquartered far away.

Interviewed by Shel in 2011, Devon Whitney-Deal, CISA's Local Hero Member Services Coordinator, noted that when the organization started tracking in 2003, there were only nine farmers markets in the Pioneer Valley—but now there are at least 40 seasonal markets plus four winter markets (a more than 400 percent increase in eight years). CISA had 199 member farmers, 50 retailers, 32 restaurants, and a total membership of 312. And in its three-county service area, reversing the farm-loss trend elsewhere, more acreage is actually in farmland now than when the group was founded.

In other words, through a massive branding campaign, this organization actually *created a consciousness about buying local.* People who in the past had not thought much about where their food comes from have made a conscious shift to buying some portion of their food supply from local sources—and that, in turn, has helped the farm economy to stay solvent.

The buy-local strategy, according to CISA's website, offers these five benefits (quoting):

- Keeps money in the local economy
- Preserves family farms
- Reduces oil-dependent transportation costs
- Protects our local landscapes
- Ensures that fresh, healthy food stays available and affordable to all[220]

This movement has spread rapidly through CISA's three-county service area, and has gone far beyond vegetables. These days, people in the region can easily obtain local fruits (some of them organic), grains (and breads made with them), cheeses, craft items, toys, jewelry, clothing, and more. And with a little help from a group called Pioneer Valley Local First, the buy-local consciousness has grown to support locally owned independent stores in other disciplines, even if the products they sell are not local. There's even a store in Amherst, Massachusetts called All Things Local, selling locally made products in many sectors.

---

220 http://www.buylocalfood.org/buy-local/, verified 4/21/15.

For independent retailers with bookstores, clothing boutiques, hardware stores, cafes and restaurants, dry-cleaners and so forth, this movement has been a life preserver in a tough economic climate.

Among other measurable results: sales of organic farm products in Massachusetts nearly doubled from $7.8 million in 2002 to $17.5 million in 2007, agritourism in the state soared from $665,000 to $5.3 million—an *800 percent increase*—in the same period, and both the number of farms and the total acreage farmed in the state increased during those years, after decades of decline.[221]

If CISA ever decides to go national, it already owns a great web address that could accommodate regional subdomains (as Craigslist.com does); find this organization not at CISA.com or .org, but at http://www.buylocalfood.com. We think CISA should consider franchising.

CISA does have counterparts in other regions, and that's part of why the local food movement is growing enormously in many parts of the US and the world. In 1990, when the very first Community Supported Agriculture (CSA) farm opened up in Berkshire County, Massachusetts, the US had about 1350 farmers markets. By the end of 2012, these numbers had grown enormously; there were at least 4570 CSA farms and 7864 farmers markets (an average of 157 per state, versus 27 in 1990).[222]

At least one national association already exists: Business Alliance for Local Living Economies (BALLE), http://www.livingeconomies.org. Founded by Judy Wicks of the White Dog Café, a successful socially conscious restaurant in Philadelphia, BALLE provides education to consumers and support to businesses around the importance of buying local. And some local Chambers of Commerce are also moving into this territory, which clearly helps their members. Businesses that can position themselves as the locally owned, locally produced alternative can harvest deeply from their local markets.

---

221 Richie Davis, , "US agriculture census sees rise in area farming," Daily Hampshire Gazette, Northampton, MA, February 19, 2009, pp. A1, B6.

222 http://GreenAndProfitable.com/csas-and-farmers-markets-note-two-decades-of-massive-growth-wow/, accessed 2/14/15.

Interestingly, small local farms can be far more profitable than big corporate ones, especially as energy prices spiral up. Writing in the New York Times, restaurant chef Dan Barber notes,

> Small farms are the most productive on earth. A four-acre farm in the United States nets, on average, $1,400 per acre; a 1,364-acre farm nets $39 an acre. Big farms have long compensated for the disequilibrium with sheer quantity. But their economies of scale come from mass distribution, and with diesel fuel costing more than $4 per gallon in many locations, it's no longer efficient to transport food 1,500 miles from where it's grown.[223]

GLOBAL AS GREEN

The flip side of the buy-local movement is that in our increasingly globalized economy, enormous opportunities are opening for nimble companies who can make sharp turns in the global arena. Mark Schapiro, Editorial Director of the Center for Investigative Reporting and author of *Exposed: The Toxic Chemistry of Everyday Products and What's at Stake for American Power*, noted in a radio interview that because environmental and safety standards for cosmetics/personal care products are much tougher in the European Union than in the United States, the few US companies that meet the stricter requirements have access to the entire EU market.

Eventually, Schapiro says, US consumers will discover the tougher labeling and ingredient standards and demand them. "There are levels of disclosure required on European products that are not required on American products. We live in a global economy. So that information is going to start making its way back here to the United States. And I think it's going to start creating some interesting tensions when people start seeing information disclosed there that's not disclosed here."[224]

---

223 Dan Barber, "Change We Can Stomach," New York Times, May 11, 2008, http://www.nytimes.com/2008/05/11/opinion/11barber.html, verified 4/12/15.
224 Interviewed on Democracy Now, February 24, 2009, http://www.democracynow.org/2009/2/24/us_lags_behind_europe_in_regulating, verified 4/13/15.

Extrapolating from that, it seems obvious to us that the first US cosmetics company to start heavily marketing its own compliance with the European standards, and what that means for consumer safety and environmental protection, could score a huge first-mover marketing coup even in the US market, and cast doubt on the offerings of many of its competitors.

In other words, the more your company holds to high ethical and environmental standards, the more you can sell in the global economy. So educate your customers on the importance of dealing fairly with suppliers in developing countries and offer fair-trade certified products they can feel good about. Sell organic clothing, craft items that benefit a women's educational co-op, natural and renewable building materials, traditional toys that are guaranteed to be safe, or even recordings of indigenous music from around the world—and show how you're giving back to the communities that supply you *and* those that purchase from you. Consumers will support you!

We'll look more closely at global marketing (both in green and nongreen sectors) in Chapter 16.

LUXURIOUS AS GREEN

One big change in the past few years is the emergence of a luxury cohort within the green world. Not so long ago, people who cared about the environment were often accused of wanting to turn back the clock on comfort; when the mass media looked at green living, they often created images of people living in deprivation—for instance, huddled in a dim living room, wearing their winter coats.

Those images were not true in the first place, except for a very few individuals on the edge. But they had become a meme in the 1970s and 1980s.

Now, instead, we have a super-luxurious side within the green world—with cars like the Tesla and the Porsche Cayenne hybrid, extravagant green mansions, elegant fashions and décor, and high-end eco-resorts. The message now is you can have all the comfort you can pay for, in pretty much any sector, but you can get those things with environmentally friendly features.

As an example, watch the 4-minute video Shel conducted with an employee of a luxury eco-hotel/resort in Taos, New Mexico: https://www.youtube.com/

watch?v=0Nj-wB1dft4.[225] As you note the lush lawns and thick foliage, remember that this is in the desert.

We won't get into a discussion of whether those lifestyle choices are actually green; that could fill another book. But we will point out that it is now quite common to market eco-consciousness at the very high end.

LESSONS

- Green can be local or global, and aimed at any demographic and economic strata
- The local economy includes both traditional businesses and hidden, "sharing economy" participants
- Organizations such as CISA have successfully changed the discourse and have had enormous economic impact; you can, as well

ACTIONS

- Define "sexy" green products in your own niche
- Find one talking point for your products or services that relates to localism.
- Find another one that relates to the global economy.

---

225 Recorded October , 2013.

CHAPTER 12

LANGUAGE, GREENWASHING, AND TRUTH

USE THE RIGHT LANGUAGE

Use the right language to get your green message across. Futerra Sustainability Communications, a UK marketing agency specializing in green approaches, studied the effectiveness of various terms in sustainability marketing.

The study found that language emphasizing empathy, personification, action, and intellect (e.g., *"smart," "conscious,"* or *"savvy"*) were highly persuasive, as were phrases that focused on connectedness and the big picture (*"one planet living"*). Terms that ranked poorly included *"eco-safe"* and *"conflict."*[226]

Language that positions the company with a friendly, human voice also works well. Consider Tom's of Maine, a natural personal care products company

---

226 Words That Sell," Futerra Sustainability Communications, as reported in Melissa Chungfat's article, "Words that 'Work': What To Write When Marketing Green," http://ecopreneurist. com/2008/12/10/words-that-work-what-to-write-when-marketing-green/, verified 4/13/15. Futerra's full report can be accessed from that link.

(now owned by Colgate-Palmolive). Tom's packaging always includes a friendly, down-home note from founders Tom and Kate Chappell. And the website's page on sourcing proclaims, "since 1981, we've proudly listed every ingredient, its purpose, and its source on our packages, so you know what you're buying."[227] There's also a prominent link to the ingredients Tom's refuses to use, again with reasons why. Green marketing expert Jacquelyn Ottman notes that this level of transparency "is unprecedented in the history of consumer goods" and points out that the detailed disclosure

> …helps get consumers over any price barriers at the point of sale. They are choosing a brand with natural ingredients and recognize that it must come with a price.[228]

As an aside—the right language is important in any marketing campaign, not just the green ones. To cite one of thousands of examples, social media strategist Chris Brogan attributes the iPod's success to Apple not getting bogged down in megabytes, sampling rates, etc.—but to position it as a player that holds 1000 songs—cutting straight to the core benefit and bypassing all the technobable.[229]

NO-HYPE ZONE

Imagine going down the road in your eco-friendly hybrid car (or better yet, your public transit conveyance or your bicycle), listening to some earnest musician's song about global warming. All of a sudden, this commercial is screaming at you:

Go green today! Act NOW to lock in your savings! Call 800-555-CASH or visit www.CashBackEnergySavings.com. That's 800-555-CASH or www. CashBackEnergySavings.com (note: phone and URL are fictional).

How do you feel about this loud, intrusive interruption?

Guess what—that's exactly how your prospects feel when they encounter hypey, in-your-face green marketing. And they tune it out. Even outside the green sector, obnoxious marketing is a lot less effective than it used to be. We

---

227 http://www.tomsofmaine.com/planet#sourcing, verified 4/14/15.
228 Jaquelyn Ottman, "The Five Simple Rules of Green Marketing," op. cit.
229 Brogan, Chris, "It's All About You," February 18, 2009, http://www.chrisbrogan.com/its-all-about-you/.

have hundreds of thousands of sources for information now, and when one of them gets annoying, we leave.

Yes, there are companies out there doing this sort of thing—but no, it doesn't work very well.

Even more than the public as a whole, many segments of the green market are turned off by screamy hype. People who are drawn to green products and green—especially the Deep Greens (more about them shortly)—perceive themselves as thoughtful and intelligent, sorting out a range of competing and sometimes conflicting benefits and demerits to make choices that are good for the earth, and also good for themselves, their family, and their wallets.

And they're hungry for tools that help them make those decisions. They will demand enough information to thoroughly evaluate for themselves whether your claims make sense and whether your offering is right for them. They will spend time reading articles, poring over back pages of websites, checking out your endorsements and testimonials, watching informational videos, scanning social media and blog feeds...and, especially, discussing planned major purchases with a cadre of trusted friends and associates.

To make it even more challenging, different sectors within that great big green market will bring different motivations and needs, and respond differently to the same marketing.

Let's look at one hypothetical typical green family. Children's health may be mom's primary concern, while her husband worries about the soaring cost of heating their home. His mother, who lives with them, has poor circulation and is cold all the time. The teenage daughter wants to make sure the workers involved are paid fair wages for harvesting the crops, but her younger brother is trying to find organic food that tastes good and doesn't seem weird to his classmates. If you try to reach all of these very different constituencies with the same marketing message, all of them will ignore you.

One way around that is to do different marketing pieces for each segment. Apple, for instance, markets one set of benefits to graphic artists, a different set to educators, and entirely different ones for musicians and film production people.

But for smaller companies, that approach may be expensive. A better alternative might be to *incorporate multiple marketing messages into the same communication,* e.g., offer multiple pages on a website or brochure.

For instance, a manufacturer of energy-efficient window quilts might create a triage-style website landing page that directs visitors to separate pages for high-end builders (looking for luxury features to differentiate their houses from others), interior designers (all about style), landlords (concerned with cost and appearance, and homeowners (balancing savings, durability, and their fashion statement). And those pages, in turn can subdivide by other interest areas.

Or, going back to our imaginary family, the company can market not only by professional affiliation but also by the particular interest. So a landing page might have links with titles like:

- How our window quilts can keep your family healthy and lower your medical bills (Mom will read that one)
- Why you're probably throwing away up to $800 every winter—through your windows (Dad)
- The inside story of why we use only fair-trade cotton and how it's working miracles in the farming villages where we work (daughter)
- Looking to have the coolest room in town? Check out these awesome designs (son)
- How to stay nice and cozy-warm this winter without putting on a second and third sweater (that page is for Grandma)

BUILD CREDIBILITY WITH THE RIGHT CERTIFICATIONS

Everyone knows that third-party endorsement is a powerful credibility builder. This is especially true in the green consumer products world, where so much of the marketing process is based on making a strong case that you have other values besides financial gain.

Certification is one way to gain that credibility. When an independent agency verifies that you are doing what you say you're doing, customer trust of you and your products go way up.

But certification raises a number of other issues:

What Does the Claim Actually Mean?

In the green marketplace, numerous products make all sorts of claims. The purchaser has to sort out what's really going on, and which claims are meaningful. Smart shoppers understand, for instance, that when a package says, "made with organic ingredients," that means as much as 30 percent of the product could be nonorganic. They don't yet have enough information to make an educated choice. What percentage of the ingredients are organic? Which ingredients were grown that way? The pesticide content of a nonfood product like nonorganic cotton will likely be much higher than the pesticide content of a fruit with edible skin, such as apples; all of this has to be factored into the buying decision. So this particular group will turn over the box and look at the ingredients list and look at which ingredients are really organic, and in what order the organic and nonorganic ingredients appear (thus, their relative predominance).

Self-Labeling Versus True Certification

Many labels claim a product is "natural" or "fairly traded"—but no standards exist for what is natural or fairly traded, and until recently, no certifying body had regulated the claims. (Journalist Debra Atlas reports on a new certification, Certified Naturally Grown, which offers a lower-cost farmer-led alternative to USDA Organic certification.[230]Consumers are at the mercy of the manufacturer and have to hope for honesty. By contrast, the word "organic" has a legal definition, and neutral-party certification such as USDA Organic in the United States or Ecocert for European cosmetics gives it teeth. And various agencies such as the 26 members around the world of Fairtrade International (from Australia to the US) certify compliance with fair trade provisions: If you see those types of certifications, you know the claim was independently verified. So as a marketer, those are the sorts of certifications worth pursuing.

Retailers are also stepping into the breach. Whole Foods, for instance, now requires certification for any product claiming to be organic. Walmart, which

---

230 Debra Atlas, "'Certified Naturally Grown' label brings trust and confidence to consumers," https://envirothink.wordpress.com/2015/02/23/certified-naturally-grown-label-brings-trust-and-confidence-to-consumers/, accessed 2/25/15.

has been ranking suppliers on a sustainability index since 2009,[231] introduced its own badge program identifying certain products as "sustainability leaders" in March, 2015, and will feature them in a sustainable products section of its website.[232]

Putting on his marketing consultant hat, Shel suggests Walmart could easily promote this: rotate badged products through front-of-store endcaps clearly labeled as the sustainability winners. Given Walmart's long-running success in selling organic foods, low-power lightbulbs and other green products (as noted in Chapter 13), this would likely create huge sales spikes for the featured products and cost next-to-nothing to implement. Shel would also advise the companies receiving this merit badge to trumpet it loudly in their other marketing.

Calling Walmart's badges a certification program is a stretch. GreenBiz.com editor Joel Makower says Walmart needs to be a lot more transparent about its criteria, and accuses the retail giant of setting the bar too low.[233] But it's still a third-party endorsement of environmental practices that companies have to work to obtain; Unilever submitted responses in seven categories, but only earned four badges.[234]

Of course in today's wired world, shoppers themselves can play a role in verifying claims. Social media allows anyone to accuse a company of making false claims, and to attract a wide audience; this is one of many reasons to be scrupulously honest in all your claims.

SPACE ON THE LABEL

Understanding the value of these certifications, some companies have obtained multiple certifications covering different aspects. For instance, a 3-ounce (66-gram) bar of Theo 91%-cocoa chocolate bears the following certifications and claims:

231 GreenBiz.com, "Walmart Unveils Phase One of Sustainability Index," http://www.greenbiz.com/news/2009/07/16/walmart-unveils-phase-one-sustainability-index, accessed 3/23/15.
232 Joel Makower, "7 reasons Walmart has given me hope about green marketing," http://www.greenbiz.com/article/7-reasons-why-walmart-has-given-me-new-hope-about-green-marketing, accessed 3/23/15.
233 Ibid.
234 Ibid.

- USDA Organic, certified by Washington State Department of Agriculture
- Fair For Life social and fair-trade certified by IMO
- Charity partner (Audubon, benefiting Costa Rican cacao farmers and bird habitat)
- Kosher
- 50% recycled packaging
- Vegan

Of the four ingredients, all four are noted as organic, and all but vanilla are also marked fair trade.

That's a lot of information, not even counting a big panel of text about the charity project. Imagine trying to fit all that on a 1-ounce (22-gram) package label.

On one hand, you want to take full advantage of all the work you've done to get those multiple certifications you painstakingly earned (and paid for). Yet you still need an attractive package with adequate white space and a great design, not cluttered up with a bunch of certification logos.

If that were our challenge, we might put text like this on the wrapper:

"Certified organic, fair trade, kosher and vegan. Benefits Audubon's forest, farm, and bird preservation efforts in Costa Rica. For more details, please scan this QR code into your smartphone, or visit www._____."

You get all the good stuff out front, provide two ways to get all the details—including instant gratification via QR code—and still keep plenty of room on the label.

DON'T GET STUCK IN THE "GREENWASHING" SWAMP

Failure to be careful about language can lead to serious backlash. If you talk to marketers who are gun-shy about green marketing, it's likely because they've been accused of *"greenwashing"*: putting a green spin on something that's not all that green when you look closely. A 2014 study by the Natural Marketing Institute showed found that 66 percent of the public thinks a green-labeled product is just a gambit to sell more of it.[235] Companies or even whole industries that try that gambit can experience serious backlash, and then it becomes much harder to convince consumers that the company has begun to work seriously on greening itself.

Look what happened to Nestlé after it ran an ad promoting one of its bottled water brands as an eco-friendly alternative in the Toronto Globe and Mail: five major environmental groups lodged an official complaint charging violation of the Canadian Code of Advertising Standards as well as environmental claims guidelines set by Canada's Competition Bureau and the Canadian Standards Association.

The legal complaint cites three problematic claims in the ad:

- "Most water bottles avoid landfill sites and are recycled";
- "Bottled water is the most environmentally responsible consumer product in the world";
- "Nestlé Pure Life is a Healthy, Eco-Friendly Choice".

In the statement, the coalition said,

"Based on our review of the representations made by Nestlé Waters in this advertisement, it is clear that they are not supported by fact—we believe this is an outrageous example of greenwashing," says Beatrice Olivastri, Chief Executive Officer, Friends of the Earth. "The truth is that many water bottles are not being recycled, a phenomena that Nestlé Waters itself—in direct contradiction to its own advertisement—admits in its 2008 Corporate Citizenship Report." Olivastri points out that Nestlé Waters states in the report that many of its own bottles end up in the solid waste-stream and that many of them are not recycled even though they are recyclable.[236]

---

235 "The State of Sustainability in America Report: Trends & Opportunities," Natural Marketing Institute, 2014, p. 88. PDF of highlights: http://www.nmisolutions.com/opt/excerpts/1502/NMI-2015-State-of-Sustainability-in-America-Excerpts-1-19-2015.pdf, accessed 2/20/15.

236 http://workcabin.ca/index.php?option=com_content&task=view&id=698&Itemid=34, July 6, 2009

Of course, Nestlé could have easily avoided the specific Canadian complaint (and resultant bad publicity) by being more careful in its copywriting. It wouldn't have helped with the growing perception that bottled water is inappropriate in most situations precisely because of its severe environmental consequences[237]—but rewriting the claims as follows could have rendered this particular complaint moot:

- "*Many* ~~Most~~ water bottles avoid landfill sites and are recycled";
- "Bottled water *could be considered an* ~~is the most~~ environmentally responsible consumer product in *parts of* the world *where tap water is not safe to drink*";
- "*Pure, clean water such as* Nestlé Pure Life is a Healthy~~, Eco-Friendly~~ Choice".[238]

In fact, bottled water has enormous environmental consequences. USA Today columnist David Grossman reports that in the US alone, manufacturing our 28 million disposable plastic water bottles each year consumes 17 million barrels of oil and three times as much water as they contain, adds enormously to our landfills and our littered streets, and eventually photodegrades into pieces small enough to harm marine life.[239] For this reason, many green consumers have switched from throwaway water bottles to filtered tap water (some popular brands are only filtered tap water to begin with—if it says PWS on the label, that stands for public water supply).

Once again, these issues provide entrepreneurial opportunities for green businesses. One company that seized on the growing awareness of bottled water's

---

237 See, for example, Corporate Accountability International's "Think Outside the Bottle" campaign, http://www.stopcorporateabuse.org/campaigns/challenge-corporate-control-water/think-outside-bottle, verified 4/13/15.

238 Even watering down the claims may not have been enough. Many environmental activists have been arguing that bottled water has serious negative environmental consequences, and that at least where tap water is safe, the environmental costs are unacceptable. See, for instance, http://www.allaboutwater.org/environment.html, among 99,600 citations returned in a Google search for ["bottled water" impact environment], April 12, 2009, verified 4/13/15.

239 Larry Grossman, "Breaking the bottled water habit," http://usatoday30.usatoday.com/travel/columnist/grossman/2008-09-19-bottled-water_N.htm, verified 4/19/15.

negative environmental impact is Hydros, which produces reusable portable water bottles *with a built-in filter.*[240]

Other consumer packaged goods (CPG) companies have also felt the sting. For example, General Mills faced multiple lawsuits about misleading packing making untrue claims that the products were natural.[241]

Honesty and Clarity are Key to Avoiding Greenwashing Accusations

Stay away from messaging that won't be believed. If you're promoting nuclear power or large-scale biomass, for example, any attempt to portray your company as green will come back to bite you. Best, of course, is not to promote those products at all, but if you have to promote them, get out of the green space and find other ways to market (or should I say, defend) these environmentally toxic technologies. Both of these have been promoted as green alternatives, and neither one passes the sniff test.

If the green content of your practices is questionable or largely unknown, be prepared to document it in your messaging—thoroughly.

I (Shel) went to a solar festival where a couple of the exhibitors were talking about "biochar." From their materials, it looked to me like just another variant on burning wood: points for renewability, certainly, but NOT for clean emissions or carbon impact reduction.

By failing to convince me that they were truly green, these companies left me highly skeptical of other claims they (or their competitors) might make.

As I learned more about biochar over the next few years, I became convinced that there actually is merit in the green argument for biochar. But these first vendors I encountered didn't make a strong enough case.

By contrast, no amount of copy tweaking could save the nuclear power industry from being accused of greenwashing. The New York Times reported on January 1, 2009 on initiatives by two different European power companies,

---

240 http://www.hydrosbottle.com/, accessed 3/5/15.
241 http://www.triplepundit.com/2012/07/responsible-company-natural-label-case-general-mills/, accessed 2/15/15.

offering so-called "green" nuclear power to their customers.[242] And this response was posted the same day:[243]

> Anyone who buys into the lie that nuclear is green needs to take a serious look at environmental impact of…
> - Mining and milling and transporting and processing uranium
> - Radiation leakage during normal operation
> - Catastrophic environmental consequences of a major accident or serious terrorism incident (and in the US, no meaningful financial liability on the part of the utilities)
> - Need to isolate extremely large quantities of toxic wastes for a quarter of a million years! (How many objects survive from even 1/10th as long ago?)

Nuclear accidents, incidentally, are far more common than most people think. This table and the linked separate list of accidents in the US reports 99 concerning accidents around the world. This is an industry that should be shut down.[244]

Still, even very mild claims can lead to greenwashing accusations. Lexus was forced by British authorities to yank an ad containing the seemingly innocuous claim that one of its cars was "perfect for today's climate." Regulators felt the ad "was likely to reinforce the impression that the car caused little or no harm to the environment and was unlikely to clarify for readers that the headline claim was intended to refer to the economy as well as the environment."[245]

---

242 James Kanter, "Utilities Offer 'Green' Nuclear Plans to Customers," http://green.blogs. nytimes.com/2009/01/01/utilities-offer-green-nuclear-plans-to-customers/comment-page-1/#respond, verified 4/14/15.

243 By Shel, whose first book, *Nuclear Lessons* (Harrisburg: Stackpole, 1980), was all about why nuclear power is a completely inappropriate way to generate electricity. But many others also raise this concern. Google returned 104,000 hits for "nuclear greenwashing" (no quotes) on April 14, 2015, including Page 1 results from such respected sites as The Guardian, Der Spiegel, and Greenpeace.

244 https://en.wikipedia.org/wiki/List_of_nuclear_power_accidents_by_country, verified 2/21/15.

245 http://storywelch.wordpress.com/2008/11/09/the-growing-greenwash-backlash/, accessed in 2009 and no longer available without a password.

To us, this is more than a bit over the top; that phrase could be interpreted in a dozen different ways that have nothing to do with climate change. It's like the lawyers who force a peanut processor to warn on the label that the package of peanuts contains peanuts. And with this kind of backlash, it's understandable that companies are reluctant to make green claims.

So how do you avoid being tarred as a greenwasher? It's very simple. Create genuinely eco-friendly innovations in your processes, sales and support structure, marketing, supply chain, and every other area of business—and don't say anything that isn't totally true and verifiable.

TerraChoice, a consulting firm specializing in environmental marketing, lists "six sins of greenwashing" on its website:[246]

- Hidden trade-offs that highlight leadership on one environmental issue while burying areas with less progress
- Lack of proof for your claims (as in the Nestlé example, above)
- Vagueness of catch-all terms like "eco-friendly," "all-natural," etc.
- Irrelevance (such as a claim that could apply to every product in the category—being free of a banned substance, for example)
- False claims
- Green claims for a harmful product that shouldn't be offered in the first place (e.g., tobacco, toxic lawn chemicals)

LESSONS
- Make sure the customer can find your true environmental message—and make that message believable
- Strict standards provide opportunities for green products that exceed them
- Greenwashing will come back to bite you—but honesty and clarity provide the best defense if others accuse you of greenwashing
- Third-party certification can add credibility

---

246 http://sinsofgreenwashing.org/, verified 4/13/15.

ACTIONS

- Identify three certifications that would help your marketing.
- Display any certifications you've earned on your website and on your packaging.

CHAPTER 13

THREE KINDS OF CUSTOMERS: ARE YOU REACHING THEM ALL?

In the last few chapters, we discussed that sexiness is in the eye of the beholder. We looked at an eco-friendly car that pretty much anyone would find sexy, and a superefficient home that only Deep Greens would find sexy.

Let's explore that further. No matter what industry you're in, you have three very different types of customers. Although some common principles apply to each—see Shel's article on GreenBiz.com, "10 Ways to Make Your Message Resonate with Green Consumers,"[247] you will almost always get better results when you treat these three classes of customers differently. As noted in Chapter 6, you have to use different framing.

After all, would you run the same ad in the New Yorker and the National Enquirer?

Who makes up these three different markets?

---

247 Shel Horowitz, "10 Ways to Make Your Message Resonate with Green Consumers" http://www.greenbiz.com/blog/2010/08/26/10-ways-make-your-message-resonate-green-consumers, verified 2/12/15.

1. THE OBSESSED

They love your niche. They read all the trade magazines, follow the websites, attend the conferences...They can cite comparative statistics on product performance, name the key people in your industry, and go head-to-head about which configuration is better, and why. Get them on your side, and they'll be not just fans but champions, ambassadors, even evangelists for you. But anger or even disappoint them, and they'll quickly become your sworn enemies.

They may or may not know your company, but they certainly know your top competitors.

Shel deliberately targeted this group when he wrote an article called "Cognoscenti vs. Hoi Polloi." Those who understood the headline, knew they were in the know, part of a "secret society."

> There's actually a lot to be said for marketing to an in-group...When you make your prospects feel special, they're more likely not only to do business with you, but to maintain an ongoing business relationship. You make them feel appreciated, you talk to them on their own level. Just as with my headline, I'm identifying you, my reader, as someone sophisticated enough to be curious about the headline and to read the article. After all, I could have said "snobs vs. the masses" or "the elite vs. the common people." But those are so...ordinary! You get no satisfaction from conquering those molehills.

Writing for the masses, make your language very accessible. But small doses of jargon and "secrets" have their place when speaking to the inner circle. Your audience feels you talking directly to them, and that *you're one of them.*

Shel's article was a response to copywriter Ivan Levison's critique of an ad with the headline,

> Can a grid leave a mark but not a footprint?

Levison wrote,

"It seems to me that this is less a headline than a secret message that needs decoding, and make no mistake. Writing an ambiguous headline like this can destroy readership of an ad, email, Web page, brochure, you name it." [248]

Involved with energy and environmental issues all the way back to the 1970s, this headline made perfect sense to Shel. The grid is the infrastructure that transmits the nation's electricity. The footprint, of course, is a carbon footprint: the impact on our environment, and specifically on climate change.

Levison is right that the headline needs decoding—but he's wrong in seeing it as ineffective. Those who grapple daily with issues of climate change and CO_2 in electricity transmission will be immediately clued in that this ad is for them. [249]

2. THE INTERESTED

They like the idea of what you do, but they're fuzzy on the details. They have no strong commitment, but if you can show that you're the best alternative, they'll come on over to your side.

3. THE INDIFFERENT OR HOSTILE

They either don't care about you, your product, or your company, or even your niche—or worse, they actively oppose your agenda. They do care about releasing a pain point or achieving a goal. Even if they hate you at the beginning, you can win them over, slowly, if you solve their problems and ease their way.

In the green world, let's call these types of buyers…

- Obsessed: *Committed Deep Greens* (focused on improving the planet)
- Interested: *Lazy, or Light Greens* (will do the right thing if it's not too much trouble)

---

248 http://www.levison.com/august_2009_cc.html, verified 3/6/15.
249 http://thecleanandgreenclub.com/cognoscenti-vs-hoi-polloi-shel-horowitzs-frugal-marketing-tip-oct-09/

- Indifferent or Hostile: *Non-Greens/Anti-Greens* (this includes everything from people who've never paid attention to the environment on up to full-blown climate-change deniers)

HOW DO YOU MARKET TO EACH?

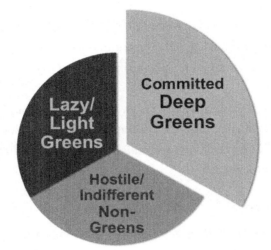

Deep Greens

They wake up in the morning thinking about how to save the planet. Green criteria factor into every buying decision: How will this lower my carbon footprint, my energy consumption, the amount of trash I generate, my water use? How will using this make me a more responsible steward of the earth?

These might not be questions you ask—but they do!

To market to the Deep Greens, answer these kinds of questions—thoroughly, but not intimidatingly.

And answer with unflinching honesty. They will like you much better if you say, "we're trying, we're not there yet, but these are the steps we're taking" than if you pretend to be more green than you really are. If they think you're greenwashing, not only won't they buy, they'll smear your company all over social media.

Here are some broad topic areas to frame your messaging to Deep Greens:

- Environment
- Social Justice
- Helping Disadvantaged Populations
- Ethics/Caring

Now, let's turn these broad topic areas into specific claims. Phrases in parentheses provide direction or alternate choices; phrases in square brackets refer to actual companies using that particular message:

Environment
- "Our facility is 83% solar (wind, hydro, geothermal…) powered." (note the specific number that leaves room for improvement)
- "Working to achieve zero waste within two years by _____." (tell them how)
- "Using only recycled raw materials since 1950." [Marcal Paper]

Social Justice
- "Poor neighborhoods have a right to local, healthy, organic food." [Nuestras Raices of Holyoke, MA, Sustainable South Bronx]
- "As a LOCAL financial institution, we support entrepreneurs and homeowners right here in this community." [most credit unions and local banks]
- "50 percent of our profits go to creating alternatives to poverty." [Dean's Beans, profiled earlier][250]
- "Reducing asthma in a polluted urban neighborhood by using clean energy." [Clean Energy Ohio]

Helping Disadvantaged Populations
- "We don't hire people to bake brownies. We bake brownies to hire people." [Greyston Bakery, mentioned earlier]

---

250 Personal email from CEO Dean Cycon to Shel September 21, 2014.

- "For every one you buy—we donate one to a needy child." [pioneered by Tom's Shoes, and widely imitated—one of our favorites is This Bar Saves Lives, http://www.thisbarsaveslives.com/]
- "Solar-powered LED lanterns provide a ladder out of poverty." [d.light, described earlier]

Ethics/Caring

- "Paying growers a living wage AND funding community development." [Fair Trade movement]
- "Microloans: Ending poverty by empowering tiny businesses." [Kiva, Grameen, Acción, and dozens of other microlenders.]
- "Vote on how we will distribute $100,000 to local community charities." [Florence Savings Bank, Florence, MA]

Lazy/Light Greens

The environment is a moderate concern to them. They recognize that the planet is at risk, but they're not focused on these issues. They probably recycle, and maybe they buy some organic products, but they haven't looked deeply, and they haven't scrutinized their own lifestyles very much.

This group is fueling the growth of the overall green sector; a small percentage move up to the Deep Green category as they get more educated (and as they find out how increasingly easy it is to live a green lifestyle)—but far more are moving from the Nongreen category into Lazy Green, as awareness of the environment has become mainstream. A 2014 Yale University/George Mason University study, *Climate Change in the American Mind*, finds that nearly 2/3 of the American public is convinced that climate change is real, and that they are much more certain of this conviction than in the past.[251] And the Shelton Group's annual EcoPulse report on green consumer behavior for 2014 notes that 70 percent of US consumers look for green products (though not all of them *demand* green—yet).[252] The home page of

---

251 http://environment.yale.edu/climate-communication/files/Climate-Change-American-Mind-April-2014.pdf, pp. 5-6. Downloaded 3/6/15.
252 http://sheltondigital.com/assets/downloads/ecopulse/EcoPulse2014_ExecutiveSummary.pdf, p. 2, accessed 3/6/15.

lohas.com puts the US LOHAS (Lifestyles Of Health And Sustainability) market at $290 billion as of March 6, 2015. If you haven't figured it out already, NOT being green is becoming a competitive *disadvantage.*

Marketing to this segment works best when you *combine self-interest with planetary interest.* Tell the lazy greens how it's going to save money, make them more comfortable, or simply work better—but also appeal to their sense of right and wrong, their desire to leave their children and grandchildren a good planet in good hands. Stress that the benefits to the user are *because* of the green design.

For this segment, the sweet spot is the intersection of doing the right thing and getting great value. So mention the green features, but focus on virtues like...

- Easy
- Cheap
- Convenient
- Durable
- Comfortable
- Luxurious
- Commonly available in regular stores
- Saves or makes money
- Convenient
- Solves or avoids problems
- Builds or creates community
- Supports a particular ethnic group or subculture

Message points might look like these:

Comfort/Convenience
- "The warmest and softest slippers you'll ever own, thanks to our special blend of all-natural fibers."
- "This powerful shower makes you feel so good, you won't believe how little water you're using."

- "Enjoy fresh veggies from our organic greenhouse all winter. Need a scrumptious, juicy tomato for your dinner? Just pick one off the vine."

Saving or Making Money
- "You'll pay only 1/3 as much for electricity as you would in most other homes of this size.
- "Earn thousands every year, selling Renewable Energy Credits to the power company."
- "Double-sided printing cuts your paper costs by 40 percent."
- "Let oil prices triple! You're protected, because you heat and cool directly from the earth."

Problem Solving or Avoidance
- "No more fussing with cranky, complicated HVAC—the earth-friendly passive ventilation system has no moving parts to break down."
- "50-year warranty, thanks to the great eco-friendly design and durable all-natural materials."
- "You'll never worry about waste disposal again. With our fully compostable packaging, you're adding nutrients to the earth instead of paying to clog up your landfill."

Community
- "You and your kids will both make new friends in the organic community garden and certified nontoxic natural playground."
- "Join an online eco-friendly social network just for residents." [Good Neighbours, Vancouver, BC]
- "We are a welcoming business that embraces the diversity of our customers and employees."

Ethnic/Subculture
- "Owned/operated by your neighbors and fellow Martians" (or whatever subculture).
- "All events signed for our deaf customers."

- "Made organically with the centuries-old family recipe our grandmother brought over from the (specifically named) Old Country."

Nongreens/Anti-Greens

They either don't care about environmental issues or actually believe that climate change is a fraud and the whole environmental movement is a government conspiracy to take their freedom away or eliminate jobs. Some of them pride themselves on doing things to bug environmentalists, like driving their Hummer a quarter-mile to the convenience store to buy chemical-crammed junk food.

You are not going to convince these people that your logic or your science is better than theirs. But don't give up! You've got plenty of ways you can reach—and eventually, change—these folks.

Some of them will begin to value green initiatives if they can be shown—on their own terms—how these measures create and maintain jobs, economic growth, and entrepreneurial success stories.

Some hunt and fish, and that gives them a strong connection to nature.

And nearly all will respond to the same kinds of personal benefits we talked about in reaching the lazy greens. Once they buy to gain greater comfort, durability, value, etc., they may shift their views if you can show them that the reason your product works better is precisely because of its green features. But wait to bring in that message until they've already bought.

You can even reach the values buyer, who acts out of conservative principles just as strong as those we in the environmental world cherish.

Here's the secret:

Talk to them as they wish to be talked to. Use their own language, their own set of passions. Never patronize them or dismiss their concerns as invalid or unimportant.

The brilliant inner-city environmental activist Van Jones has a great riff on how to talk to the Tea Partiers who come to protest his appearances about environmental issues.[253]

---

253 See Jones deliver this message at http://www.triplepundit.com/2012/06/getting-van-jones-new-economy/ , accessed February 2, 2015. This segment starts at 28 minutes, 24 seconds, and continues through 35 minutes—but the whole thing is worth watching. Or find a similar argument on pages 228-230 of his book, *Rebuild the Dream, which* Shel reviewed at http://thecleanandgreenclub.com/the-clean-green-club-february-2013/.

He goes outside to talk with them. First he respectfully asks, "what branch [of the military] did you serve in?" Instantly, he makes a human connection, citing his own family members who served.

Then he invites them to come inside from their protest, sit in the front row of his talk, and command the microphone the first time they hear him say anything unpatriotic.

And, once he's shown them that he's not the devil but a human being they can relate to, he moves in: "Shouldn't every American have the right and the liberty to power their own homes...and sell that power on that grid to anybody they want to sell it to? Why are you letting Americans be dictated to by monopoly power?"

A frequent complaint among Tea Partiers is that solar gets unfair help through government subsidies. Jones turns this belief to his own advantage; he points out that even oil companies that make $60 million in net profit every single day still receive massive government subsidies, and Jones would love their help eliminating *all* the energy subsidies.

He concludes with a double meme very close to Tea Partiers' hearts: "You close your meetings with America the Beautiful—but you got these people destroying America's beauty, and you let those little 350.org kids be the only ones defending America."

Here are a few more message points to let you reach this challenging audience:

- Be a job creator: labor-intensive clean energy produces far more jobs than the dirty, capital-intensive fossil- or nuclear-energy industries.

- The rapidly growing green sector is the next frontier of entrepreneurship. Whether you believe that climate change is a problem or not, you can certainly recognize—and benefit from—the profit potential as the green world creates whole new industries. That's why companies like Clorox, Ford, Walmart, and General Electric have jumped in whole-heartedly. In fact, some of the most successful green-company CEOs, including Whole Foods founder John Mackey, identify themselves as libertarian or conservative.

- Put more money in your pocket, because your energy and materials costs have gone down, down, down.
- Support the same kind of creative entrepreneurship and good old gumption that built this great country. The US used to be the leader in renewable energy and we let that leadership slide off to the Germans and Chinese. Isn't it time to take it back and make our country a great leader in this field once again?
- Encourage community resilience and disaster preparedness. When a storm takes down centralized power systems or an earthquake wrecks pipelines, those with solar or wind or geothermal power sources still can heat their homes, cook, and run their machines.
- Demand that those responsible take responsibility. Why should we ordinary citizens have to bear the financial and environmental costs of corporate greed? Demand that accounting procedures recognize costs over the whole life cycle, including waste disposal, pollution clean up, and all the rest of it.

As marketers in the green/socially conscious/cool and groovy/progressive activist space, we will attract the cool and groovy people—*and* we'll repel the Hummer-driving, cigar-smoking, anti-greens. They might actually speak out against us—just as WE have spoken out against THEIR actions. That, in turn, might gain the attention of uninvolved people, who may be within their orbit but hadn't thought about these issues. When they see objectively that doing the right thing helps the bottom line rather than hurts it, the business leaders in this middle group often find themselves agreeing with us—and, eventually, taking action. And their support gives us legitimacy. It was the business community that pressured Indiana and Arkansas to back off on discriminatory anti-LGBT legislation in 2015.

I (Shel) think of my experience as one of 1414 Clamshell Alliance members arrested on the construction site of the Seabrook, NH nuclear power plant, trying to keep the plant from being built, back in 1977. New Hampshire's governor at the time, Meldrim Thomson, and William Loeb, publisher of the largest newspaper in the state, the Manchester Union-Leader, called us "the Clamshell terrorists."

But we weren't terrorists. Not only had we all pledged nonviolence, we had all actually undergone training in nonviolent protest and joined small, accountable, affinity groups (which continued to function after our arrest); it was a precondition for participation. We were able to leverage Thomson and Loeb's overreaction into "marketing ju-jitsu" and build more support for our cause among ordinary people who believed in values like freedom of expression.

Governor Thomson kept the Clamshell prisoners incarcerated in National Guard armories around the state for about two weeks. When we emerged, we found we'd:

- Birthed a national safe-energy movement based in nonviolent affinity groups willing to commit civil disobedience
- Rapidly and thoroughly raised consciousness about nuclear power plant safety (and the lack thereof)
- Created a climate where, unlike previous accidents that had gotten little or no coverage,[254] the Three Mile Island meltdown in 1979 (and later catastrophic failures at Chernobyl and Fukushima) became front-page news.

Seabrook did go online, so we failed in our immediate goal. BUT in an era where former President Richard Nixon had called for 1000 nuclear power plants in the US, Seabrook was the last nuclear power plant to go on line in the US other than Shoreham, NY, which was shut down after preliminary low-power testing and never supplied the electrical grid. I believe the opposition of Thomson and Loeb to our movement helped make it a mass movement, just as the overreaction against civil rights and anti-Vietnam War protestors helped those movements gain strength, and the violent British responses to Gandhi's nonviolent mass protests built the Indian independence movement.

---

254 The two scariest (of dozens) were Enrico Fermi in Michigan, 1966 and Browns Ferry, in Alabama, 1975.

What do you think—do we need our enemies as much as our friends? Can we "ju-jitsu" their hostility into a benefit for our cause?

Smart marketers will start improving their green messaging now, so they'll be prepared and positioned when the shift happens. Here are some (among many) messages that will likely have sticking power:

- Eco-aware and eco-friendly since our founding in 1898
- We started going green in 1980, and we're going even greener today
- You save money and time because our green initiatives allow us to pass on the savings
- 66 years using recycled materials
- Every purchase you make helps fund sustainable development of indigenous farmers in (country)
- We're training tomorrow's construction workers in solar installation, so they can have jobs and you can save money
- Rethinking transportation (housing, agriculture, health care) for a sustainable tomorrow
- Small steps you can take to make big improvements in the environment
- Partner with us to save the world

Worth noting: Deep/Lazy/Non is only one way to divide things. For instance, one study subdivides environmental activists (what we call Deep Greens) into Ecological Activists, Smart Growth Reformers, and Ecomodernists; Jay and Shel put ourselves in the second group.[255]

LESSONS

- In any market, differentiate among the obsessed, the interested, and the indifferent or hostile
- Green products and services can appeal differently to three different types of consumers: deep green, lazy green, and nongreen

---

255 Matthew Nisbet, A call for greater diversity of thought in environmental studies courses, http://theconversation.com/a-call-for-greater-diversity-of-thought-in-environmental-studies-courses-39983, accessed 5/5/15.

ACTIONS

- Find at least one major green process you can call attention to within your current business framework
- Choose at least three attributes that you can turn into benefits
- Create five talking points each to reach Deep Green, Lazy Green, and Nongreen audiences—and share them with your marketing department
- Identify one or two people in your circle who have been hostile to environmental issues. Start non-threatening conversations with them and see if you can find common ground.

GETTING NOTICED IN THE NOISE AND CLUTTER: HANDS-ON WITH COOPERATIVE, PEOPLE-CENTERED MARKETING

CHAPTER 14

ADVANCED COPYWRITING

W e're assuming you already know the basics of marketing and copywriting. If this is new territory, Shel has a very strong section on copywriting in his earlier book, *Grassroots Marketing*.

WHAT PRONOUN?

When you're talking about *I, me,* or *we* and referring only to people in your own organization, most of the time, you're putting distance between yourself and the prospect. You're making it harder to get the sale.

Often, this shows up with language like "At Company Name, we stand for quality." Get rid of it. Every *I, me,* or *we* should be a very deliberate, conscious choice:

- Use *we* to include your prospects and demonstrate that you're one of them—to create community rather than distance, such as "we all know how it feels when..."

- *I* or *we* is essential in a testimonial, because someone else is talking about how you created great results for them.
- *I* can build deep intimacy in a storytelling format, if used carefully—to involve the reader in your story, the problem that you solved, or your enthusiasm for a product (use this technique only if you're a very experienced copywriter; it can backfire).

Otherwise, *you* (second-person) is the pronoun you want, except for case studies and examples. Those should be in third-person: he, she, they, him, her, them, it.

DRILL DOWN TO THE CORE BENEFITS

As we've seen, green marketers must demonstrate your superiority. Drill down and drill down again to identify and highlight the keys.

Say you manage a building with graywater recycling (a system to reuse water from sinks and showers to water lawns, flush toilets, etc.). How can you turn that feature into benefits, and then drill deeper to the core benefits?

The primary benefit is reduced water use (thus, lower water bills). Municipal water is artificially cheap in many developed countries, just as oil used to be, so that's a weak benefit. Can we go deeper?

How about this: by recycling the water, we reduce draw down on the water supply, which lets the aquifer recharge properly—and that keeps the water clean and pure.

Ah ha! Now we've found benefits! The feature (water conservation) turns into the benefits: better health and taste.

Thus, the resident saves money on bottled water, because the tap water is good enough to drink. So now we have another economic benefit.

Let's turn to the social benefits. More water is available, not only because the water is reused, but also because the considerable amount of water wasted in the bottling process is reduced—and fewer oil-based plastic bottles are needed (they have enormous negative environmental impact, by the way).

One writer says 5000 kids die every day from lack of good water.[256] So here's a major benefit to recycling graywater: *it stops kids from dying*. Add protecting the water supply for our own kids and grandkids, not squandering that resource the way we've squandered oil, and it should be easy to write powerful marketing copy.

Yes, it's work to analyze this deeply and turn your insights into great marketing. But you'll set your company apart and create powerful buy incentives.

STAY BELIEVABLE—AND CONNECTED

Because we're so barraged by marketing messages, all of us have our guard up. We have very good B.S. detectors, and if we catch a whiff of something that smells too good to be true—or just plain rotten—we're gone.

This danger signal can be subtle; Drs. Judith Sherven and Jim Sniechowski contrast *"technique acting,"* where an actor goes through the motions but doesn't internalize the character's emotions, and the much more effective, feeling-based *"method acting."* Similarly, we reject "techniqued" marketing as hype. As soft-sell marketers, they suggest, "create and maintain an authentic, heartfelt emotional connection with your customers…while preparing your customers to buy." For instance, phrase your action message as an invitation, not a command.[257]

For Sherven and Sniechowski, the best selling is spiritual—even sacred—because your connection to the customer creates mutual respect and safety. Hype would violate that carefully nurtured relationship.[258]

What happens if you're not genuine? Shel once saw a sign that claimed the store's employees were all empowered to help—but when he called to get the wording so he could put it in his next book, he was told, "I'm not allowed to give that out; please call our corporate headquarters." That store went off Shel's buy list forever.

---

256 Bill Roth, *The Secret Green Sauce: Best Practices being used by actual green entrepreneurs and businesses to grow sustainable revenues and profits*, reviewed by Shel at http://thecleanandgreenclub.com/shel-horowitzs-clean-green-newsletter-may-2011/#another

257 Judith Sherven, Ph.D. and Jim Sniechowski, Ph.D., *The Heart of Marketing: Love Your Customers and They Will Love You Back*, Morgan James Publishing, 2009, p. 35 of the unpublished advance manuscript.

258 Ibid., pp. 46-48 in manuscript.

FASCINATE—AND BUILD TOWARD THE SALE

Just because your marketing is honest doesn't mean it can't sell. Create a value proposition—the perceived difference between cost and the value to the buyer—so strong that it moves the prospect from "I'll think it over" (translation: lost sale) to "I need this NOW!" In other words, make an irresistible offer.[259]

First, create such strong value in the prospect's mind that it seems downright foolish to turn down the benefits. Two among many ways to do this:

1] Cram your marketing pieces with *"fascinations"*: teasers in the copy that hint at secrets and benefits of the product but don't tell how to implement (this is great for marketing information products such as books and special reports. Here are six (of 52) Shel wrote for a client selling audio recordings from a marketing conference.

- Where to find products you can sell at a 20,000% markup
- Should you copyright your products? The answer may surprise you!
- The secrets of putting together value-added premiums that cost almost nothing, yet allow you to charge twice as much money—while almost eliminating refund requests
- How Gary Halbert sets up his envelopes for success—right down to what kinds of stamps do better than others
- What NEVER to do at the end of a sales letter page
- What Karen Myers says to her buyers to make them feel GREAT as they part with hundreds of hard-earned dollars

2] Include add-ons—for a limited time—that increase the prospect's interest in the offer: information products, consulting and training, free trial membership in a continuity program, access to superstars…We recommend bonuses rather than discounts, or discounts that don't cheapen the perceived value, such as free shipping.

Lisa Sasevich, author of *The Invisible Close*, helped a client close 60 percent on a high-end offer with tiered incentives: sign up within a week and receive

---

259 Mark Joyner, author of several must-read marketing books, has an entire book called *The Irresistible Offer.*

a great bonus package; *sign up that same day* for an additional bonus worth hundreds of dollars.[260]

You can even use fascinations as press release headlines. Here are two that Shel wrote for his press release clients:

- It's 10 O'Clock—Do You Know Where Your Credit History Is?
- Is Your Life as Full of Holes as Swiss Cheese? Maybe That's a GOOD Thing

DITCH THE JARGON—EXCEPT...

Quick, what do these two phrases mean to you?

- "uniquely efficient stator-rotor configuration"
- "axial flux air core machine"

They're both taken from the same article about a new wind power technology. Don't feel bad; we didn't understand either.

Stringing a bunch of jargon together is even worse:

Drivers are the perceived need for audience community segmentation strategies... message volume... and/or native language requirements, among others. What should be balanced is multiple account need v. management complexity, a particularly difficult line to walk given that Twitter tools remain very fluid with functionality still evolving.[261]

That paragraph has *no message.*

It's an easy trap: you know the jargon, and you forget that others don't. Other than the special case discussed in Chapter 13 ("Cognoscenti vs. Hoi Polloi"), make your marketing pieces no-jargon zones. If you have to use jargon, explain it immediately and clearly.

---

260 "Designing Truly Irresistible Offers," Simple, Quick and Easy Ways to Boost Sales Without Spending a Dime—Day Six, email received December 23, 2008.
261 Found at https://scoopdog.wordpress.com/2009/09/03/1092/, accessed 3/5/15.

THE TRIANGLE OF EXPERTISE:
GET PAID TO DO YOUR OWN MARKETING

Marketing *doesn't* have to be a cost. It can be revenue-neutral, or even a profit center.

The Triangle of Expertise consists of three activities that can directly generate revenue, all of which also market you: Speaking, consulting/training, and writing/publishing. When you tap into this triangle, your marketing activities can not only create revenue, but also reinforce each other, and build the perception that you are the expert in your niche.

You can add media visibility for a Rectangle of Expertise—but you don't get paid to be interviewed by a journalist. However, publishing your own articles in various media can be a very definite income stream.)

So, with a for-pay speaking engagement, first of all, you're getting paid to give the speech. If you have books or other information products, you'll sell some quantity to attenders, at full price or slight discount. Better yet, negotiate a bulk sale ahead of time with the meeting planner, and send everyone—or perhaps just early registrants—home with a copy. Secondly, some attenders may buy your ongoing program or bootcamp, or hire you for consulting or other professional services—or to give another speech. Thirdly, people who consume your information products may hire you (especially if the info product made it clear that you offer these services).

People might buy your book and then hire you to perform services for them, or people hear you speak and then buy your book, or they hire you first and later decide to learn more about your skill area, so they buy the book. Or people who know of you through social media and traditional media exposure (including not just social networks but also Internet discussion groups, e-zines, and your own and others' websites, as well as print, radio, and TV) know and respect your advice, so they buy your information products or hire you to speak so they can gain more of it.

Use your book (audio, video, etc.—some kind of tangible information product) and consulting credentials to get speaking gigs, sell your books before and after the talk, and follow up—as soon as you get back to your office —with the consulting prospects who eagerly, desperately, press their business cards into your hand (annotate them before you stick them in a pocket.).

If you build your business as a speaker (paid or volunteer), that opens up many barter possibilities, too. Here are a few examples, and the names of the speakers who suggested them:[262]

- When speaking at a conference that also includes a trade show, offer an extra session on a different topic for free, in exchange for booth space (Elizabeth Fried)
- Speaking for free to a local chapter of a national organization? Prepare a contract that clearly states the dollar value of the gift, and trade for a complete list of attenders with contact information and a contact and recommendation to the national association. (Padi Selwyn)
- If there's a local nonprofit group related to the topic of your talk, get volunteers from that group to staff your sales table, in exchange for giving the group space to display and sell its own wares (Bob Ingram)

Sometimes, because of the difference in production cost and market value, barter can help leverage an enormous amount of marketing clout. Here's how it worked for another speaker (and speaker trainer), Tom Antion of http://www.GreatSpeaking.com>:

I was asked to speak at the first Wharton Business School Club e-commerce event in Washington, DC. I provided 100 of my Multimedia Internet Marketing Training CDs as "sign up premiums." They cost me $2.00 each to duplicate, but at a retail cost of $199.00 it made me a $20,000.00 sponsor. My name was plastered on many of their promotions around the world to both the public and Wharton School Graduates.[263]

---

262 All of these examples are taken from *Speaking Successfully: 1001 Tips for Thriving in the Speaking Business*, 1999 ed., edited by Ken Braly and Rebecca Morgan from tips that originally appeared in their *SpeakerNet News* e-zine. Order online at http://www.speakernetnews.com.

263 Personal email from Tom Antion (Dec. 8, 2002). Used with permission.

Martha Retallick, owner of LRP Designs, a Web design and information publishing firm in Tucson, Ariz., points out that you can draw the triangle differently depending on your own set of skills and interests. In her case, she doesn't make paid speeches—but her design services complete the triangle.

LESSONS

- Use "I" and "we" only to include; keep the focus on the prospect
- Connect to the core personal and social benefits
- Use fascinations, not jargon
- As a writer, speaker, and/or consultant, you can even get paid to do your own marketing

ACTIONS

- Pick one of your marketing pieces. Circle every time you used "I," "me," or "we" in a non-inclusive way.
- Circle any jargon.
- Rewrite to replace those problems with you-focused, benefit-oriented copy that talks to both emotion and intellect.
- Develop at least three topics you could give as presentations.

Chapter 15

GIVE THE PEOPLE
WHAT THEY WANT

WHAT GREEN MARKETERS CAN LEARN FROM RING TONES

very mobile phone comes with some ringtones built in. And therefore, nobody actually needs to purchase a ringtone. And yet, at its peak, the ringtone industry generated more than $4 billion a year (US dollars), worldwide. (The industry is declining, as text supplants voice, and as more phones carry greater options in standard ringer choices.)

$4 billion is a lot of money for something that nobody needs.

Are there lessons in this industry for green marketers? Most certainly. Here are two among many:

1. We Crave Making Our Mark

The age of individuality goes back at least as far as the Beatnik movement in the 1950s, flowered with the hippies of the 1960s, and continues to spread in our own era. As a society, we each strive to be seen as unique, different.

The conformity of the 1950s gray flannel suit is long gone. Where once there were rules of fashion, now, we have enormous latitude in what we wear. We can mix colors and patterns that would make our parents cringe. Women might wear a miniskirt over a mid-length dress, with leggings underneath. Men have added pink and lavender to their shirt choices.

And perhaps even more than in society as a whole, the green world is populated by people who declare their individuality—not just the off-grid recluse with a two-foot-long beard and a shack made from old car parts, but the suburban housewife who wears upcycled fashion jewelry made from old blue jeans and discarded CDs…the craft brewery customer who seeks out an artisan beer that uses fresh organic grain supplied by a local farmer…the college student who proudly bicycles to class…

We business owners benefit when we celebrate our customers' individuality.

Toyota had to learn that lesson the hard way. When the Prius was first introduced as a drab sedan with limited color choices, sales were slow. From the car's introduction in 1997 through the end of the original model six years later, only about 123,000 were sold.

When the now-familiar sleek hatchback with its wide variety of color choices was brought to market in 2004, sales jumped dramatically, to 1,192,000 in its 4-year lifespan. In other words, it sold nearly ten times as many, in 2/3 the time. All of a sudden, the car was considered sexy.

The trend continued into the 3rd generation, still in production and including various newer models, including the plug-in, small wagon, and midsize wagon. By September, 2014, Toyota has sold more than 3.4. million of them, with total Prius sales since the brand introduction of 4.8 million.[264]

2. We will Pay for Practical Value

There is a very practical reason why some people choose to buy a ringtone: they get tired of hearing a ring just like theirs, reaching madly for the phone, and discovering that it was someone else's.

To put this in a green context, Shel sampled some natural tooth-rinse at a green festival, and liked it enough to buy a container at the show. He was pleased with the way it made his mouth feel after daily use, and when he ran out, he

---

264 https://en.wikipedia.org/wiki/Toyota_Prius, accessed 4/16/15.

bought more. He paid $13.99 for a bottle of fluid that's basically food-grade hydrogen peroxide with peppermint oil. He could probably make his own for two or three dollars, if he could easily locate a source of food-grade peroxide. Or he could go the drug store and buy ordinary peroxide for even less. But it is worth it to him to know that they've tested the formula and got it right, to know they've gone through safety procedures and have packaged it in a way that's convenient to use.

So if you give people reasons based on convenience and practicality, they will buy from you, just as they've bought ringtones.

WHEN SATISFACTION ISN'T ENOUGH

Years ago, Jimmy Cliff had a song called "Give the People What They Want." He was referring to politics—but it works pretty well for marketing, too. Many companies talk a good line when it comes to customer service—but how many really and truly put it into practice—so thoroughly integrated delighting customers into their mission that it shapes the way they do business?

And what is the cost of not doing so? Writing on the MarketingProfs.com website, Kristine Kriby Webster cites auto-industry statistics that 85-95 percent claim to be satisfied—but only 40 percent repurchase. She also notes that up to 80 percent of customers who defect to a competitor, across all industries, expressed satisfaction with their previous vendor even right up to the point where they jump ship.[265] So how to you turn satisfaction first into delighted amazement, and then into loyalty, and finally into ambassadorship for your brand?

Timothy Keiningham and Terry Varva, in *The Customer Delight Principle: Exceeding Customers' Expectations for Bottom-Line Success*,[266] stress that merely satisfying your customers isn't enough to build even loyalty, let alone the fervent ardor necessary for customers to recruit more customers on your behalf; you have to delight them. And the bar on delight keeps getting higher, because one of the factors leading to delight is that it's unexpected.

In other words…when a new, delightful practice is successful, it is adopted by the organization, and then becomes an industry best practice—and then it

---

265 Kristine Kirby Webster, "Actions Speak Louder Than Words," November 4, 2003, http://www.marketingprofs.com/3/kwebster26.asp, verified 4/16/15.

266 New York: McGraw-Hill/American Marketing Association, 2001

goes from being delightful to merely satisfying, because the customer begins to expect it as part of a minimum service standard. So innovation plays a key role.

Want an example? Consider Dell, the computer company. Breaking almost every rule in traditional marketing of computers, Dell has specialized for years in custom-building systems to the exact specifications of its purchasers—and doing it quickly. As Keiningham and Varva might say, Dell added delight, and customization of computers became an industry standard. But then Dell failed to initiate another game-changing innovation to once again turn the PC industry upside down, and its reputation started to slide.

Keiningham and Varva's research also points out that…

- The ROI on improving delight is non-linear; certain little improvements may make a huge improvement in profitability, while others that cost more may have little effect, and the returns may shrink over time
- It's relatively easy to figure out which initiatives will offer the greatest return; just identify factors in the customer's experience that the customer sees as of critical importance, but with low current satisfaction ratings
- Profitable delight initiatives often target high-dollar-value, low-cost clients If your customer survey is self-serving and focuses on your wants rather than the customer's, you won't get the data you need to improve
- Not everyone is delighted in the same ways, so segment your markets accordingly
- Multiple touches (ways business can reach out), when handled correctly, can make a customer feel appreciated and welcomed and special
- To delight customers, you need delighted—or at least satisfied—employees
- Marketing's primary role is "to understand the wants, needs, and expectations of current and potential customers, feeding this information into the business organization to help it create and distribute products or services that more closely address and answer these inherent needs"; its secondary role is to form and nurture connections with customers

- Customer delight strategies look more at a customer's lifetime value than the current transaction
- Delighted customers not only proselytize to friends and colleagues on your behalf, they also spend substantially more

Robert Middleton, of the popular marketing e-zine More Clients, prefers the term "*inspiration.*" When you inspire your clients, he says, great things happen:

Inspiration has very little to do with "Rah, rah, you can do it!" It's not about a veneer of excitement. It's not about a tone of voice or an inspiring vocabulary. It's not even about being sincere; that's superficial, not true inspiration.

Inspiration comes from an unwavering commitment to make a difference. It's not something you do, it's a place you come from.

When you love and appreciate your clients and stand behind their vision and goals, your clients know it. They can feel it. They know you are on their team and committed to them winning.

Commitment + action = inspiration

And where does that commitment come from? You've just met a prospect or started with a client. How can you be committed so soon, let alone be inspiring? Doesn't that take a long time?

Not at all.

The source of commitment is authentic interest. If you can't get truly interested in your prospects and clients, you'll never get committed to their dreams and projects and never become a source of inspiration to them.

I've often asked my clients how much they've learned about a client in their first interview. How much did they research about this client? Did they really dig in and find out about the business or the person? Did they demonstrate a high level of excited curiosity about this prospect or client? [267]

---

267 Robert Middleton, "The Key to Inspiration," More Clients e-zine, February 4, 2008, http://actionplan.blogs.com/weblog/2008/02/the-key-to-insp.html, verified 4/16/15. His main site is http://www.actionplan.com.

COMPANIES THAT 'GET IT"

Catch A Piece of Maine

Not too many beginning loberstermen can build a $600,000 business in their first three months. But Brendan Ready did so with just one of his multiple product lines. He packaged the experience in terms of belonging to a community, making it very experiential, and also emphasized the exclusivity, the support-local, the personal touch, and the sustainability aspects as included value-adds to differentiate his company, Catch A Piece of Maine—and to charge an astonishing 12,000 percent more than most of his colleagues.

Just 25 years old when he started, he turned the commodity-based lobster industry into an exclusive private membership in which each investor received the entire harvest of one trap. With 400 memberships available during the first year, at $2995 each, he sold half the slots in the first three months. That's $600,000 not counting the additional revenues from $799 4-meal memberships, $249 full-course dinners, $19.95 calendars, t-shirts, and gift certificates. He formed partnerships with several lobstermen, and had a waiting list for more.

Understanding the experiential nature of his business, Ready piled on the extras. For example, the $799 membership included:

- DVD of your lobsterman
- Cooking instructions and recipes
- A map detailing when and where your dinner was caught
- A personal note and picture of your lobsterman
- Monthly newsletter from the wharf
- An actual phone call from the lobsterman the day your lobsters are delivered

And the site itself was full of down-home videos and blog entries featuring Ready and other loberstermen offering weather reports, discussing lobstering as well as lobster preparation, and more.

While targeting the luxury consumer, Catch A Piece of Maine filled its webpages with talk about sustainability and social responsibility, and how their customers are participating in enhancing those values. Here's a little snippet:

> We as lobsterman are all stewards of the sea; always making sure today's catch is available for tomorrow's lobsterman. Our industry exemplifies hard work, tradition, heritage, and sustainability. We pride ourselves on our eco-friendly manner of harvesting, producing little to no by-catch and enforcing strict laws to allow the release of all lobsters too small and too large. Lobstering is hard work and capital intensive, requiring boats that cost as much as a house… In the past several years the price of bait and fuel has tripled while we've watched our working waterfront slowly disappear. [268]

In fact, this venture was so successful that Ready was able to capture 10 percent of the wholesale Maine lobster market within just a few years, and actually shut down the club in January 2015 in order to focus on that sector[269]—which means that original premium retail market is wide open for someone else.

Luxury and the green market are quite compatible, as we saw in Chapter 15. How about a company that makes upcycled gift items out of used Formula 1 race car parts, such as a $1600 lamp from an exhaust pipe?[270]

Mercedes-Benz USA

One of the cases Keiningham and Varva cite, Mercedes-Benz USA, is especially interesting, because unlike many of their other examples, this wasn't about fixing a broken system. Rather, the focus was on incorporating delight into the

---

268 We thank Troy White for telling us about this innovative model. This quote appeared on the company's website when we accessed it in 2009 for our earlier book, *Guerrilla Marketing Goes Green*. Now that the company has moved to wholesale-only, that page has been taken down. However, it can be found at http://www.theghosttrap.com/inside-the-lobstering-life/get-ready-to-catch-a-piece-of-this, accessed 4/16/15.

269 http://catchapieceofmaine.com/, accessed 3/19/15.

270 http://www.mementoexclusives.com/, verified 4/16/15.

corporate culture with a true focus on serving the customer—and creating an entire business unit, in its own building, to do so.

Among other things, Mercedes integrated eleven different databases, collecting different types of customer data, into a single system that any employee could access before interacting with a client (the company stopped using the word *"customer"* and stopped referring to its franchises as *"dealers"*). It also developed a strategic separation between client acquisition and retention functions, something Keingingham and Varva strongly advocate)

Mercedes' database tracked delight factors far beyond just providing emergency road service to such amenities as pre-trip routing services similar to AAA…offered a line of branded merchandise for sale…triggered multiple touchpoints including anniversary of vehicle purchase and mileage awards at 100,000, 200,000, and 500,000 miles…

This wasn't cheap, in other words. But it was amazingly effective. After initiating the program, Mercedes was projecting an astonishing 86 percent repurchase rate. Even if their projections turn out to be inflated by 100%, a 43 percent repurchase rate on a $50,000-$100,000 item is going to look mighty good for the bottom line.

RentQuick

MarketingSherpa.com profiled a company called RentQuick.com.[271] The company offered business equipment rentals, such as laptops and projectors, to professional speakers and other business people on the go. Although it competed with much larger, more established companies in an industry that requires expensive capital purchases, RentQuick—originally based in owner Brett Hayes's home—was profitable starting with its very first month and enjoyed one of the highest profit ratios in its field.

And that's because Hayes set out from the start to make his company a place that his customers enjoy doing business with. The website copy was you-focused (on the customer) rather than we-focused (on the retailer). It asked immediately, "How can we help you?"; it used trust-building techniques (guarantee,

---

271 "Can Adding Instant Messaging Improve Your Site's Profits? One B-to-B Site's Story," August 6, 2002, https://www.marketingsherpa.com/barrier.html?ident=23047, verified 4/16/15.

testimonial, product photos) right on the home page, and clearly offered multiple ways to contact the company—on every single page. The voicemail tree had only a few levels—and then human beings quickly answered the telephone. Instant messaging and email also got immediate attention. And Hayes encouraged his support reps to answer the customer's actual question, in the first email. Hayes used these electronic communication tools to answer the easy questions, but his reps actually encouraged customers with more complex questions to switch over to telephone.

Although RentQuick was a price leader, the site didn't emphasize low prices. Instead, the company focused on providing an extremely positive experience at every point of interaction, of which competitive pricing is only one small part. "The mantra around here is 'build trust,'" Hayes said. That meant a commitment to supply the right equipment to meet the customer's needs, on time, and in full working order, and being around to support the purchase in every way.

Anticipating changes in the market—notably a shift toward much more affordable projection equipment that would reduce the rental market—and being a serial entrepreneur, Hayes sold the company in 2011 and went on to other ventures.[272]

Swedish Hospital, Issaquah, WA

Even as normally cold a place as a hospital emergency room can create a welcoming atmosphere and a customer-service home run, as Patrick Byers recounts on the Responsible Marketing blog:

> We had to take my four year-old daughter to the emergency room yesterday...
>
> We took her to Swedish Hospital's Issaquah ER and got exactly what we were looking for, and more.
>
> Though we'd never been to this ER before, instead of being handed a stack of forms and sent to the waiting room, we were in a private room in front of doctor in approximately five minutes.
>
> Seriously.

---

272 Telephone interview with Shel, March 19, 2015.

Along the way, we were helped by at least five people who were friendly, attentive and professional.

We learned my daughter has a viral form of pneumonia, were provided with care instructions and then discharged promptly.

As we left, a woman in reception asked her if she'd like a surprise and showed her a large display of Beanie Babies. With a huge smile, she picked a rainbow-colored bear and was given the chance to pick a Beanie for her brother, as well.

"My brother loves red," was her response as she pointed to 'Snort' the bull, above.

We've never left the ER with a smile on our faces, until yesterday. And with that, Swedish won one family's business for life.[273]

Pandora.com

Anticipating customer wants and needs is a sure way to create delight. Roy Williams, author of *The Wizard of Ads* books, praises companies that can anticipate your thoughts and feelings, and not just respond but be there waiting when you're ready—he calls this mind-reading "thought particle technology."[274] He cites Pandora.com, a music database that gives you your favorite artists, and other musicians who it thinks you might like. Pandora turns out to be a remarkably good guesser; Shel has bought several CDs from artists he hadn't known about.

Experience Engineering

Of course, consultants can help you. One company, Experience Engineering, has built its business by helping its clients—including some large and familiar names, as well as many smaller firms—determine exactly why customers come to them, and deliver an optimal experience based on those preferences.

EE believes that a company's brand is not just its marketing, or even its product recognition. Rather, a company brand is built on the total perception of the customer: the way that customer feels when he or she walks in, satisfaction

---

273 Patrick Byers, "No bull: Marketing lessons from the ER," The Responsible Marketing Blog, December 15, 2008, http://responsiblemarketing.com/blog/?p=755, verified 4/16/15.
274 Williams, Roy, "Monday Morning Memo from the Wizard of Ads," 3/27/2006

with both the service and the product, and how the total experience is remembered (including post-sale follow up or troubleshooting). EE attempts to anticipate and understand consumers' rational *and* emotional needs, and to set up experience management systems for its clients that enhance the customer experience—which in turn increase the customer's positive perception of the brand. EE's success is in helping its clients see the experience through their customers' eyes, and sometimes its clients find themselves moving in new directions.

Many companies claim to be customer-driven and to provide exemplary customer service. Some—not nearly as many as those who claim to—actually follow through and provide customer service that's good enough to produce fan mail and flowers. But this is something much deeper—anticipating the customer's wants and needs and meeting them *before they're even expressed*. The experience of doing business with you becomes almost an organic part of the customer's own consciousness. You achieve the result through scientific study, but it feels as if it comes straight from the heart. The thing the customer most wants is there, without being put into words.

In fact, a consistent positive experience may be *the* driving factor in repeat business, and in positive word-of-mouth. As franchise businesses or company-owned locations become an ever bigger part of the retail picture, this concern is spreading to every sector. Whether the store sells books, tires, or winter coats, executives want a customer to have a positive and consistent experience in Arizona, Abu Dhabi, or Adelaide.

Let's look at specific examples that will make sense of this rather abstract concept:

- The photocopier company Alexander Hiam described in Chapter 3 anticipated end-of-product-life issues and proactively created the loaner program
- A grocery chain, observing that many of its customers were pregnant, set aside reserved parking spaces just for pregnant women—and made CNN news
- A major office-supply chain discovered that its clients cared even more about being steered to the right technology than about price—and

changed its advertising, store signage, and other cues to bring that message forward

- A large car-rental company noticed that its customers had a lot of stress about returning cars in time to get through the longer security lines and reach their departure gates. By halving the return time for preferred customers and establishing experiential clues that their managers were with it and efficient (giving them headsets, for example), the company made it clear to its customers that smoothing the car return was a priority; this company was later named Number 1 in brand loyalty across all industries.

Even complaint resolution—which, for too many companies, is all they think of when they think of customer service—can offer a superior experience, and thus create direct revenue through upsells and saved cancellations. A MarketingExperiments.com study demonstrated additional profits of up to $110,448 per customer service rep.[275]

SHOPPING AS EXPERIENCE AND ENTERTAINMENT

Building on EE's philosophy, let's look at the experience of shopping for a moment. In recent years, shopping itself has become a tourist experience.

Consider what's happened to coffee. 35 years ago, in 99 percent of US restaurants, coffee was coffee. You had a choice of regular or decaf. It cost 50 cents a cup, but sometimes the pot hadn't been cleaned in days.

When was the last time you bought a cup of coffee like that? Coffee has been transformed into an experience. You choose among 20 or so different beans and roasts and grinds, sip it slowly in an elegant café, and pay $2 to $5 for the privilege. Even some highway rest stop service stations offer half a dozen gourmet blends.

Ever been to the Vermont Country Store, packed to the rafters with all sorts of exotic local foods? They give out hundreds of dollars worth of food samples every day, their parking lot is packed, their cash registers are ringing…and their

---

275 "Profit from Inbound Customer Service Tested," http://www.marketingexperiments.com/improving-website-conversion/profit-inbound-customer-service.html, November 28, 2005, verified 4/17/15.

prices are substantially higher than other stores, which more than covers the cost of all that free food. Once again, this is an example of a scenario with a lot of winners: the store, of course, which is constantly busy…the suppliers, who see substantially increased sales after people sample the merchandise…the local economy, which gets a big shot of tourist dollars and a number of jobs…and the hungry tourists, who can actually get lunch walking around sampling the food. By creating a tourist experience instead of just a place to shop, this store has found a formula to set itself apart from other food retailers.

If you create a craft or manufactured good, make your shop into a destination by showing the public exactly how your product is made. Shel still remembers touring the Hershey chocolate factory as a child; the image of chocolate flowing from a huge cauldron (and the wonderful smell) is indelibly burned in his brain, even though Hershey has since replaced the real factory tour with a movie. But as customers and as marketers, we still love a good plant or craft studio tour. It builds a palpable connection between the user and the product, and the percentage of tour-takers who purchase something afterward is very high. We've toured cheese plants, wineries, an ice-cream factory, glassblowers, a *damasquiña* (gold inlay) workshop in Spain, the outdoor studio of a Guatemalan man who makes giant rock sculptures, textile studios, and much more.

In Deerfield, Massachusetts, Yankee Candle has made its vast flagship store into the second-largest tourist destination in the state—with not only an enormous collection of candle shops, but also an exhibit on the history of candle making, a Bavarian Christmas theme room, model trains running above the heads of tourists in many of the shops, and eateries at several price points. Other chains that blend shopping and entertainment include Disney, Warner Brothers, Hard Rock Café, and—aimed at a very different audience— The Museum Store and Ten Thousand Villages (the latter has a charitable component that adds another benefit to the mix: helping indigenous craft artists come up out of poverty).

REPUTATION MANAGEMENT IN THE 21ST CENTURY

Once upon a time, a company's reputation had a lot to do with its advertising and traditional PR efforts; that day is long gone. Today, shortsighted, even boneheaded penny-wise, pound-foolish service experiences probably do more to undermine a brand than anything else.

Worse yet, that unhappy customer is likely to complain to friends and colleagues—and perhaps to 10,000 of your best prospects on an Internet discussion list or social media network. That's if you're lucky. United Airlines was not lucky when it broke Dave Carroll's guitar. Although Carroll and his band, Sons of Maxwell, were not exactly household names, they made a video called "United Breaks Guitars." In the first five and a half years since it was posted, 14,694,051 people watched this Youtube video.[276] And that's just one of the 289,000 results of a search for "united breaks guitars." In the pre-social-media era, by contrast, Tom Paxton, a very well-known folksinger, recorded a similar song called "Thank You, Republic Airlines (for breaking the neck of my guitar)" in 1985—and hardly anyone knows of it. A search for "tom paxton thank you republic airlines" brings up a measly 20,400 results. The Youtube video has only 692 views.[277]

If you care about your company's reputation, not only do you have to keep your company's actions squeaky-clean, but you also need to carefully watch the perceptions of others. A nasty blog entry, a post to non-company-specific gripe sites like www.pissedconsumer.com, ripoffreport.com, and www.webgripesites. com),[278] a yourcompanysucks.com website (actual examples include http://disney-sucks.com/, http://www.starbucked.com/ —dissing Starbucks since 1995— http://www.chase-sucks.com/, and multiple sites set up either to disparage or organize against Walmart), or even a conversation on Twitter can badly damage companies that are unethical, clueless, or simply not paying attention. Of course, savvy consumers have known about the Better Business Bureau's complaint logs and Consumer Reports' ad-free, unbiased product evaluations for decades—but now, it takes only a few seconds to find the dirt.

Here are five examples. The first shows what happens when senior executives are dangerously out of touch. And the second demonstrates that every single employee not only needs to understand the importance of making the customer feel special, valued, appreciated—but must be empowered with

---

276 https://www.youtube.com/watch?v=5YGc4zOqozo, accessed 3/15/15.
277 https://www.youtube.com/watch?v=mwV8ozElNjk, accessed 3/15/15.
278 All sites in this paragraph verified 4/17/15.

the flexibility, and trained to understand the need, to head off customer service disasters at the pass.

1. Blogger Jason Calacanis wrote a post with the headline, "CIGNA kills Nataline Sarkisyan." The story described a young woman whose insurance company refused and refused to cover a liver transplant, finally relenting the day she died. As Tom Watson notes in his book, *Causewired*, Calacanis's outrage included a call to contact top CIGNA executives, with their contact information. The cause went viral and was even picked up by Senator John Edwards, who made it a part of his presidential campaign in 2008.[279]

2. Bill Glazer came into a national chain food store with a $5 gift certificate. It had no expiration date, but the counter clerk and the store manager not only said they wouldn't honor the certificate because they had switched to electronic gift cards, but also refused to provide a corporate address so Glazer could send his certificates in for a gift card. Now, this kind of stupidity is completely inexcusable under any circumstances, but in this case, the irritated customer happens to publish a newsletter aimed at very sophisticated persuasive marketers, and he told the story (naming the company) to thousands of the most influential marketers in the country.

As Glazer wrote,

It has been 6 months since the incident and I haven't (and never will) stepped back into one of their stores because of this totally stupid action. Not to mention that I'm telling this story to tens of thousands of GKIC Members through this newsletter. This also doesn't help them build goodwill with their brand.[280]

That last sentence is putting it mildly. But even if he weren't a successful publisher with a large platform—it would be easy enough to trash the company online. What a public relations disaster! How many thousands of dollars did that $5 blunder cost?

---

279 Tom Watson, *Causewired: Plugging In, Getting Involved, Changing the World*, (John Wiley & Sons, 2009), pp. 124-127.

280 Bill Glazer, "The Sales PREVENTION Department," Bill Glazer & Dan Kennedy's No BS Marketing Letter, January, 2009, p. 10.

The next example:

3. Blogger and Twitter outrage about an ad by Johnson & Johnson's Motrin brand forced the company to quickly withdraw the spot.[281]

Ironically, Advertising Age and other pundits say the original campaign was actually a lot more successful because of the media storm.[282]) However, on viewing it, Shel was stunned that the company would have even considered releasing such an ad; it seems to have been deliberately designed to make mothers of babies utterly furious. What do you think? You can see the ad on Youtube (as more than 87,000 people have done) by visiting https://www.youtube.com/watch?v=XO6SITUBA38 [283]

4. When Vincent Ferrari tried to cancel his dad's AOL account and was put through over 20 minutes of clueless behavior from the customer service rep, he posted the entire recording of the call on his blog and other sites, including YouTube—where the call got 62,827 hits in the first two days.

5. CNN aired a story about Walmart's attempt to grab the insurance payments of an employee who'd been injured so badly on the job she had to go into a nursing home—an employee for whom the company had actually paid medical bills after the accident—inspiring thousands of bloggers to organize boycotts. The company was forced to relinquish its claim on the money.[284]

Companies that understand the proper use of social media, though, build a lot of trust and are much more easily seen as responsible. Here are three examples of doing it right:

- The shoe company Zappos, known for being extremely people-centered, was widely praised for the way it went about laying off eight percent of its employees—never a pleasant undertaking and often one that could result in a lot of negative feeling. CEO Tony Hsieh used his corporate

---

281 http://www.washingtonpost.com/wp-dyn/content/story/2008/11/17/ST2008111703533.html

282 http://adage.com/article?article_id=132787, verified 4/17/15.

283 Accessed 4/17/15.

284 "The Low Trust Epidemic: Why It Matters and What Communicators Can Do About It," Op. cit.

blog[285] to lay bare the facts leading to the decision (pressure from a major investor), demonstrate his concern for the laid off employees and share the details of a generous severance package, and gather support—and then Tweeted a link to his blog. Several Tweets praised his transparency. Even employees had kind things to say. One wrote to Hsieh's attention, "@zappos decisions like this are tough, I know they weren't made lightly, I don't envy any of the folks who had to make the call."[286] (Amazon.com bought Zappos for $850 million in July 2009, apparently because of its legendary customer service.)[287]

- Rubbermaid added customer reviews to its website, and yes, some products received negative feedback. But the company used that as an opportunity to find out where communication was breaking down. Rubbermaid discovered that people were using the products improperly because instructions weren't clear, immediately rewrote instructions, incorporated them into the product package, posted to the website along with an explanatory blog post, and wrote individually to those who had posted the reviews.[288]

- Tyson Foods donated 100 pounds of food to food pantries for every person who commented on its blog about the initiative—and responded directly to comments. Tyson built support for the campaign via Twitter, and filled two tractor-trailer loads for the Food Bank of Greater Boston within hours; the company also donated to other food pantries in Austin and San Francisco.[289]

Like Tyson, you can take active steps to build a positive reputation in cyberspace—before problems arise—and then, if issues develop, you'll have

285 http://blogs.zappos.com/blogs/ceo-and-coo-blog/2008/11/06/update, November 6, 2008, verified 4/17/15.

286 http://twitter.zappos.com/employee_tweets/2008/11/6/11. No longer online.

287 "Here's Why Amazon Bought Zappos," http://mashable.com/2009/07/22/amazon-bought-zappos/, verified 3/19/15.

288 Meghan Meehan, "Rubbermaid Improves Customer Experience through Ratings & Reviews," http://blog.bazaarvoice.com/2009/03/09/rubbermaid-improves-customer-experience-through-ratings-reviews/, March 9, 2009, verified 4/17/15.

289 http://frugalmarketing.com/newsletters/2008/12/16/positive-power-spotlight-tyson-foods/

a much easier time mobilizing support. In an article on MarketingSherpa. com, Andy Beal, co-author of *Radical Transparency: Monitoring and Managing Reputation Online*, suggests several steps in online reputation management:[290]

- Be honest in your self-analysis and really look at the areas that need improvement
- Control internal communication—enforce policies that prohibit dissing customers or other stakeholders
- Monitor the conversations taking place about your company and your industry—and cast a wide net for this monitoring, using such tools as Google and Yahoo alerts, Digg, Technorati, and Youtube, as well as the blogs and e-zines of key influencers (to this list, we'd add Twitter and Facebook at the least, and maybe several others)
- React strategically after analyzing the situation: ignore the problem if it's really small and not likely to grow; for bigger issues, correct rumors, issue public apologies and make-goods with "sincerity, transparency and consistency")
- Control (or at least take a prominent role in) external discourse—for example, by hosting a forum page to publicly discuss the issue
- Stay away from clueless responses such as arrogance, condescension, responding without knowing the facts, or making threats

As far back as 2005, monitoring helped Dow Jones defuse a tricky situation when a blogger got angry, perceiving a new product as a privacy invasion. Dow Jones' CMO, Alan Scott, picked up the mention and quickly wrote a personal note explaining the product's purpose; the blogger was mollified and a potential firestorm never materialized.[291]

---

290 "Protect Your Image on the Digital Highway: 7 Tips & No-Cost Tools to Prevent a PR Nightmare," http://www.marketingsherpa.com/article.php?ident=30793&pop=no, August 26, 2008, verified 4/17/15.

291 MarketingSherpa.com, "Dow Jones Steers Marketing with Plenty of Social Media Data: 7 Key Strategies," December 9, 2008, https://www.marketingsherpa.com/barrier. html?ident=30954.

SOME REAL LOYALTY PROGRAMS FROM BIG COMPANIES

Do you think a loyalty program is just a business card that gets punched for every purchase, and after ten punches, the customer gets one free? Sorry, but that's not really a loyalty program, just an incentive to come back. If the loyalty is only for the free gift, it's not solid.

Compare the punch card with some big-company approaches that really do build loyalty:

Nordstrom

How did Nordstrom become one of the largest department stores, opening numerous new locations while some of the world's greatest store names went out of business? It certainly wasn't on low prices.

Nordstrom built a reputation for excellent service—for going so far out of their way to assist customers that word spread far and wide.

Living in an area where Nordstrom hadn't reached yet, Shel first learned about the company from Guy Kawasaki's book, *The Macintosh Way*, in the 1980s. Kawasaki cited several examples of excellence, and Nordstrom was among them. The store has been known to accept returns of heavily used merchandise that probably wasn't even bought there; but instead of focusing on short-term profits, the company went after long-term consumer loyalty and word-of-mouth brand building. If you return an item of clothing that no sensible store would take back, and you get full credit, aren't you going to shop there over and over again—and tell your friends?

Stop & Shop's Two Promotions

Your collaborators in marketing don't have to be in the same market at all, or even be a business. Nonprofits or businesses from an entirely different sphere can make excellent partners.

Years ago, Stop & Shop, a large New England supermarket chain, teamed up with Apple Computer for a very innovative promotion. Many others have copied it since (and for all we know, Stop & Shop may not have been the first)—because it created huge customer loyalty for both companies and also helped the communities where it was offered.

Here's how it worked. Customers saved their register receipts, and turned them in to their children's schools. The schools counted the dollars spent toward points, and those points were redeemable for computer equipment from Apple. Of course, Stop & Shop drew customers from other stores—and Apple trained new users in its own operating system from a young and tender age. Since the Apple operating system had less than 10 percent of the market, this campaign established a vital new base of Apple-oriented computer buyers, who would be buying systems of their own in a few years.

Stop & Shop had another great win–win powerhouse a few years later: a no-fee frequent-flier credit card that earned a mile for every dollar spent, and two dollars for every dollar spent at Stop & Shop. Unfortunately, after about four years, the sponsoring bank was bought out by a large conglomerate that eventually killed the program. But many of those former airline customers stayed with the grocery chain out of habit.

Saturn

It wasn't so many years ago that buying a car was a horrible chore. You came into the dealership fully expecting a hostile, manipulative environment. But even before the Internet made it possible for consumers to be far better informed, Saturn revolutionized the way cars are sold—and sold a huge number of cars in the process.

Saturn was a part of General Motors, the largest US car maker, and one firmly rooted in the old, adversarial ways. But Saturn did a number of things differently. It created a feeling of pride and ownership among its employees that enabled the car line to quickly develop a reputation for quality. Its design standards emphasized safety but did not compromise value, economy, performance, or comfort. And the Saturn dealer network—many of whom also operated traditional showrooms selling other brands—treated the customer as a valued part of not just the sales process but the entire idea of driving a Saturn. The customer-really-counts philosophy even extended to its ads, which often featured ordinary people who drove Saturns.

When you walked into a Saturn dealer, you were given a friendly greeting and told who could answer your questions. There was no pressure. Your contact would helpfully assess your needs and suggest a vehicle that would work for you. And if you decided to go forward, the price was already set—at a level that provided very good value to the consumer and very good profit to the manufacturer and dealer.

It was all spelled out in the Saturn Consultative Sales Process, which said, among other things, "All customers shall receive a thorough interview in order for Sales Consultants to determine their wants and needs" and "All customers shall receive open and honest treatment about all elements of the transaction price."[292] Another piece of the success formula was an attitude that labor and management could be partners in creating a wonderful car built by wonderful people. Instead of the standard union contract, Saturn employees worked under a much simpler 28-page memorandum of agreement that provided a lot more autonomy.

In JD Power & Associates' annual automotive sales satisfaction study, Saturn ranked Number 1 seven out of eight years. It was the only nonluxury brand to earn top ranking in both Power's Customer Service and Sales Satisfaction indexes; the only other brand that achieved both the same year was Lexus, in 1994.[293] And the brand did extremely well in its early years, coming out of nowhere to become the third-best-selling model in America by 1994. Dealers couldn't get enough cars to meet customer demand, and only 400 were still on dealer lots when the 1994s were replaced by 1995s.[294]

Unfortunately, the brand didn't keep pace with the trend it pioneered. Since Saturn introduced its new dealership style in the early 1990s, many other dealerships followed suit. And, particularly once production moved away from the close-knit Spring Hill, Tennessee factory that pioneered the Saturn culture, reliability ratings didn't match up to rhetoric.[295] By 2008, Saturn had fallen to

292 In fairness to the old paradigm, auto industry analyst Jim Ziegler told Shel in a telephone interview on Dec. 11, 2002, that although the no-negotiation rule makes the dealerships very profitable, GM has heavily subsidized the division, driving down the price of the cars and taking a loss of about a billion dollars per year.

293 "Saturn Honors 11 Retailers for Exceptional Performance," Aug. 21, 2002 http://www.saturnfans.com/Company/2002/2002summitaward.shtml, verified 4/18/15.

294 David Hanna, "How GM Destroyed its Saturn Success," http://www.forbes.com/2010/03/08/saturn-gm-innovation-leadership-managing-failure.html, accessed 3/15/15.

295 See, for example, this letter in the The Chatanoogan: http://www.chattanoogan.com/2009/5/23/151853/Don-t-Blame-Corker-For-Saturn-Plant.aspx, accessed 4/18/15.

11th place in sales satisfaction—behind not only several luxury brands, but also Buick and Mercury.[296] As part of its massive restructuring after the economic crash and federal government bailout, GM closed Saturn in 2010. But writing in Forbes (not exactly a hotbed of radical economics), analyst David Hanna puts the blame for Saturn's closure squarely on a deliberate dismemberment by General Motors and the United Auto Workers of everything that made Saturn special as a brand, a corporate culture, and a crucible of successful product innovation—because, he says, it was a threat to the power of the status quo.[297] A similar article appeared in Newsweek.[298]

Still, even though GM closed the division, Saturn's pioneering ability to reframe the customer experience has lasted. Quality of the experience in the dealership is still crucial. J.D. Power and Associates notes that "'Hassle-free' negotiation continues to be a leading reason why buyers choose to purchase from one dealer compared with another dealership."[299]

Other Affinity Promotions

Many other businesses have teamed up with schools, offering books, supplies, training, and other benefits at certain dollar levels. And many businesses and nonprofit organizations have also benefited from affinity programs of one sort or another, from credit cards to phone plans. Working Assets was perhaps the first to team up a long-distance telephone plan with a social benefit to political organizations that its members support—in this case a pool of organizations selected by the members, each of which receives a substantial contribution. These work because they let members help the organization, just through the purchases they already make. This model has been tweaked by media companies, many of whom now offer a web page with discount offers from their advertisers.

---

296 Accessed on the original site in 2009; currently available only through archive.org, https://web.archive.org/web/20090615114930/http://www.jdpower.com/corporate/news/releases/pressrelease.aspx?ID=2008250, accessed 4/19/15.

297 David Hanna, "How GM Destroyed Its Saturn Success," op cit.

298 "How GM Crushed Saturn," http://www.newsweek.com/how-gm-crushed-saturn-77093, accessed 3/15/15.

299 "2008 Sales Satisfaction Index Study," http://autos.jdpower.com/content/study-auto/BMxNMZr/2008-sales-satisfaction-index-study.htm, verified 4/18/15.

LESSONS

- You must delight your customers; satisfaction is not nearly enough
- Make the ordinary into something special and personalized to get out of commoditization (with all its profitability problems), and turns customers into fans
- In the 21st century, reputation management is crucial
- Nordstrom and Saturn: Create win-win partnerships with consumers
- Apple and Stop & Shop: Create win-win partnerships with other businesses *and* consumers

ACTIONS

- If you run a retail store, think of two innovations to turn shopping into a destination and experience.
- If you're a service business, what can you do to translate that specialness into another venue, such as a website?
- Envision five components of a loyalty program that's deeper than just a discount after a certain number of purchases.
- Put one into place and monitor the results. If it's working out, gradually add the remaining ones.

CHAPTER 16

RUNNING A GLOBAL COMPANY

BRAND IDENTITY IN A GLOBAL ECONOMY

hat's the first thing that comes into your head when someone says "Mercedes"?

If you're in Europe, we'll guess that you think of a company that has a car, truck, or bus for every market niche. In the United States—where General Motors, Ford, and Chrysler own that positioning—Mercedes brings up images of high-end sport and luxury cars; its competitors are companies like Porsche and Rolls-Royce, not Chevrolet or Dodge. (Ironically, Chrysler was actually owned by Mercedes' parent company, Daimler, from 1988-2007.) And in many other parts of the world, Mercedes is the workhorse of taxi, truck and bus fleets, supplying durable vehicles at affordable cost. In the Spanish-speaking world, Mercedes is also a popular female name, for which the car was named more than 100 years ago.

In short, the same brand has very different associations in different parts of the world.

And this works in the green world, too: What's the first thing that comes into your head when someone says "Vitasoy"?

As a green business owner, you might be into natural foods—and you could know Vitasoy as a brand of organic soymilk, with various flavor options and a health consciousness. You might even know that the company owns several other soy-related brands, including Nasoya and Azumaya tofu products in the US and Unicurd in Singapore.

But in cultures like China, Hong Kong, and Latin America, Vitasoy's soymilks—under such names as Calci-Plus, Tsing Sum Zhan, and San Sui—are marketed as mainstream household beverages; packages I (Shel) have seen in Latin American markets that don't mention the word "organic" (*organico* or *biologico*). Vitasoy's milk is called Soy Milky in Australia—a name that would not go over well in the United States.

Let's stay with green foods for another example: natural breakfast cereals. To a shopper in the United Kingdom, Weetabix® is a well-known and diverse line of cereals: the regular kind that's similar to shredded wheat...organic, crispy minis with chocolate, strawberries, peanut butter, or fruit and nuts...baked with golden syrup...chocolate (non-mini)...crunchy bran...and then variations made with different grains, such as Oatabix. There's even an o-shaped imitation of Cheerios. But in the US, it's unusual to see anything other than the basic biscuits, sold as a healthy product.

What's the point? It's that large companies—in the green world or in the general consumer marketplace—go after different markets, and market differently, in different parts of the world, or in different market segments within the same country.

In fact, smart companies segment much more closely than by country. Within 15 miles (24 kilometers) of my house, the same supermarket chain has stores in four communities.

Walking the aisles, you'd think they were different companies entirely. Two are geared toward the adventurous tastes of healthy-living folks in the nearby college towns, with a lot of natural products, green packaging, exotic fruits and vegetables, and so on. And one of those, in a more international community, has an Asian foods section that's bigger than some Asian grocery stores. The third, in a heavily Hispanic city, has a product selection geared to Puerto Rican tastes. And the fourth, in a working-class city that hosts a large military base, is the land of packaged, bland convenience foods for a burger-and-pasta-salad crowd.

You'll find examples of this kind of segmentation in industry after industry. Even book cover design can be startlingly different for the same book in different parts of the world. The first book in the Harry Potter series even had different titles for the American and British editions: *Harry Potter and the Sorcerer's Stone* versus *Harry Potter and the Philosopher's Stone.*

These days, all of us are global businesses. As a green/social change profitability consultant, copywriter, and speaker working solo from a farmhouse in the northeastern United States, I (Shel) have not only served clients from all parts of my own country, but also Japan, Cyprus, Turkey, Israel, England, France, Germany, Belgium, Australia and Malaysia, among others.

Helping an international client incorporate deep social change or reach the US green market is easy for me. But if that client wants to reach an audience in a different market, I have to put myself in the mindset of a potential customer who thinks very differently from me.

For me, the way around this is to focus on the slices of the market that play to my core strengths. For instance, if a company wants to reach the green consumer, or market green products and services to either green or nongreen audiences, my subject knowledge is strong enough to make up for the cultural differences. (Of course, it helps that I've traveled widely.)

If you want to go into different markets, ask yourself questions like these:

- What do you offer that a customer can't find at home already?
- How will you deal with shipping, customs, and tariff costs, and will you still be profitable after factoring those in?
- What do you need to know about the culture in order to succeed?
- Do you need a local-culture expert on the ground?
- Who will sell and service your products in that country?
- How might a tweak in the product, packaging, or marketing make it more attractive in that market?

- How does entering this far-away market make the world better or address environmental and social problems—and how can you use that commitment in your marketing?

Good luck! And if you need guidance on this journey, feel free to contact me.

CREATING POSITIONING FOR GLOBAL BRANDS

What market positioning might be worth the hassle and expense of entering new countries?

Your Unique Selling Proposition, or USP, is marketing-speak for the factor that makes your offering special enough to win over buyers who either have been meeting the need elsewhere or didn't realize they needed your product or service. If you're entering a different country, your USP will have to be clear and convincing enough that people will switch.

In the green world, construct your USP based in either or both of two different themes: how the product or service improves your customer's life (solves a problem, meets a need, fulfills a desire)—and how it helps others and the world. As you already know, customers who already think green are receptive to the second—but to reach nongreens, you also need positioning points in the first category—such as:

Higher Standards

As noted earlier, cosmetics and personal care product standards are much higher than in the US. European companies—or US companies that meet the European criteria—could dominate the market with messages like "Because we're based in Spain, we have to meet European Union standards for product safety. These standards are much tougher than those in the United States, and that's your guarantee that our shampoos are safe and healthy for your children." This is a market opportunity waiting to be captured, and the early movers could have quite a leg up. Yet even European companies like The Body Shop that do have a presence in the US fail to capitalize on this in their marketing.

Standards in health, the environment (organic, biodegradable packaging, waste recapture, no animal testing, etc.), ease of use, etc. all make great positioning points.

Economic Opportunity for the Poor

If, say, your product is sourced from organic biodynamic fair-trade ingredients, that gives you bragging rights. While many consumers around the world recognize that fair trade, organic, and biodynamic are good things, they may not recognize exactly what they mean. You, as the product manufacturer, importer, or marketer, must educate them. Your customers and prospects need to know that buying from you means not only a living wage to the farmer, but also:

- Certification that child slaves are not used (an especially big issue in the cocoa industry)
- A pool of money goes to the village cooperative, which uses it for democratically decided improvement projects such as building wells—and that in turn means teenage girls are able to stay in school because they're not spending half the day carrying pitchers of water several miles
- Money that stays in the local producer communities and is not sucked away to the developed world by giant corporations
- Organic/biodynamic regenerative farming practices (such as companion planting rather than destructive monocropping) mean that the harvest will continue for many years, because the soil is nurtured, not depleted
- Consumers and farmworkers are spared exposure to harmful chemicals
- Your food product that still contains its original nutrients and thus offers both higher nutritional content and better flavor

When you present things this way, you provide good reasons to buy from you instead of some commoditized agribusiness firm, even if you represent a foreign company. Wouldn't any smart consumer want to make a choice like that?

Deeper Environmental Benefits

What do your green attributes *really* mean? Less intensive use of water, energy or materials and reduced or recaptured waste output can mean lower prices to the consumer, reduced risk of catastrophic climate change, more productive farmland, etc. Are these important enough to get consumers to switch from a home-country brand to your export? And will the differences make up for the environmental impact of shipping something halfway across the world?

THE KEY CONCEPT: MAKE YOUR STORY MEANINGFUL

When you bring a product to market in a different country, the marketing challenge is to tell "the story behind the story"—to make it come alive with your commitment to a better world that is so strong, it has brought you all the way across an ocean to do business. This kind of marketing is a good thing even in the domestic market, but with the extra challenges of going global, it's crucial. Keep asking, "what does this mean? Why is it important? Why should my customer care?"

And once again, you don't have to go it alone. People like me are happy to help you succeed.

LESSONS

- In the Internet era, every business is both local and global
- Smart companies market differently and use different product mixes to match local culture—even from one town to the next
- Opportunities abound for companies who can seize the moment and offer unique benefits
- The more you drill down to the deeper meaning, the easier time you'll have convincing people to do business with you

ACTIONS

- Analyze the global impacts, positive and negative, of bringing one of your product lines into a different part of the world.
- Create separate marketing campaigns in each market a product goes into.

PART IV

USING YOUR BUSINESS TO CREATE A BETTER WORLD

CHAPTER 17

MARKETING AS SOCIAL CHANGE, AND SOCIAL CHANGE AS MARKETING

"The man that says a task is impossible should get out of the way of the man doing it."

— Chinese proverb

"The merely difficult, we do immediately. The impossible takes a while longer."

—Author unknown

emember those discussions of framing, earlier in the book? One definition of marketing is an action or message (or series of actions or messages) that causes someone else to take an action of some kind: to buy a product, try a service, accept a new idea. In short, marketing involves persuasion.

A great persuader or negotiator embraces a mindset where both parties win. He or she is an excellent listener, able to tune in exactly on the other person's issues, whether or not those issues are verbally expressed—and to figure out how the proposed solution can help the other person. Sometimes this is a matter of persuading…sometimes, listening and responding with new ideas that move everyone forward.

Moving forward isn't always a pure business proposition. Often, it's about changing the world. Shel's earliest training in marketing was doing volunteer public and media outreach for various social change groups. His desire to free the world from hunger and poverty, heal the earth's damaged environment and the rifts that drive people to war is still a dominant factor in his marketing career, his approach to business, and, he believes, his success. Both Jay and Shel live our lives around the idea that we *can* make a difference in the world we live in. As Shel puts it, "I have both the skills and the obligation to try to make the world better in some way. "

Coming out of the corporate world, Jay reached a similar conclusion. He wrote in his book, *The Guerrilla Entrepreneur,*[300]

> Guerrilla entrepreneurs know that they are citizens of the earth and of their community…noble causes such as improving the environment, helping the homeless, abetting the US economy, teaching people to read, curing dreaded diseases, and bettering life for children are beneficiaries of their business success as well…
>
> Whatever form your altruism takes, the important thing is to nurture that sense of philanthropy, and then activate it with your business… Whoever heard of creating a small business with the idea of bettering life on earth? Well, you have now, and guerrilla entrepreneurs have been aware of this concept—even acted on it—for several decades. In this new millennium, giving back to your community or environment will prove to be less of a choice for the guerrilla entrepreneur, but a criterion for success.

---

300 Jay Conrad Levinson, *The Guerrilla Entrepreneur*, Garden City, NY: Morgan James Publishing, 2007, p. 113.

And both of us believe there is tremendous synergy between marketing and social change. When a social change message becomes mainstream, that's when the ideas take hold and the change begins to occur. Social change/environmental groups that ignore marketing will find themselves unable to reach anything more than a marginal splinter of an audience; their ideas will never become mainstream because there is no one to interpret their message for the mainstream audience. Social change advocates who make no attempt to reach the everyday world are just spitting in the wind. It may feel like taking action, but it won't accomplish much.

We also see this shift in the ways major environmental groups have begun to form alliances with the business world. Activists who once shouted at CEOs from the barricades now meet with them in boardrooms—and work out brilliant deals to advance both their agendas at the same time.

Two among dozens of examples:

- Green America led a coalition that got cocoa giant Hershey to phase out its use of non-fair-trade cacao[301]
- Greenpeace got a far-reaching agreement from Levi Strauss to stop discharging hazardous chemicals—and the clothing manufacturer's press release included this language of sweeping social change:

    Levi Strauss & Co. also commits to support systemic (i.e. wider societal and policy) change to achieve zero discharge of hazardous chemicals (associated with supply chains and the lifecycles of products) within one generation or less. Thus, our commitment includes investment in moving industry, government, science and technology to deliver on that systemic change."[302]

Activist rhetoric from major environmental groups has become much more conciliatory as environmentalists begin to understand that business is able and willing to make sweeping change—and can lead that change throughout society.

---

301 http://blog.greenamerica.org/2014/10/03/spotlight-on-herhsey-2-years-later/, accessed 2/28/15.

302 http://www.levistrauss.com/wp-content/uploads/2014/01/Levi-Greenpeace-Detox-Solution-Commitment.pdf, accessed 2/28/15.

Gwen Ruta, Vice President of Corporate Partnerships for the Environmental Defense Fund, put it this way:

> …Profit, at its root, comes from smartly anticipating and meeting human wants and needs, which include clean air, clean water, and a safe place to live…
>
> Targets for lowering greenhouse gas emissions and creating carbon markets…provide a level playing field for entrepreneurs and financiers, opening a tap of investment dollars that…could grow to be as large as the stock market…we just might fundamentally change the relationship between business and our environment, and in the process, change our very future on this earth.[303]

For generations, the most successful activists have understood marketing. Indeed, some of the most out-there social change folks were marketing geniuses, understanding fully and completely how to play on the edges of mass consciousness and instill radical changes: Abbie Hoffman and Jerry Rubin of the Yippies, Dan and Phil Berrigan and their group of radical Catholic pacifists, Martin Luther King, Jr., and Saul Alinsky, to name a few prominent examples from the 1960s.

Going decades farther back, even some of the virulently anti-capitalist Wobblies demonstrated an intuitive knowledge of marketing. Some of our Founding Fathers, notably Tom Paine, Thomas Jefferson, and Ben Franklin, were also very savvy marketers. Think about the power of Paine's pamphlet, "Common Sense" to stir people's hearts—or Jefferson's Bill of Rights to bring antiauthoritarian skeptics into the fold of the brand new government.

In our own generation, the Adbusters collective clearly understands and uses the medium it attacks. We see great examples of marketing-inspired thinking from people like Majora Carter, founder of Sustainable South Bronx, and Van Jones, co-founder of Color of Change, Green For All, and other groups—both of whom have done much to create environmental movements in inner-city communities of color.

---

303 Gwen Ruta, "The Next Frontier of Business," in *Dream of a Nation: Inspiring Ideas for a Better America,* edited by Tyson Miller, See Innovation, 2011, pp. 282, 287.

And it's not just a left-wing thing, either. The rise of the New Right in the 1980s was directly related to its marketing skills…from Ronald Reagan's successful presidential campaigns, to televangelists like Jerry Falwell who understood the enormous power the medium provided, to Rush Limbaugh and other conservative talk-show hosts, to Newt Gingrich's brilliantly crafted message: a Contract With America. The marketing mavens on the Left, incidentally, quickly dubbed that last one the Contract ON America, in the underworld hitman sense.

Successful community organizing has to be at least in part about marketing. Examine the people who have changed the direction of an entire society, from the shift against the Vietnam War and the acceptance of the Civil Rights movement to the abandonment of the safety net in the early 1980s. They did it by combining the persuasive power of top-notch marketing with the ability to organize and energize vast numbers of people. And the best organizers understand that the line between marketing and organizing is blurry, and that they need to walk both sides of it.

As we discussed in Chapter 10, the 2008 US presidential election was about both marketing and organizing. Obama's framing repeatedly prevented his opponent from backing him into a corner over and over again. His victory was the first election since Jimmy Carter's extremely narrow victory in 1976 that gave a non-incumbent Democrat more than 50 percent of the vote.[304] (Clinton, in 1992, only got 43 percent in a three-way contest.)[305]

These skills are learned. Even Martin Luther King, Jr. was not a natural-born marketer; his early sermons were less than thrilling. His biographer, Stephen B. Oates, noted that King gradually came to understand that good preaching—just like good marketing—was "a mixture of emotion and intellect":

His sermons tended to be sober and intellectual, like a classroom lecture. But he came to understand the emotional role of the Negro church, to realize how much black folk needed this precious sanctuary to vent their frustrations and let themselves go. And so he let himself go. The first "Amen!" from his congregation would set him to "whooping" with some

304 http://www.britannica.com/EBchecked/topic/97239/Jimmy-Carter, verified 4/18/15.
305 http://query.nytimes.com/gst/fullpage.
   html?res=9F0CE3DE153EF936A2575BC0A965958260, verified 4/18/15.

old-fashioned fireworks, in which he made his intellectual points with dazzling oratory.[306]

By the time he made his "I Have a Dream" speech, King had become fully aware of the marketing power of what he did, and of the impact he could have on a national and international audience. Of 86 sentences in the speech, 82 use classic marketing techniques of storytelling, analogy, and metaphor—that works out to 95.35 percent. This was the oration named the best speech of the twentieth century,[307] beating out Roosevelt's "Day of Infamy" and Kennedy's "Ask Not What Your Country Can Do for You," among others. This was the oration that catalyzed a nation to do something about ending segregation once and for all—and ensured King's own place in history—and it exemplified classic marketing principles.

This chapter focuses more on the marketing of ideas than on the marketing of products or services. Maybe you can think about how visionary thinking can relate to success with marketing tangible items, or services, in your own business.

SUSTAINABILITY IS NOT ENOUGH

In the green world, we hear the terms sustainable or sustainability quite often. Sustainability is a good first step. But is that really all we want?

Not even close. Sustainability means making sure the status quo—the existing situation—can self-replicate. But keeping the current situation from getting worse doesn't mean it's getting better.

Amory Lovins put it this way: "If you were to ask one of your best friends how their relationship was with their partner and they were to say, 'Well, you know, it's sustainable,' you'd probably say, 'Well, I'm really sorry to hear that.'" [308]

---

306 Stephen B. Oates, *Let the Trumpet Sound: The Life of Martin Luther King, Jr.* (New York: Plume, 1983), p. 56.

307 *Baltimore Sun* article, quoted in the *Daily Hampshire Gazette* (Northampton, Mass. Jan. 15, 2001, p. 1.

308 As quoted by biomimicry expert Michael Pawlyn, in his speech at the Green Cities Conference in Melbourne, Australia, March 17, 2015, as reported in Cameron Jewell, "Michael Pawlyn on the promise of biomimicry for a better future," http://www. thefifthestate.com.au/innovation/design/michael-pawlyn-on-the-promise-of-biomimicry-for-a-better-future/73061, accessed 4/18/15.

Experts put the safe level of carbon in the atmosphere at 350 parts per million (PPM). But the April 2015 figure was 403.8 PPM,[309] or 115 percent of what it should be. This is an increase of 54.62 PPM, or 15.6 percent, since the December 1987 reading of 349.18. And it's probably not a coincidence that extreme weather events (floods, droughts, intense hurricanes, tsunamis, tornados, and such) have become both a lot more common and much more catastrophic. Journalist Naomi Klein notes that global carbon dioxide emissions increased *61 percent* from 1990 (when world governments started negotiating on climate change) to 2013.[310] Clearly, we can't wait around for government to solve the problem.

The first 14 years of the 21st century included nine of the ten warmest years in the past 134 years; the sole 20th-century year in the hottest ten was 1998— almost into the 21st.

Our non-renewable resources are being depleted. Whether it's oil (used not only for energy but for most plastics), iron ore, bauxite (raw material for aluminum), or the rare-earth metals used to make products like cell phones, the raw materials that were highest quality and easiest to extract have already been harvested. The remaining materials are harder to extract, require more energy to process, and often generate more pollution.

Energy extraction methods like tar sands oil or fracking can wreak environmental devastation. Tar sands oil is dirty and low quality, scars the landscape, and requires enormous energy input. Fracking is more efficient and actually cheaper than the old methods, but puts our water supplies—our most precious resource—at risk. "Mountaintop removal" destroys whole ecosystems to get coal out of the ground.

Products and their components—even food—travel thousands of unnecessary miles. The deck seems stacked against truly local economies.

Our world takes enormous unnecessary risks by disregarding the Precautionary Principle and unleashing technologies whose effects are not known—like GMO foods—or that are known to be potentially catastrophic— like nuclear power—because we use narrow cost-benefit analyses that only

---

309 http://co2now.org/Current-CO2/CO2-Now/global-co2-board.html, accessed 5/15/15
310 Naomi Klein, *This Changes Everything: Capitalism vs. The Climate* (Simon & Schuster, 2014), p. 11.

selectively count costs (externalizing many of the real costs—pushing them back upon consumers, neighbors, or taxpayers) and disregard the complexities of lifecycle and disposal costs.

And often, this is to the detriment of our businesses. Three examples:

1. A GMO-contaminated wheat scare in Oregon led to mass cancelations of wheat import contracts or additional testing requirements of shipments from the US in Europe and Asia, with a negative impact to the farmers, wholesalers, and shippers of the United States.[311]

2. India sued Monsanto over its appropriation of local biodiversity to develop new GMO eggplants.[312]

3. By 2011, more US shoppers actively sought out non-GMO foods than sought out organic.[313] This consciousness shows up in mainstream retail. For instance, the specialty grocery chain Trader Joe's eliminated GMO foods from its supply chain all the way back in 2001.[314]

We want a world that's getting better. We want a world that's undoing the damage humans have caused to the planet. And as green business owners, we want to be part of that healing.

And we can profit from it. The Rocky Mountain Institute, the green think-tank founded by Amory Lovins, has been showing the world how to slash energy use for decades. RMI has a practical, doable plan to save the US $5 trillion while supporting a 158% bigger US economy by 2050, using no energy from coal, oil or nuclear. By 2050, the US economy can produce 84 percent more, while knocking off 9 to 13 percent of energy use, and generating 80 percent of its energy needs through renewables.[315]

---

311 http://GreenAndProfitable.com/gmo-backlash-europe-and-asia-refuse-us-wheat/
312 http://GreenAndProfitable.com/india-sues-monsanto-for-biopiracy/
313 http://www.sustainablebrands.com/news_and_views/green_chemistry/gmo-free-surpasses-certified-organic-importance, verified 2/15/15.
314 Book review of *The Trader Joe's Adventure* in Shel's July, 2014 newsletter, http://thecleanandgreenclub.com/the-clean-and-green-club-july-2014/, verified 2/16/15.
315 http://GreenAndProfitable.com/higher-productivity-without-fossil-or-nuclear-by-2050/, verified 2/15/15.

So let's reframe the conversation. Let's stop talking about sustainability—and start talking in terms like "regeneration," "restoration," and "thriving."

And let's create structures that empower businesses to combine the vision of what needs to change with the commitment to change it. Alternative business structures, from B Corporations to co-ops, are a first step. But beyond that, let's harness the profit motive to *get it done.*

BARBARA WAUGH, CORPORATE REVOLUTIONARY

In her book, *The Soul in the Computer: The Story of a Corporate Revolutionary,*[316] Barbara Waugh recounts a number of amazing stories in her career at Hewlett-Packard, where time after time, she was able to gain consent from her higher-ups to do socially conscious projects that computer companies don't usually get involved with. And interestingly, not only did she continue to get the company involved, but each time, after the dust settled, she had more responsibility and a bigger paycheck. Her initiatives not only accomplished many of HP's and her own missions, but kept getting her promoted.

Barbara Waugh epitomizes the power of positive persuasion. In her book's Foreword, Alan Webber of *Fast Company* magazine comments about people who will change your life:

> They do it by rearranging your sense of what is possible…convincing you that the only limits to your future are those you…impose upon yourself…by expressing the absolute conviction that you have within you dreams and aspirations that you've never acknowledged—and…the absolute confidence that your dreams matter absolutely…It wasn't that Barbara is a great talker, and that what she said changed my life—quite the opposite. It was that Barbara is a great listener, and how she listened changed my life.

Coming out of volunteer work in the civil rights and women's movements, Waugh was originally hired by HP in 1984 as a recruiting manager for a

---

316 *The Soul in the Computer: The Story of a Corporate Revolutionary* (Makawa, Hawaii: Inner Ocean Publishing, 2001).

manufacturing division, charged with hiring 110 new engineers. And she wasn't there very long before she began to work for small increments of change within the company. Her strategy was to do what was right and stand up for it, move slowly enough to maintain support but quickly enough to galvanize people, find "co-conspirators" who would support her within the struggle, and then find ways to change enemies into allies within the corporate structure. One of her first victories was in confronting an arrogant, belligerent colleague who didn't even realize he was intimidating most of his co-workers; he not only changed his behavior but became an important ally.

Scaling up these steps, she took on ever-bigger projects. Over time, she initiated a corporate-wide sustainability drive, started a focus group of women in technology that evolved into a series of national conferences, and eventually helped create a massive program to bring HP's technology to developing countries where it could play a major role in empowering the local populations—the aim is to serve the world's poorest 4 billion people in ways that can help bring them out of poverty and still turn a profit for the company. These are only a few of her projects over the years.

The whole focus in her odyssey is the idea that doing well is a natural consequence of doing good: make the world better, and you will be more likely to succeed personally and professionally—and the company you work for will benefit as well.

In fact, the world's most successful entrepreneurs consistently talk about some sort of higher purpose. They didn't generally start their businesses just to make a lot of money—but to accomplish a much larger social goal. Perhaps this is why even some of the corporate giants who came out of the Robber Baron period of the late nineteenth and early twentieth century were driven to massive philanthropy. Even steel magnate Andrew Carnegie funded hundreds of libraries in villages that had never had a library before.

But Waugh was not a company founder or CEO. In fact, while reviewing a draft of this section, she wrote,

> I wish we could somehow draw attention to the enormous uncelebrated, unidentified entrepreneurial initiative of the grassroots—it isn't only

or even mostly CEOs, but you'd never know it from the literature—perhaps due to the business model of consulting—the function that most amplifies what's going on inside companies—that requires the big bucks that only the top can cough up. I've advocated, with limited success, that a percent of consulting dollars spent by the top on the top be made available to the rest of the organization, as an internal consulting budget for the troops.

Barbara's book demonstrates her amazing power to persuade others—because she goes about it in a systematic way, seeking alliances and stakeholders, and clearly showing at every corner that all the players come out ahead.

She's also willing to examine herself critically, to push herself past her own prejudices. Many times in her career, she finds that someone she expected to be hostile to her ideas was actually a key ally—but first she had to overcome her initial resistance to even starting the conversation.

Like Barbara Waugh, Shel came up out of various social justice movements and had to learn how to work with mainstream people, how to be open rather than cynically skeptical, and how to accomplish change from within the power structure as well as outside of it. And like Waugh, Shel has had a few important victories. Here's an example that he's particularly proud of.

CASE STUDY: SAVE THE MOUNTAIN

In November 1999, a developer announced a plan to desecrate ridgetop land abutting a state park by building 40 trophy homes two miles from Shel's house. The original newspaper article interviewed several local conservationists who expressed variations on "Oh, this is terrible, but there's nothing we can do."

But Shel refused to accept that. Within four days, he had drawn up a petition, posted a Web page, called a meeting for two weeks later, and sent out press releases and fliers about the formation of Save the Mountain.

Note that all of these actions are marketing actions. He could have called a meeting and not told the public, and then a few friends would have shown up and realized that they couldn't do very much. But by harnessing the power of the press, the Internet, and the photocopier, and crafting a message that would resonate with his neighbors—that not only was this terrible, but that there *was* something we could do—he was able to spark something that truly had an impact.

Shel and his wife, Dina Friedman, expected 20 or so people to come to the first meeting; they had over 70. From that day until December 2000, the group fought the project on every conceivable level: technical issues like hydrology, rare species, and slope of the road…organizing and marketing components including a petition drive (over 3000 signed), turnout of up to 450 at various public hearings, lawn signs, tabling, a big press campaign with over 70 articles… working with the state Department of Environmental Management to investigate options for saving the land…

Literally hundreds of people got involved with some degree of active participation. Many, many people brought widely varying expertise to the movement, far more than any of them could have had on their own.

By using his own skills in marketing and organizing, Shel was able to convert the outrage and despair and shock that were felt throughout a three-county area when this project was announced into a powerful—and highly visible—public force. As a group, STM had about 35 core activists, all working on many levels, both public and private. The persuasion in this case was not about the desirability of stopping the project; they had near-consensus on that, community-wide. Rather, it focused on the ability of a committed group of people to make a difference even when the "experts" said it was impossible.

Within two months, STM had established itself firmly in the public eye—and had actually shifted the discourse from "There's nothing you can do" to "Which strategies will be most effective?" Collectively, the group used its powers of persuasion, and its skills at reaching the public with this message, to change the project from inevitable to impossible. The land was permanently preserved in just 13 months—four years ahead of Shel's original five-year estimate for victory.

You probably have victories in your own life as well, where you achieved a marketing success that advanced a social or environmental good (using marketing in a broad sense, not just to sell a product). If you're inspired to share them, we'll put your comments on a Web page of reader contributions on persuasive marketing. Please mail your success stories to Shel at shel @ greenandprofitable. com with the subject: Persuasive Marketing Success Story.

CONVINCE ON CLIMATE CHANGE WITH NONENVIRONMENTAL ARGUMENTS

The Guardian, a major UK newspaper, argued that activists could get more traction with nongreens on climate change by pointing out the public health consequences of failing to act.[317]

And that's certainly true—but it's nowhere near the whole story.

Earlier in this book, we discussed finding the what's-in-it-for-me factors for nongreens (hipper, cheaper, more luxurious, etc.). We even listened to Van Jones tell us how to talk about the environment to Tea Partiers.

Now we have to take that same way of thinking and shift it from the material world—products and services—to the less tangible realm of what kind of world they want to live in, what kind of world they want to leave to their children and grandchildren.

Because these folks don't generally consider human impact on the earth, save-the-planet arguments won't carry much water with them.

But we can gain converts to the clause of reversing catastrophic climate change on several grounds that are not blatant appeals to environmentalism, among them:

- Economics
- Health (as The Guardian pointed out)
- Lifestyle

Let's look at each of these in turn.

Economics

The longer we wait to reverse catastrophic climate change, the more expensive it will be. We could list dozens of economic arguments for addressing climate

---

317 http://www.guardian.co.uk/sustainable-business/climate-change-environment-health-problem, *accessed 2012, verified 2/10/15*

change NOW, and still only scratch the surface. Here are a few positive-focused and negative-focused arguments:

- We can avoid the enormous costs of cleaning up after climate-change-related storms like Hurricanes Katrina, Rita, Irene, and Sandy (many trillions of dollars)—and after disastrous oil spills like Exxon Valdez and BP Deepwater Horizon.
- When we switch to clean, renewable energy sources, we stop the transfer of wealth from individual consumers to oil barons and big banks, and from industrialized democracies to hostile dictatorships.
- Say goodbye to paying energy bills—you can harness free energy from the sun, wind, tides, etc.
- When we keep global temperatures where they belong, we lower air conditioning and heating costs.
- We can lower taxes if we no longer need the military to secure fossil fuel sources.

Health

- Getting off coal will reduce asthma, emphysema, and other breathing diseases.
- Too much heat is a public health issue. Remember the summer of 2003, when thousands of people died in Europe's heat wave?
- Natural gas fracking and tar sands oil extraction put our water supply at severe risk. Water pollution ruins not just our drinking water but also water for agriculture, medicine, food packaging, etc.

Lifestyle

- Transporting ourselves by bicycle or on our own two feet offers the benefits of cardiovascular exercise: appropriate weight, fitness, increased endurance, longevity, etc.
- Using mass transit converts stressy driving time to productivity or entertainment time.

- Crops such as maple syrup and animals such as polar bears need cold weather. At the same time, pests like mosquitoes and ticks will provide year-round misery without a frost to kill them off for the winter.
- Eating local, sustainable foods not only tastes better, it boosts the local economy.

You could easily come up with several other categories of talking points where greens can reach out to nongreens. In all of it, we need to focus on the direct benefits to the people we're talking about, who may not be committed greens. To put it another way, we need to reach each person with the arguments that resonate with that specific person.

Let's all go out and convince a few people!

LESSONS

- Catastrophic climate change, atmospheric carbon levels, irreversible GMO contamination of our food supply and other threats to our ecosystem should have us following the Precautionary Principle
- It's time to go beyond sustainability, to regeneration
- Effective social change relies on key marketing principles—whether within a community, a corporation, or a country
- The lessons of a local campaign like Save The Mountain also apply nationally and globally
- Sometimes, when we change the discourse, the social or environmental change follows

ACTIONS

- Examine your biggest social or business goal. Express it as a marketing document, with three bullet points that will convince people this is both important and achievable.
- When you don't get the results you want through other channels, consider starting a movement.

CHAPTER 18

COMMUNITY-FOCUSED AND CHARITY/SOCIAL CHANGE MARKETING

he Save the Mountain story in the previous chapter is the perfect segue to one of our favorite parts of the marketing toolbox: affinity marketing that benefits both you and a worthy cause.

In our other marketing books, we demonstrate that working with a charity allows you take advantage of free media publicity and many other marketing opportunities that are denied to strictly-for-profit enterprises. Newspapers promote your event, radio stations have you on the air to talk about it, store owners let you put posters in their windows, bloggers and Twitterers spread your message in cyberspace, libraries make space for your flier on their bulletin boards—and lots of people show up. You have a great event, and present the charity with a large check.

The reason why this works so well, of course, is that when you give back to the community, the community is eager to work with you as a partner. You gain valuable credibility and PR as a socially minded company, and attract that segment of the market that puts a high value on social responsibility. Add superior products and services for an almost unbeatable combination.

BEYOND CAUSE MARKETING TO BUILDING A BUSINESS AROUND SOCIAL CHANGE

As we've seen, donating to mission-relevant causes is an excellent first step in establishing your business as socially responsible. But of course, you can go much further. Why not design programs that can create revenue while directly making the world better?

Let's start by visiting two of the most visible socially responsible consumer-focused businesses in the world, both of which have social change in their core DNA.

The Body Shop: Turning Customers into Social Change Advocates

The Body Shop, an international personal-care products retailer founded in the UK as a home business by the late Dame Anita Roddick in 1976, embraced numerous controversial causes and used its stores to build not just awareness, but action. Customers would be asked to participate in petition campaigns, donate funds, and generally use their power for such causes as "trade, not aid"—demanding economic initiatives that built the local infrastructure, skill set, and community self-sufficiency in developing countries. The Body Shop was among the first to bring attention to such areas as ethically sourced ingredients, the conditions for farm and factory workers, and animal testing in the personal care industry.

The company was sold to cosmetics giant L'Oreal in 2006, about a year before Roddick's death. Years after its sale, it's still the second-most-trusted brand in the UK.[318]

The sale was controversial, in part because of L'Oreal's reputation for engaging in the very practices Roddick had opposed, including animal

---

318 TheInnovationStorm.com "Corporate Social Responsibility Case Study: The Body Shop," http://www.slideshare.net/Innovationstorm/csr-case-studythe-body-shop, pp. 14, 11, accessed 3/13/15.

testing and marketing through the sexual exploitation of women. However, L'Oreal promised operational independence, and Roddick expressed the belief that rather than The Body Shop being corrupted by L'Oreal, The Body Shop's values could spread through the larger entity.[319]

Ben & Jerry's and Common Cause: A Tasty Partnership

Perhaps the best-known example of a company that put social and environmental good front and center, Ben & Jerry's frequently models specific social change business practices such as

- Tying CEO and senior executive pay to the pay of the lowest line workers (for its first several years)
- Sourcing ingredients from companies with a commitment to social and environmental progress (such as Greyston Bakery, as we saw earlier, as well as Fair Trade certified farmers around the world)
- Funding renewable energy initiatives
- Partnering with human service agencies to operate scoop shops that both employ people with disabilities and fund the agencies

Like The Body Shop, Ben & Jerry's was sold to a multinational corporate conglomerate (Unilever) that promised it could retain its operational independence.

While Ben & Jerry's was known for its social activism when the company was still controlled by founders Ben Cohen and Jerry Greenfield, the company continues significant social commitment under the current ownership. Consider this note that the advocacy organization Common Cause sent to all its members in January, 2009 with the subject line, "Yes Pecan!" (To fully understand the naming of this flavor, it's important to know that in metropolitan New York City where Ben Cohen and Jerry Greenfield were raised, "pecan" and "we can" rhyme.)

---

319 "The Body Shop: Social Responsibility or Sustained Greenwashing?" http://www.icmrindia. org/casestudies/catalogue/Business%20Ethics/BECG067.htm, accessed 3/13/15.

We've got BIG news. And it's pretty sweet.

For the month of January, Ben & Jerry's is renaming its butter pecan ice cream flavor to "Yes Pecan!" and donating a portion of the proceeds from scoop shop sales of the new flavor to the Common Cause Education Fund!

We're honored to be working with Ben & Jerry's to celebrate the spirit of activism and the newfound optimism that government can work for the common good.

Here's how you can help:

1. Find your local Ben & Jerry's scoop shop and get a cone of "Yes Pecan!" Proceeds will benefit our efforts to help citizens make their voices heard in the political process.

2. Join us on Facebook! Ben & Jerry's is also donating $1 for each person who signs up on our Facebook "cause" during the month of January or who donates to the Common Cause Education Fund, up to $10,000!

3. Tell your friends about these easy (and delicious!) ways to help Common Cause. Forward this message to your friends, and if you're on Facebook, invite them to join our cause.

I'm off to get some ice cream. Best wishes for a happy and healthy new year.

Sincerely,

Bob Edgar

and the rest of the team at Common Cause[320]

Consider some of what this message accomplished:

•   Reached hundreds of thousands of Common Cause email subscribers with a time-sensitive call to action

•   Built incentive to patronize Ben & Jerry's during its winter slow season

---

320 Email from Common Cause, January 5, 2009

- Reinforced the branding for Ben & Jerry's, Common Cause, Facebook, and then-newly elected President Barack Obama, whose campaign slogan was "Yes we can!"
- Publicized Common Cause's Facebook cause page
- Raised matching funds for an organization in financial need

In short, a four-way win whose only downside (the $10,000 maximum outlay) is more than made up by the promotional value. Very strategic—and totally replicable.

Even better—the argument Anita Roddick made about values percolating up from the small, socially conscious business unit to the wider corporation seems like it's working pretty well at Ben & Jerry's and Unilever, as you'll see in the B Corp discussion in chapter xx.

HOW BEN & JERRY'S USES SOCIAL GOOD TO COMPETE

In a market crammed with hundreds of superpremium ice cream companies and thousands of ice cream companies, Ben & Jerry's has over 40 percent of the US superpremium ice-cream market; its plant is Vermont's single largest tourist attraction. Only Haagen-Dazs, with a 17-year head start and the marketing muscle of another enormous food corporation behind it, sells slightly more superpremium ice cream.[321]

In a world ruled by enormous consumer conglomerates, it's really difficult for small startups even to get shelf space in supermarkets. How did these two young guys with neither business experience nor ice cream experience start a supersuccessful company, working out of a converted garage in small-town Burlington, Vermont—and achieve 40 percent of the market?

Yes, Ben & Jerry's ice cream is delicious—and so are the company's willingness to donate 7.5 percent of pretax profits to social causes, its socially conscious

---

321 While B&J's is now owned by the multinational food conglomerate Unilever, its popularity and market share long predated its acquisition. Haagen-Dazs first started using that name in 1961; its origins trace back to a family-owned ice-cream wagon in the 1920s (Ben & Jerry's was founded in 1978). Pillsbury bought Haagen-Dazs in 1983; Nestlé owns it as of this writing—see http://www.nestleusa.com/brands/Ice-Cream/Haagendazs, accessed 4/19/15. The two brands together account for 87 percent of the superpremium category, according to B&J's board member Terry Mollner in an interview Shel conducted April 13, 2009.

purchasing and employment practices, environmentally friendly manufacturing methods, and counterculture marketing strategies. All of those behaviors and positions help consumers justify its premium prices—and provide a major differentiation point from less conscious companies.

We believe that Ben & Jerry's success was a direct result of the company's pioneering and very public commitment to greater social good. When customers chose between two brands with excellent ice cream, one of which was very public about making the world better, many of them took the socially responsible choice.

COMMON GOOD CORPORATIONS

Socially responsible investing pioneer Terry Mollner, who co-authored the original criteria for social investing and co-founded the first fully-screened social investment fund back in 1982, happens to serve on the Ben & Jerry's board. He sees the future not in the triple bottom line, but in "common good corporations," that explicitly and eagerly put social good ahead of purely profit-based approaches.

Mollner insists on a business climate where human beings make decisions to benefit other human beings, and are accountable to them—following patterns found in nature. Today's laws that force businesses to put shareholder interests above all else, and subsume humanity to what he calls "an immoral contract" between business and government, have to be changed for species survival.

He sees this shift as both a "moral imperative" on par with addressing environmental issues, and a path to immense financial returns.

28 companies moving in this direction had profits eight times higher than the S&P 500 over a ten year period...Sustained and deepening customer loyalty will naturally gravitate toward common good corporations even more than they have toward socially responsible companies. The environment movement has grown, widened, and deepened over the last 38 years because it spoke to an increasingly obvious truth: if we do not take care of our planet we could all die. The common good corporation also speaks to an increasingly obvious

truth: if each individual, group, and company does not freely choose to give priority to the common good, monopolistic behaviors and conflict could also result in us all dying.[322]

MORE CAUSE MARKETING

Smaller companies can create less dollar-intensive promotions than Yes Pecan that also benefit themselves and others. For instance, Green America's Real Green newsletter has a column that spotlights member discounts from a variety of eco-friendly firms; one issue featured three natural apparel/accessory companies and a green flooring company. How many thousands of people learned about these not-terribly-well-known companies from reading Real Green, its Green American monthly magazine, or browsing the GreenAmerica.org website? The organization claims to have redirected over $100 million toward its strategic partners just in 2008, while channeling $1 billion in donations to good works.[323]

Earlier, we talked about other campaigns where businesses assist schools, human service agencies, and other worthy causes. People are always predisposed to become your customer if doing so helps the community in some tangible way. And if your offer is good enough that it could stand without the charity tie-in, you should be able to market it very successfully by stressing the community benefit. (Of course, if your prospects don't see your offer as a benefit to themselves as well, you'll have a much harder time making the campaign work. So get your prospects to buy in to both the community benefit and their own self-interest.)

This attitude can even help for-profit businesses without a charity tie-in, under the right circumstances. Many, many local, independently owned businesses have turned to their customers for help staying afloat against predatory competitors or other adverse circumstances (such as a fire). One common strategy is to turn to

---

322 Mollner, Terry, "Common Good Investing: The Next Stage in the Evolution of Socially Responsible Investing," published in the Indian journal *World Affairs*, 13:2, 2009, available for purchase (as of April 19, 2015) at http://www.indianjournals.com/ijor.aspx?target=ijor:wa&volume=13&issue=2&article=009. As it appears here, the quote, slightly repunctuated for clarity, is taken from an unpublished advance copy supplied by Mollner to Shel in 2009. The 28-company study Mollner cites is found in *Firms of Endearment: How World-Class Companies Profit from Passion and Purpose*, by Rajendra S. Sisodia, David B. Wolfe, and Jagdish N. Sheth (Phildelphia: Wharton School Publishing, 2007).

323 "Green America Victories: Thought and Action Leadership for a Green Economy," Real Green, Winter 2009, p. 8.

your customers to raise capital, by providing scrip (money that can only be used in your own business) worth more than the cost of buying it—so, for instance, you can sell $20 scrip that can be redeemed as $25 store credit. Naturally, this only works for businesses that have had a community spirit and are known not only to treat their customers as allies, but to create a truly special environment—business owners, in other words, who have been practicing the principles of this book all along.

Charity tie-ins are also a great way to change slow times into busy times. An in-store benefit event during a normally slow period can create great foot traffic. During the annual Piece of the Pie Day in Shel's area of western Massachusetts, restaurants donated 10 percent of gross revenues for the day to a local food pantry, and all the participating eateries were mobbed. Several years in, 148 restaurants participated and raised $46,087; there were about 40 the first year. Later, the organization switched to donation checkoffs from individual diners (and grocery shoppers, rather than a percentage of the take; one promotion raised over $52,000.[324]

The possibilities range from quick, easy events that raise a small amount of money to elaborate affairs requiring months of planning. Just to provide some idea starters, here are a few possibilities:

- Invite cookbook authors or famous restaurant chefs to do dinner fundraisers
- Have local musicians impersonate famous acts and raise money for your local arts council
- Auction or raffle off artwork, memorabilia, trips, or other exotic prizes
- Donate a percentage of sales to a deserving charity
- Volunteer for a dunking booth at the fair, with proceeds going to a local agency
- Organize or participate in a bike-athon, walk-athon, skate-athon, dance-athon, etc.
- Sponsor a Little League team

---

324 Telephone interview with Meagan Finnegan, Development and Marketing Coordinator, Food Bank of Western Massachusetts, March 31, 2009.

- Take responsibility for cleaning a section of highway or park (which usually earns you a little sign, too)

Remember: people *want* to do the right thing; Shel even calls that a basic human need. If you provide a social benefit and your offerings are otherwise comparable with those that don't offer the same benefit, you will find a niche.

Many, many companies have done extremely well for themselves by being socially responsible, and then telling others about it. Ben & Jerry's may be the most well publicized among companies that act out of social responsibility, but there are thousands of others. A few examples: Seventh Generation (sells environmentally friendly products), Stonyfield Yogurt (supports community-based farming), Green America (assists worker-owned businesses and consumer co-ops),

Arts organizations can play in this sandbox, too (and you can partner with them). Here's a great example:

Give a Beat draws upon the positive energy of global dance music to facilitate empowering opportunities for foster children, at-risk youth and communities impacted by incarceration. Through active collaborations with music producers, promoters, artists and socially conscious companies, we are raising awareness of pressing issues and injustices at live music events and through online platforms. Give a Beat provides dance and world music lovers with a unique channel for activism and philanthropy, while affecting change in the face of growing inequality.[325]

LESSONS
- CSR can be a key driver of corporate identity and branding—and profitability
- Charity components—"cause marketing" partnerships—open up many new doors for marketers
- The range of possible partnership possibilities is limited only by your imagination

---

325 http://giveabeat.blogspot.com/p/about.html, accessed 5/2/15.

ACTIONS

- Think about three community-focused initiatives that would be in keeping with your organizational goals on a big-picture issue like hunger or war.
- Open up the discussion to employees and board members.
- Examine what organizations you could partner with.
- Pick an initiative and a charity partner together and get it started, using what you've learned about marketing and about convincing others. (Shel can help you if this feels difficult.)

CHAPTER 19

TAKING THE CONCEPT BEYOND MARKETING: ABUNDANCE AND SUSTAINABILITY IN BUSINESS AND IN SOCIETY

You may find this chapter a bit off topic—but to us, it's the most important part. Bear with us and read it through, even if you think it doesn't pertain to you; you'll find some of the most powerful business examples in the entire book.

This is where you may find yourself ready and willing to make an enormous difference in the larger society. By the time you've read this chapter, we hope we will have motivated you to do something to bring these ideas out of the marketing realm, and into the world at large.

It's probably worth an entire book, and Shel might write that book someday—or maybe you will.

A RECAP OF OUR CORE PRINCIPLES

Time for a quick review: let's just remind ourselves of some of the most important principles in this book, all in one place.

- Green, ethical marketing—based not only on sustainability and regenerativity but also on quality, integrity, and honesty—not only *feels* better, but *works* better
- Business can go even further and deeper, profitably addressing hunger, poverty, war, violence, catastrophic climate change and the other enormous challenges facing society
- The more people who have a vested interest in your success, the more likely you'll attain it.
- Marketing that benefits your customers, employees, suppliers, distribution/retail channels, and even competitors—and other ways to cooperate with them—are key to that success
- In the abundance paradigm, there's plenty to go around—and in the vast majority of cases, that means "market share" is irrelevant
- When you've set up the right marketing systems, selling becomes less of a concern—because by the time a prospect contacts you, that prospect really *wants* to become your customer
- To achieve your goals, you can follow numerous paths; rarely is there only one way to accomplish your agenda—and you don't have to do it all on your own if you motivate others to help

Please keep those principles in mind as we start to look at the big picture: the whole huge canvas of Planet Earth.

WHERE WE ARE RIGHT NOW

Hunger and Poverty

805 million people face severe hunger.[326] 161 million children experience hunger-related stunted growth,[327] and a million of those die preventable deaths every year.[328] Using 2011 estimates by the World Bank, 2.2 billion people live on less than USD $2 per day, and 1 billion are trying to survive on $1.25 per day.[329]

Depressing and unacceptable as these numbers are, they should give us hope—because they actually demonstrate huge progress in reducing hunger and poverty since 1990. At that time, with a smaller overall population, 1,014.5 billion were hungry and 1.91 billion were living on $1.25 per day or less. As a percentage, only 17 percent of the developing world was in poverty by 2011, compared with 43 percent just 21 years earlier.[330] The other good news is that the world has enough carrying capacity to feed its growing populace.[331]

Much of the credit probably goes to the United Nations Millennium Development Goals. This amazing initiative, passed unanimously, set "21 measurable and time-bound targets and 60 indicators addressing extreme poverty and hunger, education, women's empowerment and gender equality, health, environmental sustainability and global partnership" with a 2015 goal for the Bottom of the Pyramid to achieve a better life.[332]

While many scoff at government initiatives, especially across national boundaries, the statistics cited above, prepared by a nongovernmental organization (NGO), show that progress is indeed being made. The UN's own chart, a matrix of nine geographic regions going across and 16 targets going

---

326 World Hunger Education Service, "2015 World Hunger and Poverty Facts and Statistics," http://www.worldhunger.org/articles/Learn/world%20hunger%20facts%202002. htm#Number_of_hungry_people_in_the_world, accessed 4/19/15.

327 Ibid.

328 http://www.actionagainsthunger.org/impact/ nutrition?gclid=CMeSntqDg8UCFWRp7Aod7wMAOA, accessed 4/19/15.

329 World Hunger Education Service, "2015 World Hunger and Poverty Facts and Statistics," op. cit

330 Ibid.

331 Ibid.

332 "Millennium Development Goals: 2014 Progress Chart," http://www.un.org/ millenniumgoals/2014%20MDG%20report/MDG%202014%20Progress%20Chart_ English.pdf, accessed 4/19/15.

down, shows significant progress: out of 144 boxes in the chart, 68 have reached that goal and another 68 have made some inroads, though not enough (136 total). Of the remainder, only six have failed to make progress; the remaining two are not rated because of insufficient data.[333]

War

At least 23 countries have faced wars over resources since 1900.[334] Michael Klare, Director of the Five College Program in Peace and World Security Studies in Amherst, Massachusetts, writes,

> Competition over vital resources is becoming the governing principle behind the disposition and use of military power…a new strategic geography in which resource concentrations rather than political boundaries are the major defining features.[335]

Many of the wars we think of as religiously or ethnically caused turn out to be about resources when we look more deeply. The religious or ethnic difference is used to justify grabbing resources from the outsider group and shifting them to the one in power—and then, in the face of this injustice, hatreds seethe and violence breaks out. We see this pattern in conflicts ranging from the United States' approach to Native Americans, especially in the 18th and 19th centuries… Northern Ireland through the 1990s …Israel versus Palestine for many decades… the Chinese versus the Japanese in the 1930…and on and on it goes.

What this means is that if the resource issues get settled, the issues of race, culture, and class have at least a chance of settling down, as they did in Northern Ireland and South Africa. It's not easy; a lot of hatred on all sides has to be overcome. But it can be done.

---

333 Ibid.
334 Alanna Hartzok, "Land Ethics and Public Finance Policy as If People and Planet Mattered," in Trent Schroyer and Thomas Golodik, eds., *Creating a Sustainable World: Past Experiences, Future Struggles*, Council on International and Public Affairs, 2006, p. 245.
335 Michael T. Klare, *Resource Wars: The New Landscape of Global Conflict*, Henry Holt, 2001, p. 214, quoted in Alanna Hartzok, "Land Ethics and Public Finance Policy as If People and Planet Mattered," Ibid., p. 245.

Wars based in religious fanaticism, with no resource issues in play, are much harder to solve. We can expect achieving peace to take several generations, and to require extreme effort, active education, and breaking bread with the perceived enemy—in systems that don't like to bring in outside influences. But even the Inquisition ended eventually! In our own day, economic and technological isolation are likely to cause pressure from within for change.

And we have dozens of powerful tools in our toolkits, but most of us don't even know we have the toolkits just out of sight on our own backs. A great place to start is with Scilla Elworthy's TED talk, "How to Respond to a Bully Without Becoming a Thug,"[336] From there, read Gene Sharp, Martin Luther King, Jr., Gandhi, Dave Dellinger, Barbara Deming, Jesus, Buddha, Dorothy Day, Abbie Hoffman, Saul Alinsky, George Lakey, Ward Morehouse, Tolstoy's essays on nonviolence, Quaker peace testimonies...You 'll find some extensive bibliographies on nonviolent action at http://nonviolenceinternational.net/biblio.htm, http://www.thekingcenter.org/books-bibliography#nonviolence, and http://www.peacemakers.ca/bibliography/bib37nonviolentdirect.html[337]

Catastrophic Climate Change

For 650,000 years, atmospheric carbon dioxide stayed below 300 parts per million (PPM). In 1950, that limit was breached.[338] Since then, carbon concentration has been on a rapid upward spike, reaching 403.8 PPM by spring 2015,[339] as noted earlier. In other words, in just 65 years, levels of carbon jumped more than a third, and reached the highest level in recorded history.

The consequences of continued rapid carbon growth could be quite severe. Analyst John Holdren, Assistant to President Obama for Science and Technology, Director of the White House Office of Science and Technology Policy, and Co-Chair of the President's Council of Advisors on Science and Technology,[340] predicts:

---

336 http://www.ragan.com/Main/Articles/49612.aspx, accessed 5/5/15.
337 All accessed 5/5/15.
338 http://climate.nasa.gov/evidence/, accessed 4/19/15 and reproduced above.
339 http://co2now.org/Current-CO2/CO2-Now/global-co2-board.html, op. cit.
340 https://en.wikipedia.org/wiki/John_Holdren#Recent_publications, accessed 4/19/15.

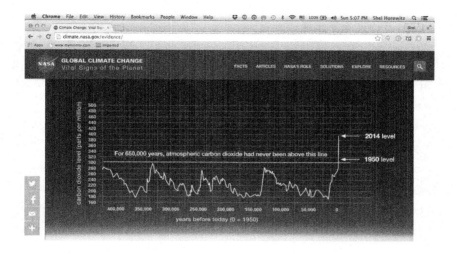

- Reduced agricultural productivity
- Increasing devastation from floods, fires, storms
- Increased ranges for tropical diseases
- Loss of biodiversity
- Property loss from sea-rise
- Drastic changes in ocean circulation patterns
- Much more rapid sea level increases than just from warming alone, 120 feet in places
- Melting near Greenland alone could raise ocean levels by two meters per century
- The submerging of low-lying areas including Florida[341]

We constantly hear similarly dire predictions of what will happen if we don't address the carbon issue right away. There's a near-unanimous scientific consensus. 97 percent of climate scientists and every major scientific organization not funded by a fossil-fuel interest group—even the American Chemical Society)—agree that humans have caused this jump, and the vast majority say we have to act.[342]

---

341 Shel Horowitz, "John Holdren: The "Roasted World" of Unchecked Climate Change: What the Numbers Actually Mean," op. cit.

342 "Consensus: 97 percent of climate scientists agree," http://climate.nasa.gov/scientific-consensus/, accessed 4/19/15.

Refuting Climate Deniers

Of course, those who deny that climate change is human-caused would argue that we don't know any of this for certain. Thus, even modest initiatives get caught in political wrangling and die a quick death. But let's use a little of that marketing jujitsu we talked about earlier.

Let's agree with them for a moment and "admit" that we have no proof. Let's say they could be right that human-caused climate change is not a problem. As the cartoon at http://politicalhumor.about.com/od/environment/ig/Environment-Cartoons/If-Global-Warming-Is-A-Hoax.1-Bh.htm shows,[343] we still get a whole lot of benefits: a cleaner environment, energy independence, more jobs, healthier kids, etc. And this cartoon doesn't even mention the economic benefit from reinvesting the money we used to spend purchasing nonrenewable fuels.

So, in other words, if the vast majority of climate scientists are right, we have to take immediate steps to stave off environmental and economic collapse. If they turn out to be wrong, we still end up fixing a lot of other problems and achieving many good things. Thus, neither proponents nor opponents have any good reasons for not doing our best to bring carbon down below 350 PPM.

Refuting "The Moral Case for Fossil Fuels"

There's one climate skeptic who needs special attention: Alex Epstein of the Center for Industrial Progress, author of a book that's gotten a lot of play: *The Moral Case for Fossil Fuels.*[344]

We give credit to Epstein for creating a well-written book that's enjoyable to read. And we even agree with some of his arguments:

- Humans live better because we've been able to harness energy—which has led to major improvements in shelter, agriculture, flood control, disaster response, etc.
- Thus, cheap, plentiful energy has saved millions of lives and improved the quality of life for billions more.

---

343 http://politicalhumor.about.com/od/environment/ig/Environment-Cartoons/If-Global-Warming-Is-A-Hoax.1-Bh.htm, accessed 4/19/15.
344 Published by Portfolio/Penguin, 2014.

- Climate activists need to be careful of our science and not make outlandish claims (he points out that the 97 percent climate-scientist consensus that climate change is real and that human behavior is a factor in climate change is *not the same* as claiming that the same 97 percent feel an immediate need to act. The number is undoubtedly high, but there are some scientists who recognize that humans have increased CO_2 levels but don't see that as a problem.
- CO_2, which plants breathe and turn back into oxygen for us to breathe, is good for plants

But Epstein ignores "inconvenient" facts that don't fit his worldview, and makes assumptions we don't agree with

- We can't rely on clean renewables to meet the power demand. Solar and wind are too intermittent, and hydro requires flooding too large an area. *Actually, we can. While, historically, solar, wind, geothermal, etc. have only generated a small sliver of our energy, they're growing exponentially, and new technologies make them more affordable and more efficient. Amazing new developments in battery technology—as well as using the electrical grid itself to store power—solves the intermittence problem. And in-line hydro can capture the power of water without the need to build dams and flood farmland. Many experts believe we can meet 50 to 80 percent of our power society with clean energy within a fairly short time, when we reduce demand through deep conservation.*
- We must examine everything from the point of view of its effects on humans. *We prefer to look at the effects on entire ecosystems, of which humans are a part. Other members of the ecosystem are entitled to life and health, too—and this helps humans as well. We don't know what cures for diseases might be lost if the wrong plant goes extinct. And we do know that removing one predator from the food chain can sometimes have disastrous consequences.*
- Government meddling has kept nuclear from playing a major role. *Actually, government subsidies and incentives (such as the Price-Anderson*

Act,[345] *which artificially lowers both the cost and the liability of nuclear insurance—switching financial responsibility for catastrophic accidents to property owners and taxpayers) are the only thing that keeps this extremely dangerous industry afloat.*

- The steep increase CO_2 levels has not caused major problems. *But the steep rise in CO_2 levels is exponential, and the planet responds in geologic time. The 65 years between hitting 300 and 400 PPM is a microsecond in the earth's time—and far shorter than the time from 200 to 300. We don't know yet what the consequences are, because the earth is still reacting. And if that exponential curve continues to shoot up (800 PPM in another 65 years?), atmospheric carbon will continue to shoot up.*

One clear and obvious rebuttal to Epstein's dismissal of clean technologies comes from Naomi Klein in her book, *This Changes Everything*:

The assertion that we have been held back by a lack of technological solutions is no more compelling. Power from renewable sources like wind and water predates the use of fossil fuels and is becoming cheaper, more efficient, and easier to store every year. The past two decades have seen an explosion of ingenious zero-waste design, as well as green urban planning. Not only do we have the technical tools to get off fossil fuels, we also have no end of small pockets where these low carbon lifestyles have been tested with tremendous success.[346]

WHAT COULD A REGENERATIVE, THRIVING FUTURE LOOK LIKE?

What kind of world would we live in if the abundance paradigm were integrated into every aspect of society? There'd be enough to go around, yes—enough food, shelter, energy, drinkable water, medical care, and so forth. But what kinds of changes would that create?

Take a few minutes to think about that, and jot down your answers. (You can email them if you like: shel @ greenandprofitable.com, subject line: Sustainable

---

345 Encyclopedia of Earth, " Price-Anderson Act of 1957, United States," http://www.eoearth. org/view/article/155347/, accessed 5/16/15.
346 Naomi Klein, *This Changes Everything*, op. cit., p. 16.

Future Ideas; we'll consider them for posting on a Web page dedicated to this topic and perhaps immortalize you in a future book.)

Here is the short version of our vision (writing from our perspective as residents of the United States):

By eliminating scarcity, we eliminate poverty and famine. Everyone has adequate food and water for survival, and access to quality healthcare. As that frees up time that had been spent on basic survival, people who have never had the luxury of education begin to build new skills and knowledge. A massive but noncoercive educational campaign not only raises the literacy rate, but lowers overpopulation worldwide. We're talking about future generations thriving, too. That drastic reduction in population growth will actually find support among the affected populations, because they will realize that nearly all of their children will live—and therefore, they do not have to have so many babies just to make sure there is someone to take care of them in their old age.

By switching the entire society from nonrenewable to renewable, clean, abundant energy—solar, hydrogen, wind, water, geothermal, wave, magnetic, etc.—we eliminate oil, coal, gas, and uranium as reasons to go to war. We also eliminate the stranglehold that certain foreign governments have on developed societies—and can deal with these countries on the merits of their actions, and not out of a need to appease or overpower them in order to maintain access to their oil. Pollution will be drastically decreased, lowering the cost of medical care for diseases like emphysema and asthma. Reforestation programs will make sure that future generations have not only adequate timber resources but adequate oxygen supplies.

The energy shift includes switching agriculture from chemiculture/GMO (Genetically Modified Organism)-based factory farming to methods that not only preserve—and often enhance—the soil, but produce significantly healthier and more nutritious food. Over time, this will raise yields, eliminate another source of pollution, and again reduce medical costs. These organic farms will produce in abundance, and the challenge will be distribution: getting food to the parts of the world where, so far, there hasn't been enough to go around. City dwellers will grow food (and collect solar energy) on their rooftops and windowsills. Most families will have access to at least a small garden.

Transportation and housing planning will lead many communities toward a village cluster model, where the buildings are relatively close together and the open space surrounding homes and workplaces is available to all. There will be a movement away from commuting long distances; many more people will either work from home or within bicycling distance.

Throughout every aspect of society, systems will be designed along the lines of John Kremer's biological model. Changes in building and transportation design will allow all of us to live more lightly on the earth, while enjoying greater physical comfort.

The communications revolution will continue; the Internet will reach into the remotest villages. This will open up vast powerhouses of learning, sustainable commerce, and global community building; every can home become its own university campus. That, in turn, could lead to locally-based, Arab Spring-style grassroots mass citizen action to bring down dictatorships around the world. Plus, this awesome, globally-distributed computer power will be able to automate a lot of the drudgery of managing corporations, schools, hospitals, and factories.

With no need to wage war for resources, and most dictators removed from power by their own citizens, the need for such a vast and powerful military apparatus will be sharply reduced. The enormous resources the military currently consumes can be channeled toward such pursuits as environmental regeneration, research to cure diseases, and perhaps even a nonmilitary exploration of space. Terrorist groups will have far fewer reasons to attack us, as these policy changes shift us away from behaviors they see as oppressive (e.g., consuming far more than our share of resources, propping up vicious dictatorships, and sanctioning exploitative labor practices abroad).

The economy will undergo some major shifts. As some of society's largest entities shrink and retract, the abundance mentality will make sure these people are not unemployed. There will be a movement toward a shorter workweek; instead of 40 hours on the job (and up to 20 more hours commuting), most people might work 20 hours or so, and would be able to maintain or expand their standard of living at that level, because so much less of their paychecks would be spent on consumption of nonrenewable resources. However, excess compensation packages in the hundreds of millions would no longer be tolerated.

This reduced work week, in turn, could lead to a major flowering of arts, culture, science, recreation, volunteering at service agencies and schools, and lifelong learning

This world is possible in our own lifetimes, if we can bring the leverage of a motivated and informed population. If you doubt that this kind of sweeping change is possible, look at just a few of the accomplishments of just the last 60 years:

- Apartheid was ended in South Africa, Rhodesia/Zimbabwe, and the American South
- Peace came to some perpetual trouble spots, such as Northern Ireland
- Water and air in much of the world are far cleaner than they were, and pollution is now considered a crime instead of the right of whatever industrialist got there first; huge strides have been made to develop safe, clean, renewable technologies that will free us from dependence on carbon-fuels
- Most countries now have a medical system that treats health care as a fundamental right—and several deadly diseases have been largely wiped out
- Women, people of color, people with disabilities, and cultural or sexual minorities have been integrated into every level of many societies, and the world has benefited greatly from their contributions

MAKING IT HAPPEN

So…How do we get from where we are to the kind of world you came up with, or the kind that we described?

For starters, we need to recognize that a lot of the ideas and technologies in that vision are already here today. We just need to alter their distribution so they're accessible to all. Here's a quick and easy example: millions of computers are replaced every year, and most of them are in fine working order. A computer that's three years old may not be able to run the latest software, but the word-processing, spreadsheet, Internet, and other applications that it *can* run would make a huge difference in the lives of people who have no computer.

So instead of creating a solid waste disposal problem and adding it to the landfill, you could donate that computer to an inner-city minority youth program, or to a college in a developing country. Years later, when it has truly worn out, materials recycling programs can take it apart and use the raw materials to make new computers—but first, computer repair training programs could use it to provide hands-on experience.

A few more ideas that have essentially no cost or lifestyle consequences but significant environmental benefits—and give you bragging rights and points of differentiation from your competitors in your marketing (as so many early adaptors have done, and benefited from):

- Switch to low-power lightbulbs. LED lights now offer much higher light quality and much lower price than in the past, and are far more environmentally friendly and longer-lasting than even the compact fluorescent bulbs that have largely supplanted the old incandescents.
- Use smart power strips to completely stop the flow of electricity to office equipment and appliances when they're not being used (such as overnight).
- Turn off unneeded lights, especially when your place of business is closed.
- Change your water consumption habits when washing dishes or brushing teeth, so the water is only running when it's actually being used, and not freely running down the drain.
- For electrical outlets, switch plates, and phone jacks on exterior walls, amazing amounts of heat and air conditioning energy can be saved if you install foam outlet insulators behind them (about two minutes per outlet and requiring only a screwdriver) and insert baby outlet protectors into unused exterior-wall sockets (about five seconds per insertion, no tools needed)

You'll find many more equally easy tips in Shel's $9.95 ebook, "Painless Green: 110 Tips to Help the Environment, Lower Your Carbon Footprint, Cut Your Budget, and Improve Your Quality of Life-With No Negative Impact on

Your Lifestyle," http://www.painlessgreenbook.com (yours free as a reader of this book).

In every aspect of our lives, these changes are possible and practical.

A PLAN TO JUMPSTART THE RENEWABLE ECONOMY WORLDWIDE

You may have read about the Marshall Plan, which restarted the economy of Europe after World War II.

With the threat of catastrophic climate change hovering over our heads, and with the economy still in tatters in many parts of the world, we suggest a worldwide Marshall Plan-style initiative. Let's stave off climate catastrophe, create jobs, put significant discretionary spending money into the hands of citizens, and lower energy prices—all at no net cost to the taxpayers, property owners, and renters.

Strategies would include lowering the price of clean technology by increasing demand…making energy-saving technology accessible to low- and middle-income people (including renters), and using the money saved to spur sustainable economic development. The plan, which we'd love to see would be adopted by national, regional, and local governments around the world, would have these components:

1. Effective immediately, starting with any plans proposed and not yet approved, any government or government-funded construction would be required to generate at least as much energy as it consumes, through clean and renewable technologies such as solar, wind, small-scale hydro, magnetic, tidal, bacterial, deep conservation, etc., rather than fossil fuels, nuclear, or most types of biomass

   If a specific project requires a waiver, aim for 10 percent or less energy consumption compared with traditional nongreen buildings serving the same purpose.

2. As prices come down due to increased demand and economies of scale, locally administered government programs make financially self-supporting renewable and clean technologies available to people who can't afford them.

For example, governments and utilities can join forces to set up lease-back programs. The company that installs an alternative energy system maintains ownership, but leases the energy back to the homeowner or tenant. Or the government guarantees loans that enable homeowners to purchase the systems and automatically pay back the loans out of the energy savings.

3. The new government buildings save government agencies enormous amounts of money in utilities. Those savings are earmarked to retrofit existing government buildings.

4. As the private sector repays the loans or buys the leased energy, that money becomes available to retrofit nongovernment buildings.

Large-scale implementation would bring down the price of clean energy… make it affordable to every homeowner…reduce or eliminate dependence on foreign oil and uranium…reduce CO_2 buildup and thus global warming. When, planet-wide, we see our rooftops as energy and food resources, and have programs in place to make these systems affordable to those without capital, we can eliminate oil dependence and reduce carbon emissions/global warming.

By outfitting every government building and providing means for low-income people to solarize, we can:

- Bring prices way down and make clean renewable energy more affordable to middle-income homeowners
- Free up funds currently spent on fossil fuels for economic development
- Create tens of thousands of new short-term jobs
- Reduce dependence on foreign oil
- Reduce pressure to "solve" our energy shortage through environmentally disastrous initiatives like tar-sands oil, fracking, and nuclear
- Slow or perhaps even reverse catastrophic climate change

Because this program is essentially self-funding, and uses the workings of the free market to create affordable alternatives for the less wealthy, it should be politically easier to accomplish than other proposals—perhaps even in time to prevent climate catastrophe.

Meanwhile, the groundwork for this kind of international cooperation has already been laid. As one example, Put Solar On It <http://putsolaron.it/>, an international initiative to get world leaders to solarize their presidential palaces, could be a natural organizing platform to expand from residences of heads of state to all government buildings. India, Chile, and the Maldives are among those who have already started solarizing their presidential palaces, and the US has finally replaced the solar panels that were installed on the White House all the way back in 1979 (unfortunately removed by the subsequent president). Expanding to the hundreds of thousands of other government buildings is a logical next step.

Some people will ask *how* we can get off fossil fuels quickly. It turns out that there are many scenarios, including these two: Amory Lovins lays out a comprehensive strategy to get off oil and nuclear, in his book, *Winning the Oil Endgame*, and in this TED talk by the same name: <http://www.ted.com/talks/amory_lovins_on_winning_the_oil_endgame#t-511003>.[347] And Tesla founder Elon Musk shows how little land it would actually take to convert all fossil fuel use in the US to solar with battery backup in his product introduction video for the Tesla Powerwall and Powerpack: http://www.teslamotors.com/powerwall.[348] Within days of Musk's announcement, his findings were validated by Forbes magazine in an article called "Why Tesla Batteries Are Cheap Enough To Prevent New Power Plants,"[349]

Let's show some initiative and gumption, put aside our cultural differences, and get this done.

HOW TO INFLUENCE PUBLIC OFFICIALS ON ENVIRONMENTAL ISSUES

Of course, the government is not going to simply decide to do this, even though a huge majority of the public in most democracies favors a rapid conversion to

---

347 Verified 4/19/15.

348 Accessed 5/7/15.

349 Jeff McMahon, "Why Tesla Batteries Are Cheap Enough To Prevent New Power Plants," http://www.forbes.com/sites/jeffmcmahon/2015/05/05/why-tesla-batteries-are-cheap-enough-to-prevent-new-power-plants/, accessed 5/7/15.

a green economy. It takes a lot of effort to turn the ship of state. Yet, Gandhi (speaking from the personal experience of defeating the world's most powerful empire) reminds us that "When the people lead, the leaders will follow." [350]

In other words, governments respond to demand. That includes citizen pressure through everything from street demonstrations to lobbying to media coverage. But the way governments actually make change has a lot to do with the minutia of regulations and laws. To make impact there, we have to speak the government's language and address governing bodies on their terms—while reinforcing these actions with those types of outside activities that change the discourse. Here's a brief strategy primer on testifying before government bodies:

As both a marketing consultant and environmental activist, I (Shel) work to convince the public to change their positions—or their brands—and to take action based on my writing or speaking.

To do this, I use my powers of persuasion and a wide range of language aimed at moving different types of people forward toward a common agenda. My arguments will typically be a mix of emotion and intellect, of appeals to self-interest and appeals to the common good.

But I've learned over the years that when the goal is influencing public officials, the rules and strategies are different.

For one thing, when government officials take testimony on an issue, they typically have a very narrow scope. In fact, they're often not even allowed to consider anything outside their purview (this is one of the reasons why change involving action by government enforcement agencies or getting new laws passed can be frustratingly slow). So big, sweeping appeals along broad issues have little effect.

In 2012, I wanted to weigh in before a government body on one of those big-picture issues. I submitted testimony to a state government agency on whether it should issue a certain permit to a nuclear power plant. I wanted to address the much wider issue of nuclear power plant safety—but I had to do it within the narrow confines of what the board could address.

---

350 http://allaboutgandhi.com/170/2013/09/07/when-the-people-lead-the-leaders-will-follow-gandhi-3/, verified 4/19/15.

I think my testimony makes an instructive example of how to influence governments—so let me point out a few things about my testimony (which I've posted at http://shelhorowitz.com/go/nucleartestimony/):

Establish Credentials and Your Standing in the Matter— Why It's Your Right To Give Testimony

Right at the beginning, I note that I've written three relevant books—and this is especially important since I'm not a resident of the state where the plant is located. Credentials don't have to be formal, though. Yours might be "resident within the evacuation zone" or "parent of a special-needs child."

Focus on the Issue the Agency can Act On

The hearing was about whether the state should grant the nuclear plant a new Certificate of Public Good. So very early, I looked at what it means to provide public good—and then I referred back to this concept several times, including the last sentence.

Use an Objective-Sounding, Intelligent Tone

Not the time for screaming hype or unsubstantiated accusations.

Respect Their Knowledge And Intelligence

I didn't explain the Price-Anderson Act; I simply referenced it with an "as you know."

Provide a Framework for Addressing the Wider Issues

By US law, the federal Nuclear Regulatory Commission has jurisdiction over the safety of nuclear power plants. But the state of Vermont can take economic factors into account when evaluating whether the plant serves a public good—so I anchored all my safety arguments in their impact on the state's economy and overtly stated that this is why I was bringing up the safety issues.

Back Up Your Claims and Cite Sources

I cite three books, the plant's own accident report, one third-party scientific report, and two top-tier newspaper articles (from the New York Times and Washington Post).

Clearly State The Desired Action The Agency Should Take, Ideally Quite Early In Your Remarks

In this case, I want the Public Service Board to deny the Certificate of Pubic Good requested by the utility, and I say so very specifically in the second sentence: "Like the majority of people who have come before you to testify, I ask that you deny the Certificate of Public Good for Entergy for the continued operation of the Vermont Yankee nuclear power plant."

Use "Social Proof"—Demonstrate that Lots of People Agree With You

The first half of that same sentence is all about social proof; the second half tells them what I want them to do.

Be Organized Ahead of Time, be Conscious of Time Limits if Speaking in Person, and be Willing to Provide Your Full, Extended Testimony in Writing

I had an outline with me of points I could make within two minutes. It would not have been nearly as complete, but it would have hit the important points.

For Maximum Impact, Make Copies of Your Statement Available to the Media and to the Public

My statement is published on my website, and thus my potential audience is a lot bigger than the three members of the Public Service Board.

Another Strategy: The Personal Appeal

Of course, we have other ways to influence governments than testifying at hearings. Here's an example of a much more informal approach: a personal letter:

A neighboring city decided to spray some athletic fields with Roundup. In addition to concerns about the health effects on the children who'd be playing on those fields, the parcel happens to directly abut a commercial organic farm—one about to receive USDA organic certification, which means that it had been chemical-free for three years.

I sent a letter to the Mayor, selected members of the City Council, the Recreation Department, and the Chair of the Board of Public Works. I also copied a reporter at the local paper.

I'm going to share the relevant portions of that email with you, then discuss why I framed it as I did—because there are many lessons in advocacy here, not only in the public sphere, but in dealing with any stakeholders on sustainability issues:

> As a customer of Crimson & Clover Farm and many other organic farms in the area...a 26-1/2-year property owner in Northampton (through this past April), and an internationally recognized expert in the marketing of green products and services, I urge you in the strongest possible terms to BLOCK the proposed spraying of Roundup.
>
> You are no doubt aware of the growing importance of agritourism and ecotourism in Northampton and the Pioneer Valley—which includes at least two lodging establishments within the City that specifically cater to a green clientele (Starlight Lama and Trailside B&Bs). Much in that sector has to do with a creating and sustaining a culture of support for local organic foods that includes both farmers and consumers. I even use the Valley as an example in my speaking and writing on green business, nationally and internationally.
>
> Spraying Roundup—a pesticide whose long-term safety is highly questionable—could have severe deleterious effects on Crimson & Clover and Grow Food Northampton. Spraying could easily drift onto the wrong fields and/or contaminate nearby water, resulting in a loss of Crimson & Clover's organic certification, a loss of customers—I am one who would not knowingly buy from a farm tainted by Roundup—and *possible lawsuits* for interfering with the livelihood of another.
>
> And did you know that in addition to selling Roundup, Monsanto sells Roundup-tolerant GMO seeds, and then sues farmers whose fields

get contaminated with them for using the seeds without permission? I have a lot of trouble with their ethics. Roundup furthers Monsanto's actions to crush local and organic agriculture…

Meanwhile, I hope you will use your influence to prevent this potential can of worms from ever being opened—and I hope to greet the three of you at the rally at Crimson & Clover tomorrow afternoon.

Why This Approach?

Paragraph 1: Establishing my credentials.

I am affected by what affects this farm, because I am a customer. I owned a home in that town for a long period of time. And I happen to have validated expertise in the subject. But if you don't have textbook credentials, you can work with what you have. For instance, you could speak as a property owner, parent, and purchaser of organic foods.

Paragraph 2: Identifying organic agriculture as an important and growing sector in the local economy.

This is critical; organic agriculture is too often seen as marginal and trivial. I shown that tax-paying businesses are affected by the city's decision—and that the region has been a model for the rest of the country and even the world.

Paragraphs 3 and 4: Demonstrating the potential negative economic consequences to the affected business, and to the city.

All municipalities in my area are strapped for cash. This city even went through a very contentious vote to raise taxes just a few months earlier, to avoid severe layoffs across many departments. Avoiding adding to that burden with preventable lawsuits is an argument to make the government pay attention.

Paragraph 5: The wider context.

In my writing and speaking, I often talk about combining messages of self-interest and planetary interest. This is the planetary part. Monsanto's frequent legal challenges to farmers whose fields were contaminated by drift is a serious problem in the organic farming world.

Paragraph 6: Offering a positive step.

I conclude the letter with something these officials can do to show their solidarity and gain public support.

Results:

One City Councilor did attend the rally. And the Mayor announced a compromise plan that put a no-spray buffer around the edge. Without the buffer on city land, the organic farm would have had to sacrifice three acres for its own buffer in order to obtain that organic certification. While it wasn't the ideal outcome, it was much better than the original plan, and shows the power of organizing along economic interest.

TRANSITION TOWNS: BECAUSE WE CAN'T WAIT FOR GOVERNMENTS TO ACT

The last three sections have all been about making change via the government. But waiting for governments to act, even when they're not paralyzed by partisanship, can be painfully slow. It took 102 years after Abraham Lincoln signed the Emancipation Proclamation before Lyndon Johnson signed the Voting Rights Act. Most climate activists and scientists today think we have a far shorter window to get off fossil fuels and bring atmospheric carbon back down below 350 parts per million.

Fortunately, an informed, empowered citizenry can start changing things right now, and governments will eventually fall in line behind them. One of many promising initiatives is the Transition Towns movement, a world-wide phenomenon that began in Totness, United Kingdom. Ordinary citizens gather together, usually in small groups, and think about how, working together, they can move their own community toward resilience and away from fossil fuels and greenhouse gases—and build a community that could survive and thrive if those fossil fuels are suddenly unavailable or prohibitively expensive.

It's very much directed by the people who participate, so projects will vary widely from place to place. Perhaps a few people form a sewing circle to make cloth tote bags for local shoppers, or plant trees, or insulate houses, or work with local government to install traffic calming, or whatever—they do it. And it's nice and small and manageable, town by town, neighborhood by neighborhood, letting people get to know their neighbors as they shift their lifestyles.

The international Transition Town website offers a 50-page PDF on how to get a Transition Town initiative going in your own town.[351] And the US branch has a nicely developed and visually pleasing website full of resources.[352]

B CORP: A MOVEMENT AROUND BUSINESS SOCIAL RESPONSIBILITY

One of the most exciting developments in the business world is the Benefit Corporation, or B Corp, movement, similar to Terry Mollner's vision of Common Good Corporations.

B Corp is a legal structure of a profit-making corporation that's allowed to promote environmental and social responsibility even if it could reduce short-term shareholder value[353]—unlike most corporations, which are prohibited from reducing profit by law and their charters. Maryland became the first of 28 US states to pass B Corp enabling legislation, in 2010.[354] It's still a new movement. Only 1203 certified B Corps exist in the world, as of late January 2015.

But at press time, news had just broken that Unilever, one of the largest consumer products corporations in the world and owner of hundreds of brands, is actively considering going for B Corp certification.[355] That could be a game changer. Unilever's tacit endorsement of the B Corp movement confers legitimacy; if one of the largest and most successful business organizations in the world can embrace it, other companies will say, "perhaps we should look into this." Unilever's Ben & Jerry's unit was one of the first

---

351 http://www.transitionnetwork.org/resources/transition-primer, verified 2/21/15.
352 http://www.transitionus.org/, verified 2/21/15.
353 http://www.bcorporation.net/what-are-b-corps, accessed 1/28/15.
354 http://en.wikipedia.org/wiki/Benefit_corporation, accessed 1/28/15.
355 http://www.theguardian.com/sustainable-business/2015/jan/23/benefit-corporations-bcorps-business-social-responsibility, accessed 1/28/15.

B Corps, back in 2012[356]—and Ben & Jerry's CEO Jostein Solheim is leading the effort, apparently with strong support from Unilever's sustainability-minded CEO, Paul Polman.[357]

The B Corp movement is still not very well known, compared to similar movements such as Fair Trade. With Unilever coming onboard, a lot more people in the business world will hear about it—and take it seriously. Pursuing B Corp will provide Unilever with substantial marketing advantages during the multi-year certification process (for such a complex entity), and longer-term if its designation is accepted. If the company is able to harness them properly, it can expect to sway many now-neutral customers to Unilever's vast portfolio of brands.

Most importantly, it will show the entire business world that corporations don't have to be rapacious; they don't have to put short-term gain above the earth and its citizens (human and otherwise). It could even provide major leverage to overturn the body of corporation law that says traditional corporations are *legally required* to put short-term profit ahead of all other considerations. And since most business people actually do want to do good in the world and many have felt burdened by this charter, this could create a seismic shift throughout the entire business community.

Of course, there are a myriad of profit-making opportunities out there for activist companies willing to create and market goods and services that meaningfully reduce hunger, poverty, war, catastrophic climate change, and other suffering—you don't need to be a B Corp for that, as you'll see in the next chapter.

LESSONS

- Once we imagine and envision the world we want to create, we can take steps to get there
- When dealing with government agencies, we do better if we follow their format

---

356 http://www.fastcoexist.com/1680771/ben-and-jerry-s-becomes-a-b-corporation, accessed 1/28/15.

357 http://unilever.com/aboutus/companystructure/executivedirectors/paul-polman.aspx, accessed 1/28/15.

- Transition Towns create a way to organize community-wide to go greener
- B Corporations provide a legal structure that allows business to work for a higher good

ACTIONS

- Write a letter to a government regulator or elected official on an environmental or social justice issue, framing your arguments in keeping with their jurisdictional authority and their district's self-interest.
- Submit this not only to the official, but tweak it and submit it as a letter to the editor of your newspaper, and post it on your blog and on social media, to significantly increase your impact.
- Consider joining (or starting) a Transition Town initiative in your community
- Form a committee to examine whether your company is a good fit for B Corp certification

CHAPTER 20

EXPONENTIAL THINKING FROM THREE PRACTICAL VISIONARIES

I f you have trouble imagining a clean planet, listen to the wisdom from three of today's greatest practical visionaries: Amory Lovins, John Todd, and Janine Benyus.[358] As you read, think not only how such changes could impact your own business, but how this harmonizes so well with John Kremer's concept of biological marketing, which we discussed earlier. Once again, the earth can show us how to do amazing things with minimal resources.

---

358   Material on Lovins and Todd is taken primarily from Shel's notes on speeches to the E. F. Schumacher Society (later renamed The Schumacher Center For New Economics), http://www.centerforneweconomics.org/ at Amherst College, Amherst, Massachusetts, Oct. 27, 2001. You'll find longer versions, along with many other great articles, in the Sustainable Business section of *Down to Business* magazine http://www.frugalmarketing.com/dtb/dtb.shtml. The webzine contains hundreds of articles on smart marketing and entrepreneurship, as well.

AMORY LOVINS: REINVENTING HUMAN ENTERPRISE FOR SUSTAINABILITY

Amory Lovins is a sweeping visionary in the tradition of Leonardo da Vinci, Ben Franklin, and Buckminster Fuller—but his focus is on how humans can fit better into this Earth of ours. As you'll remember from Chapter 11, he lives in the Colorado Rockies, where it often goes well below zero Fahrenheit (-18ºC) on winter nights. Yet, his house has no furnace (or air conditioner, for that matter)— and it stays so warm inside that he actually grows bananas. He uses about $5 per month in electricity for his home needs (not counting his home office). Lovins built his luxurious 4000-square-foot home/office in 1983, to demonstrate that a truly energy-efficient house is no more expensive to build than the traditional energy hog—and far cheaper and healthier to run.

Whether your company is looking for a huge competitive advantage, a more responsible way to do business, or both, the Lovins approach may be the answer.

The payback for energy efficiency designs in Lovins's sprawling, superinsulated home was just 10 months. The sun provides 95 percent of the lighting and virtually all the heating and cooling, as part of an ecosystem of plants, water storage devices, and even the radiant heat of the workers in his office.

Noting that energy-efficiency improvements since 1975 are already meeting 40 percent of US power needs, Lovins claims that a well-designed office building can save 80–90 percent of a traditional office building's energy consumption.

With conventional building logic, you insulate only enough to pay back the savings in heating costs. But Lovins notes that if you insulate so well that you don't need a furnace or air conditioner, the payback is far greater.

If designers learn to think holistically and harness different pieces to create something far greater than the sum of its parts, "Big savings can cost less than small savings, because you also save their capital cost—which conventional engineering design calculations, oddly, don't count." Look for technologies that provide multiple benefits, rather than merely solving one problem. For instance, a single arch in Lovins's home serves 12 different structural, energy, and aesthetic functions. This mirrors nature, where many components have multiple functions. A mouth processes food, water, and air, communicates, and kisses. A hand can pull, push, hold, lift, manipulate, write, type, draw, paint, sculpt, fasten, unfasten, dress, undress, check the weather, provide sensory feedback, point, speak sign language... And we discussed 13 functions of a tree in Chapter 6.

Lovins consulted on a 1656-square-foot tract house with neither heat nor air conditioning in Davis, California, where temperatures can reach 113 degrees Fahrenheit. Replicated on a mass scale, construction cost would be $1800 cheaper than a comparable conventional house, and maintenance costs would drop $1600 per year. While it's easier to achieve these dramatic savings in new construction, even on a retrofit, the savings can self-fund these improvements.

Lovins' Rocky Mountain Institute was also one of several companies involved in the massive "deep energy retrofit" of the Empire State Building, discussed in Chapter 9. Built in 1931, when fossil fuel efficiency was not a consideration, the iconic skyscraper received remanufactured windows, new temperature controls, and a host of other improvements.

Just by switching a factory from long, narrow, pipes with turns to short, wide, straight ones, Lovins was able to cut energy costs for that process by 92 percent—and slash maintenance costs and operating noise, too.

Lovins has also looked long and hard at transportation. He and his associates have developed amazing car designs, under the service mark Hypercar.[SM]

Again, it's a whole-systems approach. By changing everything from the construction materials to power source to the aerodynamics to the possible uses of a parked car, Lovins's team designed an SUV that not only can hold a whole family (or two people and their kayaks), but weighs 52 percent less than a Lexus SUV, can go 55 miles per hour on the energy the Lexus uses just for air conditioning, achieves the equivalent of 99 miles per gallon (except that it runs on hydrogen fuel cells—330 miles on 7.5 pounds of hydrogen), offers greater safety than a heavy steel SUV (even if it hits one), is undamaged by a 6-mph collision, emits only water, and is so well made that its designers expect to offer a 200,000 mile warranty.

When parked, the Hypercar vehicle "could be designed to become a power plant on wheels"; plug it into the electrical grid and watch your meter spin backwards, eliminating any need for nuclear or coal plants.

Lovins says cars like this could be in production within five years, dominate the market within a decade, and essentially wipe out today's steel-bodied internal combustion-fired, polluting cars within 20 years. (Hypercar, Inc. spun off from Lovins's Rocky Mountain Institute as a separate business in 1999.)

But for Lovins, even this is not the true big picture. "We still have to look systemically at land use, alternative modes, virtual mobility, and transit; we need to drive less or run out of roads and space." Even a super-advanced car can still get stuck in traffic, after all.

Lovins has developed a few key principles over the years:

- Design whole systems for multiple benefits, rather than components for single benefits
- Redesign production to close all the loops in a system and eliminate both waste and toxicity
- Reward service providers and customers who do more and better, with less, for longer
- Reinvest the resulting profits in scarce natural and human capital

The regeneratvity model can have a huge impact not only in developed countries, but in areas of deep poverty, too.

Lovins described an effort by the Zero Emissions Research Initiative to grow houses out of bamboo, in a developing country with an acute housing shortage. The houses cost only about $1700 each, can be located where they're most needed, and can finance themselves by selling excess bamboo to carbon brokers for energy or other uses. And of course, if the bamboo is cut back (rather than cut down) to build the houses, the plant can regenerate and maintain an ongoing income stream.

Curitiba, Brazil, was a struggling city with deep-rooted problems. But when city planners began to look at its needs as a system, they were able to shape the agenda and pull the city out of crisis. Rather than building superhighways, they increased road capacity along several parallel routes; this was both much less costly and far less destructive to the neighborhoods. Then they provided density bonuses so that the arteries best suited to large traffic volumes could support more residents. Then they reinvented mass transit, with a bus system that moves people as efficiently as a subway, but at a fraction of the cost. The fully integrated approach to changing from a dying to a thriving city is told in Lovins' book, *Natural Capitalism*—and can be read online at <http://www.natcap.org/images/other/NCchapter14.pdf>.[359]

Using nature as a model and mentor, Lovins encourages companies to rethink their waste streams, too. In many cases, the waste of one system can become a nutrient for another process. Closing these loops is both cleaner and more efficient. (See the next section, on John Todd, for more on creative reuse).

One of the great things about the Lovins approach is that it relies on the private sector to do well by doing good. Companies that adapt to the systemic approach will be highly profitable key players in the new economy. "Early adopters will enjoy a *huge* competitive advantage," Lovins says.

JOHN TODD: "WASTE STREAMS" INTO "FISH FOOD"

In downtown Burlington and South Burlington, Vermont, you'll find a very unusual industrial park: a place where brewery wastes turn into a growing environment for mushrooms—and in the process create an enjoyable biopark, a green and vibrant ecosystem in the middle of the business district, where downtown workers can enjoy a unique natural setting.

Welcome to the Intervale, 700 acres of sustainable enterprises and ecofriendly public spaces.

This project is one of many lasting gifts to the earth—*and* to the business world—from John Todd. Todd defines ecological design as "the intelligence of nature applied to human needs": a new partnership between the ecological needs of the planet and the physical and commercial needs of human beings that can "reduce negative human impact by 90 percent."

Todd described a project on Cape Cod to save a pond that was receiving 30 million gallons of toxic landfill waste a year. His staff remineralized the pond by adding a rock floor and brought the dead bottom water up to get light with floating windmills. They installed *restorers*: solar and wind-powered biosystems that process the contaminated water through a series of cells, each with different

---

359 Verified 4/19/15.

ecologies—integrated networks of microorganisms, higher plants, snails, and fish. Each of these mini-ecosystems removes specific toxins from the water. Designed to work as a system, the restorers—nine cells in this case—digested 25 inches of sediment within two years—and the water is clean enough to drink now. "This pond was constipated; we uncorked it," says Todd.

In Maryland, Todd worked on a project to clean up waste from a large chicken-processing plant. The highly concentrated waste was being dumped into a lagoon that flowed directly into Chesapeake Bay. "We planted restorers with 28,000 different species of higher plants and animals. It grew very quickly. Each was designed to break down or sequester different compounds. We reduced the electrical power to convert the waste by 80 percent and cut capital costs in half." This kind of system is "very effective in agriculture, because it's cost-effective enough for farm use."

One of the underlying principles in this work is sharing resources among different pieces of the system and changing the paradigm about what's left over. Instead of disposing of a waste stream, Todd encourages people to think about how to use that material as an input. The goal is zero emissions: no waste generation at all. If wastes are considered as inputs, they can lead to new commercial enterprises—for instance, a mushroom farm. All of a sudden, the cost of waste disposal turns into capital for a new revenue stream.

This is how the natural world works, at least when undisturbed by human pollution. When these systems are integrated together, they not only eliminate waste, but also provide shared synergy, reduce costs, spread technical and legal expertise, and create both economic and environmental improvements—as occurred at the Intervale, where biowastes feed a commercial fish farm that also cleans the water, and the waste heat from a wood-fired power plant is recaptured to heat the complex. "I begin to see a model for college and urban food production. We can begin to think of strengthening our own food security in these troubled times. We're creating a new culture based on earth stewardship."

These concepts can also work easily in developing countries. Todd designed a water treatment sustainability project for a refugee camp, using a long transparent pipe to expand and contract gases. The range of temperatures and conditions is so great that it kills viruses.

Todd notes, "The biotech industry looks for magic bullets—single solutions to complex problems. Nature is a symphony"; it doesn't work that way.

JANINE BENYUS: MOTHER NATURE, CHIEF ENGINEER

Think about this: *Whatever engineering challenge we face, nature has probably already solved it.*

Imagine the fortunes awaiting companies that can roll out a construction material as strong and lightweight as spider silk…a desalination process as cheap and effective as the one that mangrove roots use…a water collection method as powerful as the one used by the Namib desert beetle. John Kremer talked about "biological marketing"—so why not biological engineering, also known as biomimicry? It's just as miraculous—and just like biological marketing, the results can be outsized. Nature has figured out Zero Waste, and figured out how to do pretty much anything that humans feel a need to do: housing, transportation, flood resistance…

These technologies have been around for thousands, maybe millions, of years, and they outperform what we humans have come up with.

Meet Janine Benyus, TED speaker and author of several books on biomimicry. When she walks you through Lavasa, India, where native vegetation has not grown for 400 years, and tells you that the area gets 27 feet of rainfall during the three-month monsoon season and basically nothing the rest of the year, you know that maintaining a thriving city here will be challenging.

Yet, immediately abutting this city, she finds proof that nature knows quite well how to handle this environment: a hilly wilderness area that, despite the alternating torrents and droughts, experiences zero erosion. As she walks us through this wilderness, she shows us adaptations like an anthill built with curves and swales, so that it doesn't get washed away in the flood. She walks us through a sacred grove there, cool and delightful even in the dry season, and lets us understand that our cities could be just as pleasurable to live in.[360]

360 "Cities that Function Like Forests," speech by Benyus to ESRI, January 30, 2014, accessed 2/8/15 at http://video.esri.com/watch/3158/cities-that-function-like-forests-biomimicry-maps-a-sustainable-future. Her work has clearly influenced the city's thinking; evidence can be seen in Lavasa's visionary "Smart City" plan, which incorporates a plethora of cutting-edge technologies to create an eco-city that will be attractive to western investment: http://indiasmartgrid.org/en/resource-center/Conference%20Presentations2/Lavasa%20A%20

She shows us a 1500-year-old live oak tree in Louisiana that has designed itself to withstand hurricanes, and points out that only four of New Orleans's hundreds of live oaks were killed in Hurricane Katrina.

And whether it's in India, Louisiana, China, or New York City, she captures metrics like carbon sequestration, energy and water use from those neighboring wilderness areas—things no one has bothered to measure in the past—and then cheerfully announces, "Because this is happening in the wild land next door, no one can say it's impossible. A city that does this, that's generous in its ecosystem services, is going to be great to live in." She describes ecosystems in terms like "generous" and "competent," and reminds us that the human species, at 200,000 years old, is still a baby, and we can learn much from our "elders" in the plant, animal, insect, fungal, and bacterial realms.

Her approach combines human-built infrastructure and nature-built ecostructure together to provide "ecological services" that contribute to meeting per-acre and per-block metrics, carried in part by the buildings and in part by the landscapes.

Species adapt and evolve over time, growing more able to influence their environment while being influenced by it in turn—and most of these adaptations are positive both for the organism and the ecosystem. Maladaptations create room for better-adapted species to move in. Species that fail to provide these ecological services are maladapting, and will be replaced by those that do contribute, she says. She remains optimistic that humans will learn to positively adapt, and be welcomed by other species.

A lot of her work is based on the idea that because each place is unique, the technologies we use should be matched to each place, as they are in nature. In nature, organisms ensure the survival of the species by protecting the survival of their habitat; they can't directly take care of offspring many generations in the future, but they can protect the place where those future generations will live.

How can biomimicry change our patterns of design and construction? Thousands of ways. Here are just a few projects Benyus and other biomimicry researchers are working on:

Smart%20City,%20Scot%20Wrighton,%20MYCity%20Technology%20Ltd.pdf, accessed 2/8/15.

- Concrete that sequesters CO_2 rather than emits more of it (Bank of America did a building this way, and the exhaust air was three times as clean as the intake air)[361]

- Altered wind patterns through urban rooftops, modeled after the reverse-hydraulics of an Indian forest[362]

- Artificial leaves that—just as real leaves do—convert sunlight to energy far more efficiently, and using far less expensive inputs, than today's solar panels[363]

- A robot hand with more agility and dexterity, because it was inspired by cockroaches' spring-like feet[364]

- Desalination systems that not only create drinking water from the sea at a fraction of the energy requirement, but can green the desert at the same time.[365]

- GeckSkin™, an ultra-powerful adhesive developed at the University of Massachusetts after studying the way gecko lizards climb walls[366]

- The Biomimetic Office Building, whose designers encourage starting not with reality, but with the ideal, and then seeing how close they can come to it. They "found inspiration from spookfish, stone plants and brittlestars for daylighting; bird skulls, cuttlebone, sea urchins and giant amazon water lilies for structure; termites, penguin feathers and polar bear fur for environmental control; and mimosa leaves, beetle wings and hornbeam leaves for solar shading."[367]

---

361 "Cities that Function Like Forests," op. cit.
362 Ibid.
363 Jaymi Heimbuch, "14 Best Inventions Using Biomimicry in 2011," http://www.treehugger.com/clean-technology/14-best-inventions-using-biomimicry-2011.html, accessed 2/8/15
364 Ibid.
365 Michael Pawlyn, "Using Nature's Genius in Architecture," TED talk available at http://www.ted.com/talks/michael_pawlyn_using_nature_s_genius_in_architecture?language=en, accessed 9/1/14.
366 https://geckskin.umass.edu/, accessed 2/8/15. Similar research has been conducted at Stanford (http://news.sciencemag.org/biology/2014/11/gecko-inspired-adhesives-allow-people-climb-walls) and elsewhere.
367 Cameron Jewell, "Michael Pawlyn on the promise of biomimicry for a better future," op. cit.

PROFIT BY THINKING LIKE LOVINS, TODD, AND BENYUS

It doesn't surprise us that Lovins, Todd, and Benyus focus a big portion of their social change work through the business community, not just the academic and government worlds. Their innovations are not in a vacuum, but designed quite consciously to make a profit. They've found ways to integrate profound social change into a traditional capitalist business—as have Barbara Waugh, John Kremer, Bob Burg, and countless others.

These models of sweeping social change within the business context can change the world. If their stories can inspire you to create a business whose ultimate purpose is a significant betterment of the world, then we've done a very good job with this book. I hope that many of you will write to us and tell us how you've put the ideas in this book—not just the last couple of chapters—into practice. Perhaps we'll be able to gather so many success stories that we can write a sequel all together, sharing your successes with the world.

Any kind of verifiably green enterprise—that holds up to thorough scrutiny and isn't just greenwashing—appeals to a much less price-sensitive, more caring market. In a 2014 study, 29 percent of the population was willing to pay up to 20 percent more to get a green product.[368] When you add innovations that remove the old ways of thinking and the old processes entirely, like building a house that doesn't need a furnace, purifying water by using nothing more than a pipe running through the desert, or reducing air resistance by adapting innovation from birds and whales, you combine higher prices and lower costs, and profits soar. The demand for truly planet-improving products is high; those who harness these sweeping efficiencies toward a greater social and environmental good can profit handsomely.

With the right kind of green initiatives, big savings are there for the taking. The Asian green business site eco-business.com estimated that switching to a circular economy where "waste" is recycled into something else could generate more than a trillion dollars in global materials savings by 2025.[369]

---

368 "The State of Sustainability in America Report: Trends & Opportunities," Natural Marketing Institute, 2014, p. 28. PDF of highlights: http://www.nmisolutions.com/opt/excerpts/1502/NMI-2015-State-of-Sustainability-in-America-Excerpts-1-19-2015.pdf, accessed 2/20/15.

369 Eco-Business.com, "The circular economy: How do we get there?," http://www.eco-business.com/opinion/circular-economy-how-get-there, accessed 3/11/15.

Here are a few more among thousands of examples of both profit-seeking and nonprofit ventures:

- The Kenguru, a tiny electric car, even smaller than a Smart or a Mini-Cooper, can transport a person in a wheelchair. Instead of needing a huge van with complex and energy-drinking lift systems, a hatchback and simple ramp allows the driver to roll into place through the back of the car.[370]

- Earthship, a community just outside Taos, New Mexico (and replicated elsewhere), has built a 70-family deep-eco-village using primarily recycled materials (including used tires). The community generates all of its own power and most of its own water (a scarce commodity in Taos, which gets a mere eight inches of rainfall in a typical year). Read Shel's blog post about touring this community, which he describes as looking like "a mating between the Taos Pueblo adobe of 1000 years ago and Starship Enterprise," at http://greenandprofitable.com/earthship-redefining-sustainable-housing/

- Wattsaver, marketed to hotels, turns off AC and lights when guests have left their room[371]

- The amazing book *Influencers* (see Resources) describes how a dreadful parasitic worm was pretty much eliminated just by changing the way water was gathered and stored in a remote African village.

- Mr. Ellie Pooh is an innovative venture that produces a toxin-free fine-art/gift paper line made of—are you sitting down?—75 percent elephant poop and 25 percent post-consumer recycled paper! The project accomplishes a number of interlinked objectives: lowering carbon output by reducing the need to produce virgin paper, preserving elephant habitat, and reducing the problem of elephant conflict with agriculture (which has caused the destruction of thousands of elephants).[372]

---

370 "Four Wheelin'," *Utne Reader*, November-December 2008, p. 17, verified 4/19/15.

371 http://wattsaver.com/english/wattsaver.php, accessed 4/21/15. Shel was informed of this via a Twitter post, incidentally.

372 Quoting from http://mrelliepooh.com/pages/our-paper as of April 19, 2015:
"According to 'The State of the Paper Industry (2007)' a report by the Environmental Paper Network, 50% of the world's forests have been cleared or burned, and 80% of what's left

- Science Daily reports on very promising technology that uses bacteria and solar power to capture carbon waste and turn it into plastics and other useful products, using green chemistry.[373]

LESSONS

- Like Amory Lovins, John Todd, Janine Benuyus, and other practical visionaries, we can develop the greenest *and* most profitable solutions by looking holistically
- Often, it takes no more resources to make big, sweeping, game-changing shifts than it does to make little ones
- Nature can show us affordable, practical technologies for solving tough problems while keeping energy and resources in balance

ACTIONS

- Think about how your company or some other entity might use three different byproducts that you now throw away
- Determine how much their disposal is costing you, and budget it instead toward their reuse or elimination
- Select one product or service you currently offer. Brainstorm for ten minutes on how it could be reengineered on biomimicry principles.

---

has been seriously degraded. If the United States cut office paper use by just 10% it would prevent the emission of 1.6 million tons of greenhouse gases—the equivalent of taking 280,000 cars off the road. http://www.greenpressinitiative.org/documents/StateOfPaperInd.pdf" [greenpressinitiative URL verified 4/19/15].

"Compared to using virgin wood, paper made with 100% recycled content uses 44% less energy, produces 38% less greenhouse gas emissions, 41% less particulate emissions, 50% less wastewater, 49% less solid waste and—of course—100% less wood."

373 http://www.sciencedaily.com/releases/2015/04/150416132638.htm

CHAPTER 21

PROFIT BY HELPING THE WORLD

eyond going green and marketing green—can business actually help create the regenerative, thriving future we previewed in Chapter 20? Could you create a profitable business whose core mission was creating a better world?

Good news: you can.

HOLISTIC, SYSTEMIC THINKING

Have you noticed a common thread running through the many "practical visionary" examples we've seen in these pages?

Whether it's closed-loop energy systems, biomimicry in industrial design, permaculture gardens, or even biological marketing, these people think holistically. They think in systems—even in ecosystems and microclimates. They look at the whole picture.

They have a clear sense of what resources are needed, and they compare the full impact of each system. They understand that if they count time from door to door rather than gate to gate, train travel is often just as fast as air for trips under 300 miles or so, once you factor in traveling an hour to your local airport, getting there two hours early, and then traveling another hour from the destination airport to the center of the city. (Sometimes, even a bicycle can be faster![374]) They analyze the entire nuclear fuel cycle to prove that nuclear has a very destructive carbon impact (among other serious problems).

That's why they're able to design elegantly simple multi-purpose systems, like the single arch performing 12 functions in Amory Lovins's house and the d.light lantern addressing poverty, environmental degradation, and personal safety all at once—or enormously complex ones, like John Todd's dozens of different restorers working together to clean up pollution.

ONE PRODUCT, MULTIPLE BENEFITS

Just like Lovins and d.light, you can achieve multiple purposes with a single item. The item could be a product, a component, a service, or maybe even an idea. Systems that incorporate this principle are generally much more sustainable, need fewer components, and are therefore also more economical.

Does that sound like a bunch of abstractions that's a bit too complicated to puzzle out? Two more examples might make the concept more real:

Purus Pavers: Old Soda Bottles Solve Water Runoff Problems

Green builders are discovering eco-friendly substitutes for the traditional asphalt paving area. Asphalt prevents water from seeping into the ground and diverts it—usually into sewers, but sometimes into places where it causes harmful erosion.

By contrast, a paving system that allows the water to drain back into the ground right there and yet insulates vehicles from the problems of parking or driving directly on the ground can maintain the water table, reduce concentrations of toxic contaminants, eliminate the erosion problem, and even allow for plantings that grow close to the ground—thus adding oxygen and reducing CO_2 emissions, which in turn help preserve the earth in the face of catastrophic climate change.

These pavers create a latticework of support above an open area, so the water can freely drain, right where the rain falls.

---

374 http://GreenAndProfitable.com/when-bicycles-are-faster-than-planes/

We've seen concrete pavers like this, and they're very cool. A company called Purus[375] took things up a notch, making the pavers out of recycled polyethylene from old soda bottles. This adds several more benefits: longer lasting landfills, avoiding toxic fumes from incineration of plastic (which should NEVER be burned), reuse of materials, among others.

Organic and Biodynamic Farming: Benefiting All Stakeholders

You're probably already familiar with organic farming. You may have even heard of its more tightly regulated cousins, Demeter Certified Biodynamic agriculture http://www.demeterbta.com/ and veganic http://www.goveganic.net/ (grown without any animal-based fertilizers), or of the growing permaculture movement, all of which go much further than mere organic certification.

You already know that organic foods not only eliminate harmful chemicals but also typically produce tastier foods. But you might not know that organic agriculture can sequester 7000 pounds of carbon per acre...that agriculture can raise a significant portion of our energy needs through oilseed crops like sunflowers (yes, we're aware there are issues in using cropland for energy)...that a good organic diet of grasses and flax can significantly reduce the (very troubling greenhouse gas) methane emissions from cow burps...and that a cow fed an organic diet will be far more profitable for farmers, because she is likely to live up to three times as long, have many more lactation cycles, and even yield 20 percent more beef.[376]

But we don't have to stop there! Consider the biodynamic Hawthorne Valley Farm, in Columbia County, New York. The farm uses synergistic marketing to attract people to a wide range of offerings—for instance, attracting kids to its summer camp through its yogurt packages reaching parents a thousand miles away—and regularly brings in 600 children and teens a year, many of whom are inner-city children with no previous exposure to nature. Martin Ping, Hawthorne Valley's Executive Director, describes what happens:

375 http://www.purus-plastics.de/en/ecorasterr/ecorasterr-s50.html, verified 4/22/15.
376 These statistics are taken from Shel's report on the 2011 Sustainable Foods Summit held in San Francisco, http://GreenAndProfitable.com/its-about-tradeoffs-part-1/

We find nine years old is the sweet spot for education. You pull out a carrot and they say, "whoa, food comes out of the ground!" You get them mucking out a stall, taking care of another sentient being–a chicken, a goat, a cow—for the first time in their lives. Kids are not standardized. They're individual and spiritual…They get a sense of the relationships, that it doesn't magically appear. There are 100 pounds of milk in 10 pounds of cheese. Kids get a lesson in economics, in food miles, in the relationships of the whole food system.

The farm was founded to counterbalance the domination of farming by large-scale agribusiness while at the same time, kids were more and more isolated from nature. The farm's mission:

Founding the seed of a living organization: agricultural, artistic, educational. The goal is to become full human beings…renewal of society and culture through education, agriculture, arts. It's a food shed, a watershed. We think of the whole farm as a living organism.[377]

And You?

These are just two of thousands of examples. How can you incorporate holistic, systemic thinking to create multiple benefits with one innovation? The next section will give you a big hint.

SIMPLE ELEGANCE

If your goal is to let astronauts write in deep space, you could spend millions of dollars researching, designing, and prototyping pens that will work without gravity—or you could simply hand out a box of pencils. Maybe they could even be special pencils that make a deeper, darker writing imprint and don't fade quickly (such pencils already exist).

Just as in the space program, in the world of complex environmental problems, the best solution is often surprisingly simple and very elegant. And we

---

377 Martin Ping, speech to the Slow Living Summit, Brattleboro, VT, June 6, 2014, as documented in Shel's June, 2014 newsletter, http://thecleanandgreenclub.com/the-clean-and-green-club-june-2014/.

as green business people need to find those solutions, bring them to consumers—
and market their benefits.

The massive consumer products company Procter & Gamble understands
this concept and has capitalized on it. Company engineers realized that one of
the biggest consumers of energy in households is heating water, and one of the
largest uses of hot water is laundry. You could attack that problem with complex
solutions such as heating the water with solar systems—or you could market a
detergent that works perfectly well in cold water.

P&G chose the latter course, and developed Tide Coldwater, as we saw in
Chapter 10.

Tide Coldwater's big lesson here is the simple and elegant solution. For the
average householder, it's going to be far easier to heat 30 percent less water than
to install a greener hot water system—and the savings start immediately, with
no big cash outlay to pay back first. For tenants who would never pony up a big
capital investment to improve a property they don't own, cold-water washing is
an extremely sensible choice.

Two of the practical visionaries we met earlier, John Todd and Amory Lovins,
are especially good at solving complex problems with simple elegance:.

Decades ago, Todd grasped the simple and elegant concept that the
waste from one production process could almost always be raw material for
another one. And you can create an ecosystem of several of these processes
layered together.

For Lovins, the three simple and elegant ideas are:

1. You can design for such deep conservation that you don't need to buy
   big expensive systems like furnaces and air conditioners—and the
   savings on these capital costs, along with the savings on energy, pay for
   the improvements.
2. Enormous amounts of energy are wasted in transmission losses. If you
   generate power where you need it, you need considerably less than if you
   transport it across great distances.
3. One design component can achieve multiple purposes, as we've
   already noted.

Here are a few more examples of simple elegance addressing other environmental issues:

- Pole-mounted solar collectors allow the ground underneath them to be used for agriculture
- Pedal-powered vehicles can transport surprisingly large quantities of people and goods
- Simple mesh nets keep birds from devouring our berry crops—no pesticides needed or wanted
- Algae-covered buildings generate ethanol more cleanly than corn, and without taking away cropland[378]

Simple innovations like these create huge market opportunities for pioneering green entrepreneurs. What simple innovation can create a big market for your company?

SQUARING AND CUBING THE PARETO PRINCIPLE

Here's one way to harness those big-picture holistic insights, courtesy of Perry Marshall, a well-known Internet marketer, in his book, *80/20 Sales and Marketing: The Definitive Guide to Working Less and Making More*: Remember the Pareto (80/20) Principle? Pareto tells us that 80 percent of results will come from 20 percent of the effort, or the customers, or the money.

And Marshall tells us that the *Pareto Principle is fractal*. In other words, after you identify the top 20 percent, you rinse and repeat. You take the top 20 percent of that 20 percent—the top 4 percent of your original sample—to get 16 times the results.[379] After you've run this up a few more iterations, you have a crystal of pure power. You can get things done that others only dream of. You can change the world, and you can achieve enormous personal success.

---

378 GreenBiz.com/SustainableBusiness/com, Algae industry moves beyond research to commercialization, http://www.greenbiz.com/article/algae-industry-moves-beyond-research-commercialization, accessed 4/6/15.

379 Perry Marshall, *80/20 Sales and Marketing: The Definitive Guide to Working Less and Making More*, Entrepreneur Press, 21013, p. 37.

LESSONS

- Thinking holistically typically yields better results than thinking piecemeal; it means counting *all costs and benefits*, even non-obvious ones as power transmission losses over distance
- Often, the solutions you want to monetize can be surprisingly simple and elegant, just like providing astronauts with pencils
- The Pareto (80-20) Principle can be magnified if you "rinse and repeat"

ACTIONS

- Think of a way to streamline and simplify one process in your business.
- Road test it, watching for unintended consequences.
- If it's working, roll it out.

CHAPTER 22

IMPOSSBLE IS A DARE: BUSINESS FOR A BETTER WORLD

"The desire to leave the world better than you find it is as basic a drive as needing to eat, needing a home, needing a purpose and a career... It's a biological need, just like food and sex and shelter. Many people shut that down because it feel too scary—but we don't feel whole unless we're somehow making the world better."

—Shel Horowitz

WE ALREADY KNOW HOW TO FIX THE WORLD

ell into the 21st century, isn't it time to finally say goodbye to the big crises that hold our whole society back? We should no longer have to put up with hunger, poverty, war, violence, and catastrophic climate change.

"But we've always suffered with these things. It's impossible to make them go away."

Well, guess what: we actually already know how to eliminate or greatly reduce most of the biggest problems the world faces. In fact, *we do hundreds of things every day that were considered "impossible" not all that long ago.*

When my (Shel's) house was built, in 1743, we assumed that humans couldn't travel faster than the fastest horse. Yet the International Space Station hurtles astronauts through space at 17,247 miles per hour. When I was born, in 1956, most people who even had one at all shared one phone, tethered by a wire to a wall, for a whole household—or sometimes several households. Most people had never even seen a computer, let alone owned one. Music came into our houses on big vinyl platters or over a scratchy, low-fidelity radio. Apartheid reigned over South Africa, Rhodesia, and the American South, while communist dictatorships ruled Eastern Europe. And life expectancy was decades less than it is today.

Those are just a very few of the thousands of shifts we've made, in just 60 years (a microsecond relative to human history, a nanosecond in the history of the earth).

In short, "impossible" is a mindset, a self-imposed limitation—and we can change it.

We've known this for years. Henry Ford said, "Whether you think you can do a thing or think you can't do a thing, you're right."

Muhammad Ali put it this way:

"Impossible is just a big word thrown around by small men who find it easier to live in the world they've been given than to explore the power they have to change it. Impossible is not a fact. It's an opinion. Impossible is not a declaration. It's a dare. Impossible is potential. Impossible is temporary. Impossible is nothing." [380]

This quote struck me so deeply that I built my entire TEDx talk around it: http://www.business-for-a-better-world.com/tedtalks/ Spend 15 inspirational minutes listening to it.

---

380 http://www.goodreads.com/quotes/121663-impossible-is-just-a-big-word-thrown-around-by-small, accessed 2/12/15.

After all, I have first-hand experience achieving several "impossible" things, including the Save the Mountain campaign you've already read about. While the "experts" were wringing their hands, we went out and got it done.

Let's restate a key insight: when you look deeply, a lot of the causes of hunger, poverty, war, violence, and catastrophic climate change turn out to be about resources: who uses how much, whether they're taken sustainably, how fairly they're distributed.[381] When we address resources systemically, we're able to transform hunger and poverty into sufficiency, war and violence into peace, and catastrophic climate change into planetary balance.

We actually know how to do this. Passive-energy construction expert David Bainbridge estimates that not only can we reduce the typical building's energy footprint by 90 percent on new construction, but we can even cut the footprint on existing buildings by 50 to 70 percent.[382] We knew how to build near-zero net-energy buildings at least as far back as 1983, when Amory Lovins built his house. We understand how to significantly increase crop yields without using chemicals and without compromising quality.

We know how to replace nearly all our fossil and nuclear fuels with the combination of clean, renewable energy and deep conservation, thus reversing the increase in greenhouse gases. We even know how to imitate nature's best engineers to achieve zero waste while developing stronger, lighter materials and incredible processes to do things like extract water out of fog.

On the peace side, we've developed all sorts of conflict resolution techniques that don't involve shooting each other. We also have wonderful ways to frame alternatives to violent conflict, such as Anthony Weston's concept of "delightism" as the opposite of terrorism: "The *opposite* of a terrorist might be someone who is an ever-present disruptive possibility like the threat of terror, except in the other direction." He envisions secret flashmob armies spreading joy in the world by stealth:

---

381 Tom Standage, in his book, *An Edible History of Humanity,* argues that we can trace most sweeping societal change to one resource in particular, food, over thousands of years. See Shel's review at http://thecleanandgreenclub.com/the-clean-and-green-club-april-2014/.

382 http://www.triplepundit.com/2012/11/resilient-design-buildings-be-designed-change/, accessed 2/15/15.

Roving bands of youth, maybe, who transform people's yards while they're out. Or paint magnificent murals on freeway underpasses or leave flowers on whole neighborhoods' doorsteps, or stage unplanned Shakespeare performances…vanishing away afterwards as quickly as they come. Anonymous companies or congregations that give away subway tokens, or food or art, "targeting" the weakest and must vulnerable.[383]

He takes the metaphor further, advocating that we preemptively spread peace—using South Africa's Truth and Reconciliation Commission as one possible model.

We also know the tremendous profitable business opportunities at the intersections of two or more of these problems. We saw this, for instance, with d.light, in Chapter 9. Let's take d.light's concept further and look at a way to power homes with solar for an initial cost of just $10—this is happening now, in Kenya. Users pay the remaining cost out of savings, and at $80, they own the unit free and clear.[384] This article appeared in the very conservative UK magazine, *The Economist*, back in 2012. The times, indeed, are a changing.

Now, slash energy needs by switching to equipment that can use solar-generated DC power directly, without converting it to AC. When we eliminate the substantial power loss of converting the energy, and tap the inherently greater efficiency of direct current, we can cut back dramatically on power. Even a super-efficient 15-inch LED AC TV consumes 15 watts, while a 50-inch plasma model chomps down 300 watts.[385] When you power a DC television with just 5.5 watts,[386] and obtain similar savings on other energy hogs, you need less generating capacity. It's the Amory Lovins principle all over again.

Using technology to address poverty isn't always about renewable energy, either. The Grameen Phone project has changed the way Bangladesh

383 Anthony Weston, *How to Re-Imagine the World: A Pocket Guide for Practical Visionaries*, New Society Publishers, 2007, p. 40.

384 "Starting from scratch," *The Economist*, May 3, 2012. Online at http://www.economist.com/blogs/babbage/2012/01/solar-energy, verified 2/16/15.

385 "Electricity usage of an LCD/LED Display or TV Screen," http://energyusecalculator.com/electricity_lcdleddisplay.htm, accessed 3/22/15.

386 Helene Smertnik, "DC Power for the Off-Grid Market," http://www.gsma.com/mobilefordevelopment/dc-power-for-the-off-grid-market, accessed 3/22/15.

communicates. A profit-making enterprise, the company took the country from one landline phone for every 500 residents in 1993—3/4 of them in the capital city—all the way to about one mobile phone for every three residents by 2005. Even cooler: Every 10 percent increase in cell phone penetration correlates with a .8 percent increase in the country's GDP. Within just 12 years, the company grew to 250,000 retailers, 22 million subscribers, and 50 million cell phones (many of them smart phones that bring computing power to these remote villages).[387]

The nonprofit venture One Laptop per Child is changing lives in places like Uruguay, Cambodia, and Afghanistan by providing kids with cheap, rugged, *Internet-connected* laptops.[388]

We could list hundreds of other examples—but we think you understand the idea.

WHAT KIND OF ROLE CAN GOVERNMENT PLAY?

So, if private enterprise is going to step up to these challenges, is there still a role for government?

Absolutely. Government policies had a lot to do with creating the problems we face. Tax and development laws have favored the non-renewable economy: oil depletion allowances, subsidized highways and airports (at the expense of rail and ship traffic), limited-liability subsidized insurance for nuclear plants…

And these policies, tax structures, and subsidies, have also allowed polluters to socialize the costs of polluting while privatizing the profit—an inequity that has to be addressed. Business must be held accountable for true costs, and not allowed to treat them as externalities that someone else has to pay for.

One way to start addressing this is a tax on pollution—a carbon tax. Several countries in Europe and Asia, at least one Canadian province, a nine-county area around San Francisco, and the city of Boulder, Colorado have instituted carbon taxes.[389] Perhaps the biggest success story is Sweden, which instituted its carbon tax back in 1991, only a year after Finland pioneered the tax—and provided

387 Talk by Iqbal Quadir at Boston Book Fair, October 24, 2009, as reported in Shel's blog post, "Negroponte/Quadir: How Laptops and Cell Phones Attack Systemic Poverty in Developing Countries," http://GreenAndProfitable.com/negropontequadir-how-laptops-and-cell-phones-attack-systemic-poverty-in-developing-countries/
388 Talk by Nicholas Negroponte, *Ibid.*
389 https://en.wikipedia.org/wiki/Carbon_tax, accessed 4/13/15.

help in switching to cleaner technologies, as well as other incentives like vehicle congestion fees in Stockholm. By 2006, Sweden had already cut carbon 9 percent compared to pre-carbon tax 1990, while growing its economy 44 percent.[390]

The President of the World Bank, Jim Yong Kim, called for an immediate end for all fossil fuels subsidies and implementation of carbon taxes in April, 2015.[391] Many environmentalists agree, including Randy Hayes, co-founder of Rainforest Alliance:

> A carbon tax is to penalize the polluter…the polluter pay principle. If you internalize those pollution externalities into the price of things, the cleanest processes become the cheapest. And when the cleanest is the cheapest, we can save the planet.[392]

Yet, governments around the world have helped us make tremendous progress. The United States federal government has been a major player at least as far back as the Supreme Court's Brown v. Board of Education of Topeka decision of 1954 outlawing segregation, and continuing through the Civil Rights Act and Voting Rights Act in the 1960s, the establishment of the Environmental Protection Agency and the passage of the Clean Air and Clean Water Acts in the 1970s. Many European and Asian governments have had a large role in the drastic reduction of domestic fossil fuel use. And as we saw in Chapter 19, the United Nations Millennium Development Goals have created major reductions in poverty.

True, national governments in many countries are so polarized as to become paralyzed. We can't rely on them to get the job done. But they can still come to our aid—and, much more easily, so can smaller entities like state and provincial,

---

390 Gwladys Fouché, "Sweden's carbon-tax solution to climate change puts it top of the green list," http://www.theguardian.com/environment/2008/apr/29/climatechange. carbonemissions, accessed 4/13/15.

391 Larry Elliott, "Scrap fossil fuel subsidies now and bring in carbon tax, says World Bank chief," http://www.theguardian.com/environment/2015/apr/13/fossil-fuel-subsidies-say-burn-more-carbon-world-bank-president, accessed 4/13/15.

392 Randy Hayes, interviewed by Harvey Wasserman on Solartopia Radio, April 7, 2015. Both the link to the podcast and an explanation of Hayes' "nine planetary principles" can be found at http://prn.fm/randy-hayes-9-planetary-boundaries-to-ensure-a-healthy-planet/, accessed 4/13/15.

county, and municipal governments. Of course, we as business owners in the green sector need to advocate for our needs at least as strongly as the lobbyists for fossil, nuclear, and polluting technologies.

Green Scissors: A Green/Red Coalition on Government Waste

Interestingly enough, we can make common cause with people with very different beliefs. A wonderful example in the US is the Green Scissors movement.[393] Left-wing environmentalists join with right-wing opponents of government waste to demand an end to wasteful government programs with an anti-environmental agenda. The unlikely coalition includes Friends of the Earth and Public Citizen—but also Taxpayers for Common Sense and the Heartland Institute, among others. Together, they've outlined nearly a trillion dollars in potential savings.

Where we've gotten stuck, in other words, in not in the technology. It's in finding the personal, social, and political will to implement all this great stuff.

But now for the good news: we don't have to wait around for governments to get it done. *We can motivate the private sector, the business community, by showing them how to make a profit.* We've tried for too long to motivate social change through guilt and shame. Let's try the profit motive instead.

No less an authority than Sir Richard Branson, billionaire founder of the multifaceted and always innovative Virgin empire and an expert both on entrepreneurship and on the environment, sees enormous opportunity in solving the climate crisis:[394]

> I have described the increasing levels of greenhouse gases in the atmosphere as one of the greatest threats to the ongoing prosperity and sustainability of life on the planet…The good news is that creating businesses that will power our growth, and reduce our carbon output while protecting resources is also the greatest wealth-generating opportunity of our generation.[395]

393 http://www.greenscissors.com/, accessed 2/20/15.
394 Among dozens of examples, see Branson's essay, "A sustainable future is the biggest prize of all," http://www.virgin.com/richard-branson/a-sustainable-future-is-the-biggest-prize-of-all, accessed 4/2/15.
395 "Climate Change—Good for Business" by John Friedman, http://www.sustainablebrands.com/news_and_views/articles/climate-change-good-business, verified 2/16/15.

Similar opportunities exist in solving the other major problems.

A NEW BILL OF RIGHTS FOR THE PLANET AND ITS INHABITANTS

Consider the following wish list a global Environmental and Social Change Business Bill of Rights; adoption would rapidly move us forward toward the kind of world described in Chapter 25:

We, the people of Planet Earth, hereby declare that every nation and the planet as a whole have certain inalienable rights, including Life, Sufficiency, Peace, and Planetary Balance. To these ends, we call upon the governments of the world, at all levels, to establish these rights through mandating the following policies:

Manufacturers shall take full responsibility for their products at all stages in the product lifespan, including manufacturing, distribution, use, collection, reuse, disassembly, recycling, and disposal. Retail and wholesale channels shall accept used products and convey them back through the supply chain to the manufacturers.

Passing off costs to others, as externalities, is not acceptable. Pollution, waste, destruction of others' property, etc. will be paid for by the entity that causes it.

All new construction or major renovation shall meet minimum standards of energy, water, and resource conservation, as well as fresh air circulation. Such standards shall be incorporated into local building codes, meeting or exceeding LEED silver[396] and stretch codes.[397]

All newly constructed or significantly renovated government buildings shall be Net Zero or Net Positive in energy and water use, producing at least as much energy and water as the building uses. Private developers shall receive incentives to meet this standard.

All subsidies for fossil (including but not limited to oil, petroleum-based diesel fuel, airplane fuel, natural gas, propane, and coal), nuclear,

---

396 http://www.usgbc.org/leed, accessed 2/14/15.
397 http://www.mass.gov/eea/docs/doer/green-communities/grant-program/stretch-code-qa-feb10-2011.pdf, accessed 2/14/15.

or other nonrenewable energy sources shall be phased out as soon as practical, to be completed within a maximum period of three years.

All subsidies that promote fossil-fuel-powered vehicles over cleaner alternatives, including subsidies to infrastructure exclusively or primarily for their use, shall be phased out as soon as practical, to be completed within a maximum period of ten years.

Average fleet vehicle mileage standards shall be increased to 70 MPG for passenger vehicles carrying up to six people, and to 40 MPG for trucks and buses within ten years. Non-fossil-fuel vehicles shall be designed to make a contribution to stationary power needs.

Add your name to this manifesto at http://business-for-a-better-world.com/bill-of-rights

CENTURIES OF WISDOM FROM OTHERS

The world we wish to create (and live in) is getting stronger and more possible all the time. For centuries, our smartest thinkers have been easing the door open inch by inch. Long before Amory Lovins, there was R. Buckminster ("Bucky") Fuller. Before Fuller, Thomas Edison said back in 1931,

> We are like tenant farmers chopping down the fence around our house for fuel when we should be using Nature's inexhaustible sources of energy— sun, wind and tide... I'd put my money on the sun and solar energy. What a source of power! I hope we don't have to wait until oil and coal run out before we tackle that.[398]

Two hundred years before Edison, Benjamin Franklin prevented millions of homes from burning to the ground by inventing the lightning rod, and conserved thousands of acres of forests by inventing the Franklin stove, which produced the same heat with far less wood than a fireplace.[399] Three hundred

---

398 In conversation with Henry Ford and Harvey Firestone (1931); as quoted in *Uncommon Friends : Life with Thomas Edison, Henry Ford, Harvey Firestone, Alexis Carrel & Charles Lindbergh* (1987) by James Newton, p. 31. Accessed at http://en.wikiquote.org/wiki/Thomas_Edison, 5/3/15.

399 "Benjamin Franklin's Inventions, Discoveries, and Improvements," http://www.ushistory.org/franklin/info/inventions.htm, accessed 5/3/15.

years before Franklin, Leonardo Da Vinci experimented with biomimicry as he tried to design a human-powered airplane.[400]

On the peace side, Martin Luther King, Jr. was heavily influenced by Gandhi...who was directly influenced by Tolstoy (they corresponded)...who was influenced by Jesus...who was familiar with the story of Abraham bargaining with God to spare Sodom and Gomorrah[401]—a tradition of nonviolence going back at least 2500 years.[402]

These ideas of solving hunger, poverty, war, and the environmental crisis have been bubbling up from hundreds of springs. Some of these springs become great gushing rivers of nonviolent political and social change: the struggle for Indian independence from Britain, the Civil Rights movement, the campaign to create a free South Africa, the massive movements for peace in Vietnam and Iraq, the Arab Spring...

In our own time, one thing that's different is that many of these voices are coming from the business community. As you've seen in these pages, thousands of entrepreneurs and big companies have found ways to make a real difference. Harnessing that perhaps-unstoppable force may be the ingredient that's been missing for so long, and may be the secret to finally achieving these very big, audacious goals. This may be the first time in history that such a large percentage of businesses have chosen deliberately to leverage their standing as forces for social change.

We invited a few entrepreneurs to share their social change work with you, in their own words. Please spend a few minutes with our Practical Visionary friends Cynthia Kersey (author of *Unstoppable!* and *Unstoppable Women*, Frances Moore Lappé (author of many books on food and democracy, including *Diet for a Small Planet*), Ken McArthur (author of *The Impact Factor*), and Yanik Silver (author of *Evolved Enterprise*).

---

400 "Leonardo Da Vinci Inventions: Flying Machine," http://www.da-vinci-inventions.com/ flying-machine.aspx, accessed 5/3/15.

401 Genesis 18:20-32, available in a modern translation at https://www.biblegateway.com/ passage/?search=Genesis%2018&version=NIV, accessed 5/3/15.

402 Wikipedia dates the writing of the Book of Genesis to the 5th or 6th century BCE: https:// en.wikipedia.org/wiki/Book_of_Genesis; the stories, of course could actually be much older; if we follow the timeline laid out in Genesis itself, Abraham would have had this argument with God about 4083 years ago: http://biblehub.com/timeline/old.htm

THE GIFT OF GIVING: WHY I HAVE BEEN CALLED TO SERVE: THE STORY OF AN UNSTOPPABLE WOMAN!
By Cynthia Kersey

Who knew that when my husband of 20 years and I separated in December 1999, 21 months after my first book, *Unstoppable*, was published, my pain would open the door to my greatest purpose?

We had planned on spending the holidays with my parents in Florida. Now my son and I were going alone. I felt devastated and overwhelmed, but somehow in the midst of my pain, I made a promise to myself that the next Christmas would not find me at my parents' house feeling sorry for myself. I would instead dedicate myself to doing something for someone else.

As soon as I got home, I called my mentor and friend Millard Fuller, the founder of Habitat for Humanity International. I'd met him when I interviewed him for *Unstoppable*. He said "Cynthia, when you have a great pain in your life, you need a greater purpose." He told me about his recent visit to Nepal, one of the poorest nations in the world, and suggested that building a house for a Nepalese family in need could be a great project for me.

As I sat with his suggestion, I asked myself, 'how many houses would I need to build that would be bigger than this pain in my life.' When I finally got to 100, that felt bigger than my pain. Although I'd never been to Nepal and had no idea how to pull something like this off, I felt invigorated by that greater purpose and grateful to have something to take my mind off of my problems. Throughout the year when I was grieving the loss of my marriage, there were times when I felt so depressed that I didn't even want to get out of bed. At that moment, I'd think about these families who didn't even have a decent place to sleep at night. And I moved forward.

By December 2000, a year after my separation and subsequent phone call to Millard, I had raised $200,000. I brought a team of 18 people to Nepal and we built the first three of the 100 houses that would get built over the following year. I'll never forget the connection I formed with Chandra, a single woman who was supporting seven other family members including her parents, brothers and sisters. They all lived together in a tiny one-bedroom shack.

Although Chandra diligently saved money each week for 18 years from her job at a biscuit factory to buy the land for her potential home, she never would have been able to save enough to get the home built without the help of our project. Even though we didn't speak the same language, our connection ran deep. When it was time for me to leave, both of us in tears, she begged me to never forget her. As we hugged I thought "Forget you? How could I ever forget you? You were the purpose that got me through the most difficult year of my life!"

Not only did I get through that painful year, but I had been forever changed. I experienced for the first time the transformational power of giving. And that year, I earned more money than I had earned in a very successful corporate sales career. My success in my new career was skyrocketing without my even focusing on that! I was starting to understand the spiritual axiom, "Give, and it shall be given unto you." Not "Give when you have money in the bank," or "Give when you have some extra to spare." Just "Give."

Over the next few years I continued to engage in all sorts of philanthropic projects while running my business.

Fast-forward a few years to the fall of 2006. I had just written my second book, "Unstoppable Women," and I was looking for my next philanthropic project. Out of the blue, I received an invitation that would change the trajectory of my life forever. An invitation I said "yes" to right away, even though I didn't know why at that point.

They were looking for solutions to fundamental problems -- things we never have to think about and take for granted in the United States, like how to get access to clean water for their family. How to feed their children in times of persistent drought.

And the number one question, their greatest concern and their greatest hope, was how to get their children an education. Because without it, nothing would change and their children would have little hope to do more than to eke out a meager existence for themselves and their families.

I couldn't imagine what it would be like if my child would never learn how to read or write his name, count money, or have no hope of an inspiring future.

Suddenly, I became clear about the reason I'd been drawn halfway around the world, and a purpose birthed within me that I could not ignore. I knew I had to help.

There was just one problem. I had no idea what to do.

I started with research. The more I learned about the power of education, the more determined I became. Education has a larger impact on the eradication of poverty than any other form of help we can give. Education changes everything!!!

At the same time, I was shocked by number of children around the world who were denied access to the basic human right of even a primary education. That's where I decided I would focus.

So, fast-forward two years later and my birthday seemed like a perfect opportunity to start. We raised enough money at my party to help build two schools in Uganda. It was hugely inspiring to know that we were changing the lives of every child who would attend those schools for generations to come.

But that night also changed my life.

I initially thought I was doing something great for these children, but I realized that supporting them was doing something great for me, and for everyone who attended.

That unusual BD party was the greatest gift of my life… and an even greater purpose emerged within me to do a whole lot more.

So I began asking people to join me in this vision to ensure every child received an education. And what I discovered is that people really care about others…whether they're in their own communities or half way around the world.

And so they gave. They had fundraisers. Their children had fundraisers. They asked their friends and community to write checks. They gave up their birthday parties.

And the results have been amazing. Together, in just a few short years, we've helped over 8,000 children in 3 countries in Africa to receive an education every day through a proven model called Sponsor A Village. With this model, we work with established partners on the ground who work side by side: men, women and children who are committed to freeing themselves from poverty.

Partnering with these communities, we have built schools AND provided access to clean water and sanitation, food and nutrition, healthcare, and income and empowerment training for parents to over 30,000 community members.

The result…thriving communities with the tools to help them stop the cycle of poverty in their villages.

We have accomplished so much in just 7 short years, but the truth is…we are ready to take it to a whole new level with the numbers of children and their families that we're impacting.

And we have to!

But there are still thousands of children and their families waiting for an education.

It costs only $1 a day to educate a child through our Sponsor a Village model for one year. Every $25,000 raised supports approximately 70 children and 350 family members with the 5 pillars of sustainability.

We have promised the children and elders that *as long as they work hard* and lead this effort to raise their community out of poverty, we *will not leave them*, until *every child* and *every community in their entire region* receives access to these life-saving services.

We will not stop. We are unstoppable!

The best-selling author of Unstoppable *and* Unstoppable Women, *Founder & CEO of the Unstoppable Foundation,* **Cynthia Kersey** *funds the education of over 7,000 children every day. Cynthia's passion is showing how simple individual actions can solve the world's most seemingly impossible challenges. http://www. UnstoppableFoundation.org*

HUNGER AND DEMOCRACY…HUH?
By Frances Moore Lappé

Many ask me, "What does hunger have to do with democracy?"

Just about everything, I believe. Yet, rarely do we hear the two words in the same sentence.

To grasp the connection, I start with two simple observations: 1) enough food exists for everyone on Earth to eat well; 2) no one chooses hunger.

Thus the very existence of hunger belies the heart of democracy. In a democracy everyone has a voice. And, more specifically, democracy carries within its heritage a commitment that citizens' voices will be heard by the body politic. Today, living in the United States under what I call "privately held government" without the right to be heard, citizen voices are virtually drowned out by "megaphones of great wealth" that dominate popular media, especially during election season. Thus, those speaking in at a normal volume cannot be heard.

Philosopher Henry Shue argues that freedom to secure essentials of life—a healthy diet, for example—is the most basic freedom of all. For without it, he argues, one cannot enjoy any other freedom supposedly guaranteed by the state.

The existence of hunger in any society, especially on the scale we see today, is proof that the essence of human freedom—democracy's core value—is being denied.

From this understanding of the root cause of hunger, it becomes clear that ending hunger is possible *if, and only if,* we create polities in which…

1. Private wealth is barred from control of the electoral process.
2. Citizens have multiple channels to be heard, by ballot box and beyond. This means understanding the Internet and the TV airways to be a public good, not mere commodities to be exploited for economic gain.
3. Democratic values of transparency and mutual accountability are extended into economic life, understanding that enterprise and commerce serve social functions—not the other way around. In this way, the phrase "free market" must be understood as the freedom of all to access not only social freedom, but economic freedom from the struggles of poverty and hunger.

With these three shifts, all of us become free to choose *not* to go hungry.

Even in some countries that are far from having these conditions in place, however, considerable progress is being made as citizens step up to make nutritious food a human right. Roughly 25 years ago, citizens of Brazil began organizing toward this end. In 2010, the right to food became part of the country's constitution. Since 1990, in Brazil the number of hungry (defined by calorie deficiency) has been cut in half.

Where the three conditions assuring a real voice for citizens are more nearly met—including, for example, Scandanavia, the Netherlands, and Germany—measures of hunger such as infant death are typically about half that of the United States, which ranks far below them on electoral integrity.

Democracy capable of ending hunger is what I love to call Living Democracy, meeting our physical needs—certainly—but also the deep human needs for meaning, connection, and power.

Frances Moore Lappé *has written 14 books, including the three-million-copy bestseller* Diet for a Small Planet. *The co-founder of two national organizations focused on food and democracy, she is only the fourth American to receive the Right Livelihood Award. Her most recent book is* World Hunger: 10 Myths. *http:// smallplanet.org*

UNTIL YOU TAKE ACTION, YOU HAVE NO IMPACT—DO THE MATH
By Ken McArthur

"How much impact do I really have?" and "What do I do about it?" I'm trying to answer those two questions with the Impact Factor Movie Project.

You make a difference, whether you want to or not. If you don't do something, thousands will be impacted by your inaction.

You have a choice, and it's bigger than any choice you've imagined. You can choose to leverage art, science and technology in the ways that the most powerful people in the world have used it to impact millions.

How can one person make a difference in a noisy world? Here's the answer: "The Impact Factor."

Ideas change the world, but just thinking about something is not enough. Our small actions create an overwhelming flood of impact. These small actions move us beyond what we can imagine into measureable results that meaningfully address huge problems and even bigger opportunities to alleviate hunger and poverty, prevent wars—and yes, even mitigate the effects of nature upon us and our effects on our environment by not measuring what harm we cause.

Yes, we can profit and grow along the way.

When you take the time to measure your impact, you'll live your life differently and run your business differently. That's just a fact.

It's an exciting and challenging world we live in. We have art, science and technology beyond anything imagined a century ago. Those resources allow us to impact exponentially more people in a "power law curve" effect I call "The Impact Factor."

It's not the "Butterfly Effect." And this is not a "feel good" idea—because if you don't take action, thousands will be impacted by your inaction. The Impact Factor is the exponential result of all of the choices you make.

It's math, just like the balance in your checking account is math. But, instead of addition and subtraction, it's the direct results of your actions raised to the power of the leverage you create.

Your personal and business leverage is the exponential impact created by how quickly you start, the value you bring, how many people you connect with, the clarity of your message, how rapidly and effectively they spread your message and how concentrated that leverage is in time.

On one level there is no choice. You DO have an impact, whether you want to or not.

The reason you don't realize how much impact you have is because you don't measure it.

You know how much money is in your checking account. Why not keep track of your Impact Account?

Start with a simple Impact Journal. Ask the people around you and the customers and clients you attract what kind of impact you've had on them and write it down each day as you impact thousands more. Put it into numbers and you will be amazed at how many people you're impacting right now.

The Impact Factor is a call to action.

Why?

Because if you don't take action thousands will be impacted by your inaction. Because if that impact isn't positive, the potential negative impact is enormous. For more people to feel good and do good, we need positive impact created by the countless small actions we can take right now and leveraged by what we know about art, science and technology.

The time to start is right now.

Ken McArthur, best-selling author and producer of "The Impact Factor" movie, was selected by Fast Company as one of the 20 Most Influential People Online. He can be reached directly via e-mail at ken@kenmcarthur.com

BUSINESSES WITH SOUL: 11 EVOLVED ENTERPRISE™ IMPACT BUSINESS MODELS
By Yanik Silver

Imagine a whole new way for your venture to align purpose and profits, merging head and heart (and maybe even your inner child).

This counterintuitive blueprint creates a *'baked-in'* impact across your entire company: delivering an exceptional customer experience, creating a culture of fully engaged team alignment and driving your bottom line!

It's a transformative moment…

What worked before is no longer an option. Maverick entrepreneurs, visionary creators, change makers and impactful leaders must rewrite business rules for the 21st century as Evolved Enterprises™.

By law, a corporation is its own entity. If it has a 'body,' can't it also have a soul?

Enhance your bottom line with a bigger, distinctive, mission. These 11 models create that bigger purpose—consider combining several.

Model #1: Buy One Give One (B1G1)
For every item purchased, the company gives one away.

- **TOMS Shoes**, a $300 million operation, popularized its trademarked "one for one" model—and partners with larger companies that want the "halo effect." TOMS' eyewear funds surgery, glasses, or medical treatment—and every bag of coffee from TOMS Roasting provides one week of clean water to a person in need.

- **Warby Parker** has sold more than 1,000,000 pairs of glasses, direct-to-consumer online.
- **One World Futbol** has distributed 1.5 million balls (with help from corporate partner Chevrolet).
- **Happy Blankie project** (Everythinghappy.com) donates blankies to children in orphanages and hospitals in Africa, Thailand, China, and Haiti—and US hospitals and Ronald McDonald houses—with the slogan, "one to love and one to give"*—re-framing B1G1 with a bigger benefit.
- **B1G1.com** is a membership community connecting companies to 900+ giving opportunities. The site has tracked 51,320,157 small business donations.

Model #2: Direct Impact

Authentic, understandable direct donations. If customers and fans "grok" the relevance, they'll spread your marketing message.

- Every **FEED** (feedprojects.com) slogan-imprinted bag feeds one child for a year (84 million meals globally, so far).
- **BioTrust** sells supplements and meal replacements—and feeds a hungry child with every order. This increased sales 15 percent, and fed 659,000 children.

Model #3: Percentage or Dollar Amount

Donate a percentage or dollar amount. Give more—make more.

- **Brett Fogle** split tested his sales page with and without a donation certificate. The certificate raised conversion 10 percent on a $2,000 product, generating thousands in sales—and a $40,000 charity check.
- **Sevenly** (Sevenly.org), donates $7 per purchase toward the week's featured cause—and has donated over $3,000,000 in 2.5 years.

80 percent of new buyers come through social media—so instead of spending on marketing, Sevenly plows more money into social good.

Model #4a: Donate What You Want
Give consumers the power to donate what they want.

- **Humble Bundle:** Humble Bundles are limited-time (i.e., two weeks) packages of software or games. Several bundles generated $1million+ in revenue. By, 2013, over $50 million in sales and $20 million in donations.
- Community Cafes have no fixed prices for their menus. oneworldeverybodyeats.org/other-community-cafes

Model #4b: Donate Where You Want
The impact changes based on the product chosen.

- **Project7** lets consumers support seven charities, depending on their gum or mint flavor.
- Each of **Marie Forleo**'s for-profit training product supports a different nonprofit initiative (marieforleo.com/giving-back/).
- **1 Face Watch company** (1face.com) sells brightly colored watches, each with a different direct impact. Five yellow watches fund a year's education through Pencils of Promise. One white watch feeds ten people through Faces of Change.

Model #5: 'All In'
Give away all profits (after salaries/expenses) to charity.

- **Newman's Own** had given over $400 million by 2015.
- **Greyston Bakery** donates all profit to low-income housing, community day care, a medical center for AIDS patients, etc.

Model #6: Source Matters

Many clothing and food companies disclose the full impact of their supply chain.

- **Patagonia** switched from conventional to organic cotton in 1996—and co-created the Sustainable Apparel Coalition, influencing companies like Walmart and Levi.
- **Icebreaker**, lets you trace back your clothing to the source…the sheep
- **Elvis and Kresse** turns abandoned fire hoses into bags, wallets, belts, etc., donating 50 percent of profits to a firefighting charity.
- Artisan tea company **Teakoe** (teakoe.com/pages/sustainability) uses compostable packaging—and examines manufacturing, recycling, waste byproducts, low-emission delivery vehicles and responsible business practices.

Model #7: Experience the Good

Add celebrity firepower to charity auctions.

- **Charity Buzz**, an online auction marketplace for unique experiences, gives 80 percent to charity, raising $100 million+ since 2005.
- **Omaze** offers sweepstakes with prizes like riding in a real tank with Arnold Schwarzenegger. A recent experience with comedian Seth Rogan offered entries from $10 (personal video message) to $25,000 (guaranteed sit-down lunch with Seth).

Model #8: Empowered Employment

Companies directly hire marginalized workers—and increase consumer value; workers employed despite disability or personal history are deeply committed.

- **Samasource** (samasource.org) addresses poverty and builds skills through its Microwork™ model–breaking complex data projects into small tasks.

- Actress and singer/songwriter, Caitlin Crosby, founder of **The Giving Keys**, sells necklaces of old keys engraved with a word: 'hope,' 'strength,' 'believe.' She asks people to give their necklace to someone who needs that message—creating stories and shared connections. She employs those who are looking to transition out of homelessness and partners with **Mirakle Couriers** in India to use deaf drivers.

- Similarly, **Signs Restaurant** in Canada (signsrestaurant.ca) hires deaf servers. To facilitate dialogue, menus come with ASL cheat sheets!

- **ULTRA Testing** (ultratesting.us) sees "disability" as a competitive advantage, employing onshore teams of individuals with Autism Spectrum Disorders for software testing.

- For nearly 30 years, nonprofit **Homeboy Industries** has served high-risk, formerly gang-involved men and women. It operates seven job-training social enterprises spanning printing, groceries, baked goods, diners and apparel.

- With revenues topping $24 million, **Delancey Street** (Delanceystreetfoundation.org) operates food/hospitality, handcrafted furniture manufacturing, ironworks, car services, printing, landscaping and moving businesses. The typical resident has been a hard-core substance abuser, been in prison, is unskilled, functionally illiterate, and has a personal history of violence and generations of poverty. Residents stay two to four years—drug, alcohol and crime-free—earn GEDs, and learn marketable skills.

- **Opportunity Village** (opportunityvillage.org) is driven by individuals with cognitive disabilities. They provide skill training and run their own business units: package inserts, shredding, document imaging, button creation, wholesale baking... Participants even sell their artwork and keep 50 percent of the profits.

Model #9: Co-Development

Connect directly with producers to enhance experience (and impact) for everyone involved.

- **Good Eggs** enables online orders directly from farmers/manufacturers. Producers know exactly how much to make—reducing waste and spoilage.
- Fair trade fashion jeweler **Aid Through Trade** employs over 75 women artisans in Nepal, connecting them to consumers in the West and paying additional benefits such as retirement and healthcare.
- **I-DEV International** helped Peruvian farmers build new global food, pharmaceutical, leather, and pet-food applications from tara, a native fruit tree; 200 Peruvian farmers organized a co-op generating nearly $7 million in revenue.
- **Equal World TV** (Equalworld.com/) is the first-ever profit-with-purpose TV shopping channel exclusively marketing global social enterprises.

Model #10: Ethical Opportunity

Having reps distribute your products—door-to-door, through house parties, and via other channels—creates a new breed of Evolved Enterprises™.

- **Living Goods** modifies Avon's model to lower costs, increase profits, and improve rural reach for social enterprises. Over 1,000 agents in Uganda and Kenya franchise received microloans, initial inventory, and business tools. .
- **VisionSpring** leverages direct agents to target four billion consumers at the Bottom of the Pyramid (BoP) with $3,000 maximum annual income. VisionSpring's mutually supporting hubs and spokes—optical shops and sales agents—conduct vision screenings and educate about eye care and vision correction. High-end sales subsidize basic eyewear for BoP customers.
- **Soul Purpose** recruits women of from underserved communities and ethnicities to direct-market natural beauty and wellness products"

Model #11: Ecosystem

An **ecosystem** is a mutually dependent community of living (plants, animals microbes) and nonliving (air, water minerals, soil) components, interacting as a system.

Natural ecosystems include reefs, rain forests, organic farms—and the planet. Man-made ecosystems include communities, cities and networks.

- **Zingerman's**, a deli, chose to grow not by opening new locations, but building an integrated ecosystem of related businesses—from a bakeshop to a mail order facility to a training and seminar company, sharing the Zingerman's name and administrative functions (IT, HR, PR, marketing, payroll)—and buying from/selling to each other.
- Nonprofit **Planeterra** is funded by a for-profit travel adventure company G Adventures; the local community works with both. Combining these three sides of the triangle creates a sustainable advantage *and* delivers a deeper travel experience. In Bolivia, they got locals who'd been fighting each other for generations to build an ecolodge for the travel company's tours.

Each of these models showcases how business can become a huge lever for good—while aligning purpose and profits, merging head and heart.

Yanik Silver redefines how business is played in the 21st century at the intersection of more profits, more fun and more impact. He is the founder of Maverick1000, a private, invitation-only global network of the top entrepreneurs and industry transformers that's raised $2 million+ for cause partners.

This excerpt is condensed from his new book Evolved Enterprise™: http:// yaniksilver.com/evolvedenterprise/

In 2016, we should no longer put up with a world full of misery. Isn't it time to reward businesses that are working meaningfully to end hunger, poverty, war, and climate catastrophe while penalizing those that are stuck in the rapacious practices of the past? I (Shel) intend to spend the next 10 to 15 years of my life co-creating this incredibly exciting world where humans can reach our potential without fear. Will you join me in this incredible journey?

Please visit:

- *Changemakers in the corporate, academic, NGO/nonprofit, or government sectors:* http://goingbeyondsustainability.com
- *Entrepreneurs who want to incorporate social change and business success into the core of your business:* http://impactwithprofit.com, for help in discovering and monetizing the ways you can make deep social change a core (and profitable) part of your business
- *Entrepreneurs looking for help greening their business in cost-reducing, profit-building ways:* http://greenandprofitable.com, for help going green, marketing green, and making a good green living
- *Business as a force for social change:* http://business-for-a-better-world.com, where you'll find the beginnings of resources to address and *solve* these issues, including the chance to nominate your favorite socially conscious business project so others can work on it too.

You'll find our contact information in the Resources section. Don't hesitate to get in touch.

May you be inspired, ethical, and successful, may you find deep satisfaction in the work you do, and may you never lack for abundance in your life.

LESSONS
- Once something has been done, we've proven that it's not impossible
- Solving hunger, poverty, war, and catastrophic climate change are not impossible; we've done harder things already
- The private sector can accomplish some kinds of change best; other kinds can be helped by government involvement

ACTIONS
- Take the social change business profitability self-assessment at http://impactwithprofit.com/self-assessment/
- Take the green business profitability self-assessment at http://greenandprofitable.com/self-assessment

- Add your name to the Environmental and Social Change Business Bill of Rights at http://business-for-a-better-world.com/bill-of-rights, and circulate it widely
- Contact Shel http://goingbeyondsustainability.com/contact/if you need help thinking about or implementing any of the concepts in this book
- Make use of the free 15-minute phone consultation Shel is offering you as a reader of this book, and read the additional resources you can download at http://impactwithprofit.com/giftsforreaders

RESOURCES

If you feel *this book* is a superior offering that you'd like to share with others, Shel can arrange discounted bulk sales. We can even arrange for custom editions with your company or organization name printed right on the book cover. Contact Shel and explain your needs: shel @ GreenAndProfitable.com.

If you'd like to earn commissions for marketing Shel's consulting, speaking, and copywriting, also contact Shel.

MORE HELP FROM GUERRILLA MARKETING
AND FROM SHEL HOROWITZ

Jay Conrad Levinson passed away in 2013, but his organization still exists:

> http://www.gmarketing.com
> http://www.guerrillamarketingassociation.com

Shel Horowitz

> http://GreenAndProfitable.com/contact/
> shel @ GreenAndProfitable.com
> shorowitz @ GoingBeyondSustainability.com
> 413-586-2388
> Twitter: @shelhorowitz
> Country/Time Zone: US/Eastern

Services include:

- Strategic consulting on profitably integrating social change into your business
- Strategic consulting on greening your business and making your green business profitable
- Strategic marketing planning, with emphasis on ethical, affordable, and effective methods
- Copywriting: individualized marketing plans, book jacket and cover copy, news releases/press releases, media pitch letters, blogs, newsletters, Web pages, direct-mail, print/radio/online ads (display or classified), brochures, etc....for businesses, nonprofits, authors, publishers, and community organizations
- Intensives, retreats, and mastermind groups—at your location, or at Shel's mountainside solarized antique farmhouse in Massachusetts
- Analysis and quick tune-up of your existing marketing
- Social media /Web 2.0 marketing: Twitter, Facebook, LinkedIn, blogs, and more
- Coaching and training on socially conscious/green business, meeting facilitation, and more
- Training in media relations and/or public speaking:
  a. Be comfortable, authentic, friendly, approachable—and authoritative...
  b. Get your message across in ways that make sense to each audience... and stay on message
  c. Develop sound bites that you can use on TV and radio and when speaking live.
  d. Make your slides much more exciting—with almost no effort...
  e. Increase your impact before, during, and after your talk...
  f. Attract more and better media coverage.
- Book shepherding: turning you from unpublished writer to well-published, well-marketed author
- Naming: products, companies, domains, campaigns, etc.

- Dynamic, interactive, *results-oriented* presentations to get attenders to take action. Talks on green/socially conscious business success, book marketing and publishing, and general marketing. Sample topics include:
  a. Making Green Sexy
  b. Impossible is Not a Fact—It's a Dare!
  c. Leading with a Green Heart
  d. "Peopletalk": Finding the No-Jargon Zone
  e. Selling Your Self-Published Book to a Larger Publisher
  f. How to Get Past "Market Share" to What's Really Important

Visit http://GreenAndProfitable.com/have-shel-speak for lots more talk topics

WEBSITES:

Profitable Social Change for Enterprise-Level Organizations
   http://GoingBeyondSustainability.com
Going Past Mere Sustainability—to the World We Want
   http://GoingBeyondSustainability.com
Profitable Social Change for Entrepreneurs, Small Businesses, Nonprofits, and Community Organizations
   http://ImpactWithProfit.com
Greening Your Business and Running it Profitably
   http://GreenAndProfitable.com
Business as a tool to transform hunger and poverty into sufficiency, war and violence into peace, and catastrophic climate change into planetary balance
   http://business-for-a-better-world.com
Directory of Shel's Websites and Social Media Profiles
   http://ShelHorowitz.com

BOOKS AND OTHER OUTSIDE RESOURCES

Here are a few wonderful books that help our culture expand its idea of the possible. We also suggest the capsule reviews of 53 more books included in our older book, *Guerrilla Marketing Goes Green*, posted at http://impactwithprofit.com/bookresources. That list on the Web includes many by people we've cited in this book, such as *Javatrekker* by Dean Cycon of Dean's Beans, *Winning Without Intimidation* and *Endless Referrals* by Bob Burg, and Keiningham & Varva's *The Customer Delight Principle*.

Business Creating Social Change

Paul Polak and Mal Warwick, *The Business Solution to Poverty*. Read Shel's review at http://thecleanandgreenclub.com/the-clean-and-green-club-june-2014/)

C.K. Prahalad, *The Fortune at the Bottom of the Pyramid*. Read Shel's review at http://www.principledprofit.com/subscribe-2#fortune)

Anita Casalina with Warren Whitlock and Heather Vale Goss, *Billions Rising: Empowering Self-Reliance* (see Shel's review at http://thecleanandgreenclub.com/the-clean-and-green-club-january-2014/)

Profitable Green Business

Andrew Benett, Cavas Gobhai, Ann O'Reilly, and Greg Welch, *Good For Business: The Rise of the Conscious Corporation*. Read Shel's review at http://thecleanandgreenclub.com/current-issue-december-2010/.

Andrés R. Edwards, *Thriving Beyond Sustainability*, New Society Publishers. Read Shel's review at http://thecleanandgreenclub.com/the-clean-and-green-club-february-2015/.

Al Iannuzzi, *Greener Products: The Making and Marketing of Sustainable Brands*. Read Shel's review at http://thecleanandgreenclub.com/the-clean-green-club-may-2012/.

Gareth Kane, *The Three Secrets of Green Business: Unlocking Competitive Advantage in a Low Carbon Economy*. Read Shel's review at http://thecleanandgreenclub.com/the-clean-and-green-club-december-2013/.

Joel Makower with Cara Pike, *Strategies for the Green Economy*, http://www.makower.com/strategies

Jacquelyn A. Ottman, *The New Rules of Green Marketing: Strategies, Tools, and Inspiration for Sustainable Branding*. Read Shel's review at http://

thecleanandgreenclub.com/shels-clean-green-newsletter-march-2011/#book.

Peter Senge, Byran Smith, Nina Kruschwitz, Joe Laur, and Sara Schley, *The Necessary Revolution: How Individuals and Organizations Are Working Together to Create a Sustainable World*. Read Shel's review at http://thecleanandgreenclub.com/the-clean-and-green-club-september-2015/.

Bob Willard, *The New Sustainability Advantage*. Read Shel's review at http://thecleanandgreenclub.com/the-clean-and-green-club-december-2014/.

Environmental Issues

Thomas L. Friedman, *Hot, Flat, and Crowded: Why We Need a Green Revolution—and How It Can Renew America*. Read Shel's review at http://thecleanandgreenclub.com/the-clean-and-green-club-december-2013/.

Building Movements

Judah Freed, *Making Global Sense: How One Billion Awakened People are Creating World Enlightenment*. The author's personal journey in search of a better future for himself and the planet. http://hokuhouse.com/making-global-sense/

Van Jones, *Rebuild the Dream*. Read Shel's review at http://thecleanandgreenclub.com/the-clean-green-club-february-2013/.

Naomi Klein, *This Changes Everything: Capitalism vs. The Climate*. Why we can't wait to tackle climate change, and how we can organize a people's movement around it. http://thischangeseverything.org/

Dalya F. Massachi, *Writing to Make a Difference: 25 Powerful Techniques to Boost Your Community Impact*. Read Shel's review at http://thecleanandgreenclub.com/the-clean-green-club-march-2012/#book

Robbin Phillips, Greg Cordell, Geno Church and Spike Jones, *Brains On Fire: Igniting Powerful, Sustainable, Word of Mouth Movements*, p. 95. Read Shel's review at http://thecleanandgreenclub.com/the-clean-green-club-february-2012/#brains

Amy Showalter, *The Underdog Edge: How Ordinary People Change the Minds of the Powerful...and Live to Tell About It*. Read Shel's review at http://thecleanandgreenclub.com/the-clean-green-club-june-2012/

INDEX